T0281809

FIFTY KEY IMPROV PERFORMERS

Fifty Key Improv Performers highlights the history, development, and impact of improvisational theatre by highlighting not just key performers, but institutions, training centers, and movements to demonstrate the ways improv has shaped contemporary performance both onstage and onscreen.

The book features the luminaries of improv, like Viola Spolin, Keith Johnstone, and Mick Napier, while also featuring many of the less well-known figures in improvisation who have fundamentally changed the way we make and view comedy – people like Susan Messing, Jonathan Pitts, Robert Gravel, and Yvon Leduc. Due to improv's highly collaborative nature, the book features many of the art form's most important theatres and groups, such as The Second City, TJ & Dave, and Oui Be Negroes. While the book focuses on the development of improvisation in the United States, it features several entries about the development of improv around the globe.

Students of Improvisational Theatre, History of Comedy, and Performance Studies, as well as practitioners of comedy, will benefit from the wide expanse of performers, groups, and institutions throughout the book.

Matt Fotis is an Associate Professor of Theatre at Albright College, where he teaches improvisation, comedy studies, and writing for performance. He is the author of *Satire & The State: Sketch Comedy and the Presidency* (Routledge 2020), *Long Form Improvisation and American Comedy: The Harold* (2014), and co-author of *The Comedy Improv Handbook* (Routledge 2016). He has published or presented on various topics, including improvisational theatre, new play development, political theatre, solo-performance, comedy studies, folklore studies, popular culture and more. His work has appeared in *Theatre Journal*, *Theatre Topics*, *Theatre/Practice*, *The Journal of American Drama & Theatre*, *Academic Minute*, *The Encyclopedia of Humor Studies*, *The Encyclopedia of American Studies*, *McSweeney's*, and MLB.com, among others. He is an award-winning playwright and the co-founder and co-executive director of The First Thursday Comedy Series in Reading, PA.

Routledge Key Guides

For a full list of titles in this series, please visit: https://www.routledge.com/Routledge-Key-Guides/book-series/RKG

FIFTY KEY IMPROV PERFORMERS

Actors, Troupes, and Schools from Theatre, Film, and TV

Matt Fotis

Routledge
Taylor & Francis Group

NEW YORK AND LONDON

Designed cover image: Matt Fotis, adapted from JackF at Getty Images via Canva.

First published 2025
by Routledge
605 Third Avenue, New York, NY 10158

and by Routledge
4 Park Square, Milton Park, Abingdon, Oxon, OX14 4RN

Routledge is an imprint of the Taylor & Francis Group, an informa business

Library of Congress Cataloging-in-Publication Data
Names: Fotis, Matt, 1979– author.
Title: Fifty key improv performers : actors, troupes, and schools from theatre, film, and TV / Matt Fotis.
Description: New York : Routledge, 2025. | Includes bibliographical references and index.
Identifiers: LCCN 2024021377 (print) | LCCN 2024021378 (ebook) | ISBN 9781032414225 (hardback) | ISBN 9781032414218 (paperback) | ISBN 9781003359692 (ebook)
Subjects: LCSH: Improvisation (Acting) | Comedians | Comedy. | Stand-up comedy.
Classification: LCC PN2071.I5 F475 2025 (print) | LCC PN2071.I5 (ebook) | DDC 792.02/8—dc23/eng/20240524
LC record available at https://lccn.loc.gov/2024021377
LC ebook record available at https://lccn.loc.gov/2024021378

ISBN: 978-1-032-41422-5 (hbk)
ISBN: 978-1-032-41421-8 (pbk)
ISBN: 978-1-003-35969-2 (ebk)

DOI: 10.4324/9781003359692

Typeset in Bembo
by codeMantra

To Jeanette, my favorite scene partner in the whole wide world.

CONTENTS

PREFACE

This list is not definitive.

Any list invites discussion, debate, and criticism.

This list is no different.

I hope this list will spark interest in those included and, more importantly, lead to more lists, more scholarship, and more attention given to this incredible art form.

Undoubtedly, there will be omissions – some from hard choices and some from my biases and blind spots. While reading this book, you will think to yourself, "Why on Earth is X included but not Y?" (see #50). For instance, my wife is furious that I have not included Mr. Rogers, the king of make-believe and making the invisible visible. Few people more fully embody the improvisational philosophy of curiosity, active listening, and being present in the moment. So, you know, she's not wrong.

Because there is a wealth of interview-based resources – Jeffrey Sweet's *Something Wonderful Right Away,* Jimmy Carrane's extensive interview library via the *Improv Nerd* podcast (see #35), Feña Ortalli's interviews in *Status,* the dozens of Improv-Interview-style podcasts and blogs, etc. – I have structured the book around the impact of each entry, rather than as an edited interview. I have focused the book on three main styles: Theatresports, The Match, and Chicago-style long form improvisation. Global improv in this book falls into two categories – Anglophone or Francophone. Anglophone improv tends to follow either the Theatresports model based on Keith Johnstone's work (see #2) or Chicago-style long form based on the work of Viola Spolin (see #2) and Del Close/Charna Halpern (see #7). Francophone improv is based on *le Match d'improvisation théâtrale* (commonly referred to simply as The Match), developed by Robert Gravel and Yvon Leduc (see #15). There is crossover between the styles, and all three rely on the same basic principles of improvisational theatre. There are plenty of Match-style improv shows in the US, just as there are dozens of long form shows in Paris. While I have included some groups and improvisers from around the globe, a more comprehensive global accounting is an area that future scholars can more fully and successfully address.

Okay. Enough about what this book is not.

This book *is* a collection of incredibly important, interesting, and influential improvisers. You will also probably notice that this book is a collection of people, theatres, and groups rather than only individual improvisers. Improv is by nature a collaborative art form, so it was contrary to the core principles of improvisation to isolate 50 individuals. While there are still individual entries, I have also included theatres and groups that have been instrumental in the development of improvisational theatre. Similarly, in some cases, I have grouped individual improvisers to highlight their shared experiences and contributions. For instance, Susan Messing and Jonathan Pitts (see #24) are not an improv group or duo, but their work has had a similar impact in shaping and spreading improvisation within and beyond Chicago. I have structured the list this way because I feel it best reflects the reality of improvisational performance. It also allowed me to include more than 50 people in a series featuring Fifty Key People in Field XYZ. Improv has drawn the short straw enough times that we deserve the win on this one.

While the book is in roughly chronological order, it is not structured precisely in terms of time/chronology – some things intersect in different sections. When we get to the 1990s and what Amy Seham deems The Third Wave of Improv, there is simply too much overlap to continue a straight-line chronology. Similarly, the development of improv on screen overlaps much of what is happening in live performance. Additionally, global improv is developing at different rates. While places like the US, France, Germany, the UK, and Australia have well-established improv scenes, other places like India, Kenya, and Indonesia are still in what would be their country's first wave.

Another aspect of the book that leaps out and differentiates improv from other artistic genres is the masters of improvisation on stage and screen also tend to be the best improv teachers. Many of the entries in this book are now or were at the very pinnacle of performance improv. Many of those same people are also at the pinnacle of improv pedagogy, which is important because improv classes and workshops are among the primary ways improv has spread and evolved. In many artistic fields, the folks at the tippy top of the profession rarely teach…or rarely teach regularly … or frankly, rarely are particularly good at teaching. Improv is different because the same skills and traits that make someone an excellent improviser – active listening, curiosity, empathy, adaptability, the ability to fail spectacularly, and an open mind – are the very same things that make someone a great teacher. Improv and teaching are about giving, building community, and helping others achieve their potential. As such, there are performers who are equally amazing teachers throughout the book. Maybe I should have included Mr. Rogers.

Before we get too far – what exactly is improv? If you're reading this book, chances are you are an improviser or know something about improv. If you're new to improv, let me briefly overview improvisational theatre. Let's start with what improv is not. Improv is not "winging it." Improv is not showing up to a presentation totally unprepared and then just "seeing what happens." Improv is not just saying or doing whatever you want in front of an audience. Contemporary improvisation is an art form – it has its own theories, philosophies, structures, movements, aesthetics, and styles. *It is an art form*. As such, improv requires preparation. Improv requires rehearsal. An athletic team practices skills and plays even though they don't know exactly what will happen so that they can be best prepared to react and respond during the game. Improv is no different. Improv is not inherently silly, wacky, or frivolous – it can be serious and dramatic. At its best, improv can mix silly, fun, and profound.

At heart, improv is a system of collaborative, spontaneous creativity. There are many applications of improv (see #37), but this book focuses on comedic improvisational theatre. The core tenet underlying all of improvisation is agreement. If you know nothing else about improv, chances are you've heard the term "Yes, And." That's about agreement. In improv, the actors agree to play collaboratively, to accept and build upon one another's offers, and most importantly, agree that they are going to work together to build one another up rather than to tear one another down (or exploit, embarrass, or otherwise take advantage…though as we shall see, this has not always been the case). Long story short, improv is playing along. When you were a kid on the playground and someone was pretending to be a dinosaur, chances are you joined in – whether you were another dinosaur, an asteroid, or something else in that world – you agreed to the reality, recognized the structure of play, and added something to it. That's improv.

Comedic improv exists in two main forms: the very cleverly titled short form and long form. Short form improv is based on games and can be seen at Theatresports (see Loose Moose Theatre Company #14), ComedySportz (see #17), Match-style improv (see #15), and on television via *Whose Line is it Anyway?* (see #27) and Wild 'N Out (see #28). Short form is built around independent 2–7-minute games, each with a particular gimmick. For instance, any guessing game relies on the premise that a set number of players do not know a key piece of information that everyone else – including the audience – knows. In Party Quirks, for instance, one player is hosting a party, and the other three players are all portraying a quirk given to them by the audience. The host does not know those quirks and must figure them out from clues given by the players. Much of the humor then rests on the fact that the audience knows the answer, and they find humor in the players' clues and the host's attempts to figure it out. There are hundreds of short form games, most of them based on the exercises and theories of Viola Spolin and Keith Johnstone (see #2).

Long form improv is more scenic based, often focused more on the relationships and connections between characters than on a structural gimmick. You'll never guess, but while short form games tend to be shorter in duration, long form tends to be longer. Some staple long form structures provide scenic improvisation frameworks, such as the Harold, ASSSSCAT, the Armando, Deconstruction, the Movie, and more – but all are rooted in scenic-based improv. Whereas the humor in short form is often based on playing the structural gimmick of the game, the humor in long form tends to come from how players tie together narrative threads or make callbacks and connections throughout a performance. Long form can be seen at theatres like ImprovOlympic (iO) (see #16) or The Upright Citizens Brigade (see #20), or in the Netflix special *Middleditch & Schwartz* (see #34).

The third main form of improv (I know I said there are only two; stay with me) is sketch comedy, which is scripted but often devised using improvisation. The *product* is not improv; however, improv is vital to the creative *process*. Places like The Second City (see #11) or The Brave New Workshop (see #13) produce sketch comedy but rely heavily on improvisation, teach improv classes, and consider improvisation central to their identity. For parts of improv's history, there has been tension and clashes over which of the three genres is real improv – the most famous between Second City producer Bernie Sahlins, who felt improv was best used as a tool, and iO's Del Close, who thought improv should itself be the sole product. At the current moment, that argument has somewhat abated. Perhaps we've finally stopped fighting amongst ourselves, or maybe it will arise anew from the ashes. Time will tell.

Allow me one more tangent, a pre-list of sorts, before we jump into the actual list. I refer to the theories of Bertolt Brecht throughout the book. While not an improviser, his theories enormously influenced many of the earliest improv pioneers. Just in case you need a slight reminder on Brechtian or Epic Theatre, let me start the list early with:

0. BERTOLT BRECHT

Improv has its own theorists and theories, but much of their work builds on the theories of Bertolt Brecht. A German theatre artist working in the first half of the 20th century, Brecht advocated for a theatre of ideas performed in a cabaret-style venue that allowed the audience to engage intellectually with what was happening rather than engage emotionally[1] or simply sit in the dark passively. Let me be clear: Brecht was not an improviser, nor did he advocate for improvised theatre. His theories, however, became vital to creating contemporary improvisational theatre. Brecht's main theory – *verfremdungseffekt,* or the Alienation Effect – was a conscious technique to engage theatrical audiences in new ways. First articulated in his essay "Alienation Effects in Chinese Acting" (1936), he described it as performing "in such a way that the audience was hindered from simply identifying itself with the characters in the play. Acceptance or rejection of their actions and utterances was meant to take place on a conscious plane, instead of, as hitherto, in the audience's subconscious."[2] By maintaining a distance – by being alienated emotionally from the characters – audiences would be able to engage intellectually with what was happening on stage, a kind of intellectual empathy. They would be able to understand how the character's choices, combined with their so-cial and cultural conditions, created the play's outcomes. As such, Brecht theorized that audiences could similarly apply that reasoning to their sit-uations and choices and adjust accordingly.

Brecht believed theatre could catalyze meaningful social change by engaging audiences intellectually and critically analyzing the conditions of the play and their outcomes rather than emotionally engaging with the characters ("I feel so bad for X"). Brecht employed many techniques to achieve *verfremdungseffekt,* often rooted in making the familiar strange. One such way was employing a particular acting style that required actors to break the fourth wall and maintain a triangular relationship between themselves, their character, and the audience – what Ian Wilkie has de-scribed as a "reflective practitioner."[3] In other words, the audience (and the actor) should never lose sight of the fact that the actor is *playing a part.* As such, the actor can critically analyze and comment upon the character in a way that helps the audience do the same. This detachment is also a constant reminder to the audience that this character is not real and that they are watching a theatrical performance. The intentional highlighting of the play's construction encourages the audience to view other "famil-iar" things and ask in what ways those "normal" things might also be social or cultural constructions.

You might be asking, "Okay, but how does this apply to improv?" In three ways. First, the founders of The Compass Players (see #9) and The Second City (see #11) were *deeply* influenced by Brecht. David Shepherd was actively trying to create a Brechtian theatre in the United States, while Paul Sills often employed Brechtian techniques in his directorial work (and directed the US premiere of Brecht's play *The Caucasian Chalk Circle*). They repeatedly reference and call upon Brecht in their work with The Compass Players and beyond. One of the significant rifts between Shepherd and Sills that helped lead to The Compass Players' downfall was their different applications of Brechtian Theatre (political vs. aesthetic). In addition to the beginnings of improvisation, another thread we will see carry through the history of improvisation is using improv to enact change. Whether it is in a similar vein, a la the work of Augusto Boal (see #5), or via Applied Improvisation (see #37) – from helping businesses be more creative, to assisting doctors to become better listeners, or to helping everyday people cope with social anxiety.

The second major influence is Brecht's idea to re-imagine the audience experience. For starters, Brecht wanted to attract a new audience of regular people rather than the traditional theatrical audience of the economic and cultural elites. He wanted an audience of everyday people watching theatre about their lives, problems, and experiences. As such, the theatrical space was hugely important to Brecht. Rather than a passive audience, Brecht wanted the audience to be critically engaged and felt that the environment played an enormous role in achieving that end. As such, he advocated a cabaret-style performance venue in what he deemed a "smokers' theatre." A theatre "where the audience would puff away at its cigars as if watching a boxing match, and would develop a more detached and critical outlook than was possible in the ordinary German theatre, where smoking was not allowed."[4] The desire to create a new type of audience experience (and audience composition) runs through much of improv's history. Shepherd, Sills, Boal, Johnstone, Gravel and Leduc, and so many more sought to change how audiences related to theatre by making them a more central and active part of the process. They likewise wanted to attract different audiences from traditional theatre and give them a different theatrical experience. As with Brecht's comparison to a boxing match, to achieve this new audience and new experience, many improv theatres and styles have been structured to mimic the experience of attending a sporting event.

The third Brechtian influence is in the actor-character-audience relationship. As we will see, the first set of formal rules for improvisation explicitly calls for a similar triangular relationship: in "an improvisation, where there are no lines, or given actions, or dramaturgical 'spine' to set a character in motion, *you* are your character ... All characterization or 'acting' comes from an exaggerated or intensified rendition of yourself called by another name."[5] An improviser, even one with absolutely no Brechtian training or motivations for social change, must maintain a distance between themselves and their character because *they do not know what will happen.* An improviser must bring themselves to the role because they must use their brain, skills, and body to react and respond *in the moment.* As such, Brecht's impact on improvisational theatre is immense. We see his influence via the application of his theories – The Second City is arguably the most successful Brechtian theatre in history – and the ways his theories simply permeate the art form's fundamental relationship between the performer and the audience.

Now you know something about Brecht. But you still might ask yourself, "Why is this book necessary?" In the United States, improv has become the most important comedic performance and training style. Vaudeville (see #1) was the dominant American comedic influence in the first half of the 20th century and stand-up in the second half. Improv has become the most dominant influence of 21st-century American comedy. So many of the leading comic figures and voices working today have an improv background, several of whom are highlighted in this book. Contemporary improv might have begun in a settlement house in Chicago in the 1940s, but it has become one of the world's most important performance styles and techniques. This book aims to document some of the most important figures in improv's evolution from Chicago's Hull House to the forefront of comedy.

Notes

1 Brecht did not advocate for no emotional engagement, rather he prioritized the audience's intellectual engagement and critical analysis over emotional investment.

2 John Willett, ed. and trans., *Brecht on Theatre: The Development of an Aesthetic* (New York: Hill and Wang, 1964), 91.

3 Ian Angus Wilkie, *Performing in Comedy: A Student's Guide* (London: Routledge, 2016).

4 Willett, 8.

5 Janet Coleman, *The Compass: The Improvisational Theatre that Revolutionized American Comedy* (Hyde Park: University of Chicago Press, 1990), 225–226.

PART 1

INTRODUCTION

DOI: 10.4324/9781003359692-1

1. THE FORERUNNERS

This book focuses on the development of improvisation over the last 75 years. Yet, we cannot ignore improv's origins. All the theatre history books tend to omit one significant fact: improvised performance is historically the most dominant form of popular performance. Sure, the Greeks wrote some fantastic plays, and some guy named William had a few hits in England, but for most of human history, performance has been improvised. While contemporary improvisation has a very particular structure and style that is relatively new (emerging in the 1950s), it is imperative to take a moment to look at the improvisational roots found in storytelling, commedia dell'arte, and vaudeville – all of which have had a profound effect on both improvisation and Western performance.

Humans have been telling stories orally longer than we have told them on the page. We have communicated our culture, values, and beliefs through oral storytelling for centuries. Since we've only been writing things down for a few centuries, it is more likely than not that a lot of these stories featured frequent improvisations. If you've ever played the game "Telephone," you know how much a story can change from one listener to the next. So, it is fair to assume that our ancestors used some improvisational techniques to heighten their stories, to follow the game of the scene, and to make their performances more entertaining. While we tend to think of storytelling as an individual act, some researchers argue storytelling is collaborative – that narratives are co-constructed improvisationally.[1] If you've spent time in a kindergarten classroom, you will observe children building worlds together – the playground might be the world's most creative and collaborative place. There are more formalized collaborative storytelling traditions, where the performers intentionally collaborate, but also those where the audience or spectators take an active role in collaborative storytelling, whether through call-and-response or other means.

There have been several more formalized improvisational modes of performance. One of the oldest forms of improvised performance in the Western world is the Atellan Farce. Influenced by Greek New Comedy, Atellan Farces (also known as Atellanae Fabulae) emerged in the 3rd century BCE and were largely improvised comic performances about life in the Roman countryside. Featuring masks, stock characters, bawdy humor, and extreme comic exaggeration, the Atellan Farce represents one of the earliest forms of structured improvisation. They were short performances and usually performed as entr'actes or as after-pieces to more traditional scripted plays. The plots could be wildly complicated or incredibly thin but usually revolved around mistaken identity, lust, and greed. They featured five stock characters in masks that pop up repeatedly in different guises throughout the history of comedic performance. The most popular was Maccus, the typical clown or fool type. The other four were Pappus, the easily deceived older man; Bucco (often called Fat Cheeks), who was a long-winded gluttonous braggart; Dossennus, a hunchbacked character who was a crafty cheat; and Manducus, who some scholars believe was an alternative name or type for Dossennus. Lasting for hundreds of years, the Atellan Farce demonstrates the enduring popularity of improvised performances. Not only were they popular, but they were also influential. William Beane argues, "We have reason to believe that in the life of common people, from early times to the end of the Roman Empire, popular farce played a greater part than all the literary forms of Roman drama put together."[2]

The Atellan Farce's most significant impact on contemporary improvisation would be its influence on commedia dell'arte. Borrowing stock characters and the physical performance style that marked the Atellan Farce, commedia rose to prominence in Italy during the 16th century. Over the next two centuries, commedia troupes would perform across Europe, becoming the most influential form of popular comedic performance and forming the bedrock of characters and plot structure of contemporary Western comedy. Much like the Atellan Farce, commedia troupes worked improvisationally from a basic outline or plot. This structure, which would come to be known as scenario plays, would provide the working blueprints for The Compass Players in the 1950s. They wrote down many of these scenarios, as were the most popular Atellan Farces, but they all originated in improvisation – a model that The Second City would later borrow.

Audiences and performers knew the basic story structure from the beginning, but it was up to the performers to invent the dialogue in the moment and move the performance from plot point to plot point.[3] In addition to the scenario play structure, commedia relied heavily on stock characters. Three main categories were Masters, Servants, and Aristocrats (or non-masked characters). These stock characters often find their way into contemporary improv scenes and have become a staple of modern scripted comedy – stock characters such as Pantalone, the miserly older man (Mr. Burns on *The Simpsons*); Dottore, the know-it-all who knows nothing (Michael Scott on *The Office*); Capitano, the cowardly braggart soldier (Gilderoy Lockhart from *Harry Potter and the Chamber of Secrets*); or Harlequin, the tricky servant (Bugs Bunny). A typical plot follows two young lovers who were forbidden to marry by their parents, but with the help of the servants, the two young lovers can live happily ever after – pretty much a happy *Romeo and Juliet*. Much like a contemporary romantic comedy or Hallmark Christmas movie, the plot itself was less important than the actors and their performance. Audiences were not biting their nails, wondering if the two young lovers would get together. Instead, they were delighting in the antics of Harlequin and Zani or laughing at the back-and-forth bickering and brinksmanship between Pantalone and Dottore.

Performers almost always played the same part, and nearly every commedia plot followed a similar structure. In many ways, most contemporary comedic animated series – *The Simpsons, SpongeBob SquarePants, South Park,* etc. – are good examples of commedia's style and structure. They each feature the same set of stock characters wholly defined by their roles, playing out those roles in a relatively set and oft-repeated plot structure. Rather than become bored by Patrick's stupidity or Squidward's pessimism on *SpongeBob,* audiences *delight* in these repeated character tropes. These stock characters and stock plots relied on commedia's other structural contribution to comedic performance: *lazzi,* or what we'd call bits. These bits were any independent comedic action guaranteed to elicit laughter, usually repeatable and easily recognizable (traditionally tied to a stock character's dominant trait). Nearly all short form improv games have a *lazzi* built into the game to guarantee laughs. For instance, the short form improv game New Choice (or Ding). In the game, an improviser must change whatever they just said or did when the host/emcee says 'new choice.' The immediate switch in tone and tenor, not to mention the dexterity and adaptability of the players to completely change the scene on a dime becomes the game of the scene – it's the *lazzi* – and guarantees a laugh. In long form improv, The Upright Citizens Brigade's "the game of the scene" (see #20) is *lazzi* – any repeatable action the performers use and exploit to get laughs and progress the scene.[4]

Repeated bits, stock characters, and exaggerated verbal and physical comedy would form the bedrock for contemporary improvisation's subsequent major influence – vaudeville. Influenced by the minstrel show, music hall, and other earlier forms, vaudeville became the dominant form of popular performance during the first half of the 20th century. Akin to a variety show, vaudeville "was the United States' first modern mass entertainment."[5] Vaudeville was everywhere – purposefully so – and its stars were some of America's first celebrities. While vaudeville featured all kinds of acts, the comics and singers were the true stars. Vaudeville comedy was broad, bawdy, and filled with puns and double entendre. Comics did not completely improvise the sketches and bits of vaudeville. Instead, they were performed with an improvisational style and passed down through an oral tradition. Comics embellished, stretched, switched, and personalized stock bits. Because of this improvisational performance style, very few complete written scripts from vaudeville exist. Performers rarely looked at scripts, instead learning the bits through repetition and by developing their own twists. Much like the Atellan Farce and commedia scenario play format, vaudeville comics knew the basic parameters of each bit but did not have a set script.

What made vaudeville unique was that each comic, duo, or team performed a bit differently. As Andrew Davis argues, "the scripts that exist were aids to the rehearsal process. Comics usually talked through the scenes before going onstage, then came up with their own line of dialogue in performance."[6] Once again, The Compass Players would borrow this format for their improvised performances in the 1950s, taking audience suggestions, going backstage to plot out scenes, and then improvising the dialogue in performance. One common semi-improvisational technique in vaudeville was joke switching. Joke *stealing* was rampant in vaudeville, with comics stealing jokes from one another and producers heading to Broadway to watch comic revues and then insert them into their shows. Joke switching, however, was a standard technique comics use to personalize bits. The basic idea is that a comic will use the same setup for a joke but deliver a different punchline (or vice-versa, though less common). This technique was used at both the macro level – switching the punchline for a sketch based on a previous or widely used premise – and the micro level, where a comic switched a single joke. Forgive me, but the most straightforward contemporary example is "Yo mama" jokes. They all have the same setup – Yo mama is so _____, she [insert punchline]. Similarly, at the macro level, Hallmark Christmas movies all have the same setup (and ending) but use different characters and scenarios. It's not precisely improv, but it demonstrates the performance style, where comics constantly changed and adapted their material, often without ever writing it down.

Vaudeville's reach was so long that there were hardly any comics in the first half of the 20th century who did not perform in vaudeville, and certainly, none who were not influenced by its style – both in content and in its creative process. American culture and life were similarly influenced. By 1900, "there were 2,000 vaudeville houses, half of all theaters in the country— [and Americans] understood that vaudeville meant the best, or at least the most energetic, form of live entertainment."[7] Its style permeated the culture. Nearly all early 20th-century American comics "learned the ropes," so to speak, in vaudeville and carried its traditions, rhythms, and jokes into early radio, film, and stand-up comedy. Even though vaudeville on the stage died in the 1930s, comics like Jack Benny, Fred Allen, and Bob Hope went from vaudeville to the radio, bringing the improvisatory aesthetic with them, which would carry into early film and television as well. Fanny Brice, Abbott and Costello, Laurel and Hardy, Burns and Allen, the Three Stooges, Buster Keaton, Charlie Chaplin, and many more film, television, and stand-ups started in vaudeville.

Another aspect of vaudeville that carried through American comedy was segregation. Being America in the late 19th and early 20th centuries, vaudeville was mostly segregated and featured mostly white performers entertaining primarily white audiences. While Black comics did appear on vaudeville, such as the comic super team of Bert Williams and George Walker, doing so was both rare and potentially dangerous. Williams and Walker regularly changed their routine, making it less funny because white comics would pressure owners not to re-hire Black acts who were funnier than them. They also made sure their characters did not undercut too many social or cultural norms (e.g., a Black character couldn't out-smart or outwit a white character without there being some later come-uppance). At the same time, Williams and Walker's act directly tried to undercut stereotypes. Their act was a subversion of the minstrel charac-ters Jim Crow and Zip Coon, with the two men donning blackface to caricature the idea of blackface: "what could better symbolize the artifice of the minstrel character than a black man blacking up to play himself?"[8]

In their act, Williams played a sort of slow-footed, oafish character who was always down on his luck (his song "Nobody" stems from this character). In contrast, Walker played the slick-talking dandy type char-acter, who usually tried to take advantage of his friend. Most Black com-ics, however, including Williams and Walker, performed on the Chitlin' Circuit, which was technically called the Theater Owners Booking As-sociation (TOBA), also colloquially known as Tough On Black Asses (or Actors). These venues across the country featured Black performers, pri-marily musicians and comics, performing for Black audiences (for much less pay and in much harsher conditions). Scores of incredibly well-known and influential singers and comics got their start on the Chitlin' Circuit, including Moms Mabley, Mantan Moreland, Hattie McDaniel, Stepin Fetchit, Count Basie, Boots Hope, Bessie Smith, the husband-and-wife comedy duo Butterbeans and Susie, Redd Foxx, and David "Pigmeat" Markham.

A common question in contemporary improv is, "Why is improv so white?" Part of the answer lies in the history of American comedy and entertainment. For centuries, white producers, institutions, ven-ues, and performers intentionally excluded BIPOC performers (Black,

Indigenous, People of Color), making all-white casts and all-white audiences the American standard. BIPOC performers, especially Black comedians, have been exploited, appropriated, stereotyped, ridiculed, tokenized, and "othered" throughout the history of American comedy. Why is improv so white? In part because improv exists within this historical framework. There are absolutely issues specific to improvisational theatre that have resulted in an overwhelmingly white and male system, many of which are detailed in this book, so I don't say this to absolve improv in any way. Still, it is important to acknowledge that improv is not alone in its demographics, nor are its systems/structures uniquely problematic.

Notes

1 Keith Sawyer, "Improvisation and Narrative," *Narrative Inquiry*, Vol. 12:2 (2002), 319–349.

2 William Beane, *The Roman Stage* (Cambridge, MA: Harvard University Press, 1951), 129.

3 Performers often spoke in a gibberish language known as Grammelot, which was a common "language" for physical comedy performance.

4 Matt Fotis and Siobhan O'Hara, *The Comedy Improv Handbook: A Comprehensive Guide to University Improvisational Comedy in Theatre and Performance* (New York: Focal Press, 2016), 7–19.

5 David Monod, *Vaudeville and the Making of Modern Entertainment, 1890–1925* (Chapel Hill: University of North Carolina Press, 2020), 2.

6 Andrew Davis, *Baggy Pants Comedy: Burlesque and the Oral Tradition* (New York: Palgrave Macmillan, 2014), xii.

7 "History: Vaudeville and Broadway," *Make 'Em Laugh*. 2 December 2008. https://www.pbs.org/wnet/makeemlaugh/comedys-evolution/history-vaudeville-and-broadway/31/

8 David Suisman, "Bert Williams and George Walker—Victor Releases (1901)," *Library of Congress*, 2003. https://www.loc.gov/static/programs/national-recording-preservation-board/documents/WilliamsAndWalker1901Recordings.pdf

PART 2

THE ICONS

As Part 1 demonstrates, comics and performers had been using improvisation for centuries – to tell stories, to fill in plots, and to personalize material. Yet, *improvisational theatre* as a distinct and independent style of performance did not yet exist. As Sam Wasson argues in *Improv Nation*, improvisational theatre "had to be invented."[1] While improvisation had been used in performance, the distinct art form of improvisational theatre was not created until the mid-20th century. The forms, styles, and rules of contemporary improvisational theatre did not exist until Viola Spolin and Keith Johnstone began creating the philosophical, theoretical, and practical framework for this new art form.

The practitioners that appear in the following entries are indispensable in the creation and development of improvisation. Without their work, contemporary comedic improv would either not exist or look completely different. Many of them had no roadmap or examples to follow. While it is easy to say they "made it up as they went along," doing so undermines the deep-rooted theories and philosophies that underpin the creation of improvisational theatre. The artistic theories of Bertolt Brecht (see #0), combined with Neva Boyd's research and implementation of the sociology of play, were vital to creating contemporary improvisation.

The social, political, and cultural climate of 1940s and 1950s Chicago (and America) are likewise fundamental to the foundations of improv. The revolutionary act of performing onstage without a script during the 1950s' "American normalcy" is an essential framework for understanding how improv developed and why it appealed to audiences and performers. Young, hip, cool, intelligent people getting onstage to talk about politics, culture, sex, and drugs – and doing it without a script!!! – against the backdrop of a white picket fence American suburban utopia where "one simply did not talk about those things" made improv unique and incredibly attractive. The same "what are they going to say" aesthetic, at

DOI: 10.4324/9781003359692-2

times dangerous and at times silly, is still at the heart of improv's appeal. Some of that story is in the following pages, but anyone interested in a more detailed account should read Janet Coleman's *The Compass*, Jeffrey Sweet's *Something Wonderful Right Away*, and Sam Wasson's *Improv Nation*. Long story short, improv didn't spontaneously emerge at a random time or place.

2. VIOLA SPOLIN AND KEITH JOHNSTONE

All the icons are important, but let's face it: the rest of this list would not exist without Viola Spolin and Keith Johnstone. Working independently, the two would develop the theories and practices that would create and continue to shape improvisational theatre. Spolin is the dominant theorist for American improvisation, while Johnstone is the most influential theorist for the rest of the Anglophone globe. Spolin's *Improvisation for the Theater* (1963) and Johnstone's *Impro* (1979) remain the art form's most vital texts. Yet, arguably, the most influential figure in the creation of improvisational theatre was a sociologist named Neva Boyd.

Boyd loved games. She believed games held tremendous power to transform lives and set about doing just that – using games as the centerpiece of her educational program at Hull House in Chicago. A settlement house for European immigrants, Hull House was co-founded by Jane Addams and Ellen Gates Starr in 1889. It became a model for the settlement house movement, which aimed to alleviate poverty by having middle and upper-class volunteers living and working with low-income residents, usually comprised mainly of recent immigrants. Hull House and other settlement houses had extensive educational programs. Boyd inherently understood the importance of play in education and understood that games were more than physical exercise. In her essay "The Theory of Play," Boyd wrote, "Play involves social values, as does no other behavior. The spirit of play develops social adaptability, ethics, mental and emotional control, and imagination."[2] She was "among the first to emphasize the important relationship between play and the social education of children."[3] Beginning in 1920, Boyd headed the Recreation Training School at Hull House, a one-year program designed to train educators and facilitators in her game-based pedagogy, which in 1927 would become part of Northwestern University. One of Boyd's students was a young actress named Viola Spolin, who, beginning in 1923, would study with Boyd for three years at Hull House. Boyd was the predominant influence on Spolin's theories, with Spolin writing "The effects of her inspiration never left me for a single day."[4]

Spolin loved games and would use the foundation Boyd gave her to create a system of theatre games that would revolutionize American theatre and create contemporary improvisational theatre. Spolin got married, had two children, and then divorced in a relatively short time frame. During this time, she began hosting informal gatherings featuring improvisations at her home, an unexpected way to workshop what would become her pedagogical philosophy. She trained at DePaul University and left Chicago briefly to study with The Group Theatre in New York before returning to Chicago, where she lived and worked communally with other divorced mothers in what they called The Educational Playroom. Spolin continued honing her theatrical pedagogy based on play, and in 1939, she became the drama supervisor for the Works Progress Administration's Recreational Project on the recommendation of Neva Body. In a letter to her sister in 1937, Spolin remarked:

> I am beginning to make a name for myself in creative dramatics.... Everyone made such a big fuss about the unusual results I got. I used the charades a good deal as a means to teach acting techniques, and I realize that I have learned an amazing lot in the last years— both by my training under competent people and my awareness of living and the necessity to help people become more creative as a real justification for living.[5]

The young students in her workshops were often immigrants with limited English language skills. So, Spolin improvised.

Spolin began creating games to teach lessons about acting and life. She brought some prepared games into the rehearsal room but made up on the spot many of the games that would form the bedrock of her acting – "The games emerged out of necessity. I didn't sit at home and dream them up. When I had a problem [directing] I made up a game. Then another problem came up, I just made up a new game."[6] For instance, the Gibberish game came about to sidestep language, a common problem considering that many of her students spoke limited English or none. The two players perform a scene in the game but are only allowed to speak in gibberish. As a result, the players naturally default to other means of communication, using their environment, bodies, faces, and vocal tonality to convey meaning. Spolin used these games to teach but also to develop performances. Some of the earliest improvisational-based performances happened with her students at Hull House, including 1939's *Halsted Street*. Writing about a 1940 performance, the *Sunday Times Magazine* wrote:

> Organized recreation for children takes many unique forms, none more unique than what is being done at Hull House. Aimed at stirring creative ability inherent in all children, it's a program of unorthodox drama that hews to no lines, knows no cues, and never heard of a rehearsal. The youngsters are given a bare idea, characters are chosen and the impromptu play begins ... Are these young thespians good? They're the finest ad-libbers the stage has seen, says Director Viola Sills Spolin.[7]

After World War II, Spolin moved to California and founded the Young Actors Company in Hollywood, where she continued teaching, directing, and developing her revolutionary system of games.

Spolin's impact extends beyond her work at Hull House and the Young Actors Company. She would also go on to train the actors in the world's first contemporary improvisational theatre – The Compass Players (see #9). All of it is rooted in Spolin's games. Her system transformed complicated dramatic techniques and conventions into a series of games focused on spontaneity, physicality, intuition, and imagination designed to make play the catalyst for creativity, self-expression, and self-awareness. First published in 1963, Spolin's *Improvisation for the Theater* introduced the broader world to her pedagogical theory of learning through play. The book's famous opening lines have provided a philosophical framework for contemporary improvisation: "Everyone can act. Everyone can improvise. Anyone who wishes to can play in the theater and learn to become 'stageworthy'."[8] Spolin's system was revolutionary, creating a revolutionary new art form, but it also had a revolutionary philosophy. Rather than tapping into high art aesthetics or deep wells of emotion or focusing on "talent," Spolin focused on what we'd now call experiential learning: "Acting can be taught to the 'average' as well as the 'talented' if the teaching process is oriented towards making the theater techniques so intuitive that they become the students' own."[9] This philosophy that everyone can improvise and has a talented artist inside of them has become foundational to nearly every theory of improvisational theatre.

Across the Atlantic, Keith Johnstone was growing dissatisfied with the traditional theatre in Britain in the 1950s and 1960s. Johnstone's own educational experience proved foundational for his theatrical philosophy. Frustrated with what he saw as an education focused more on memorization than imagination, Johnstone struggled in school but, like Boyd and Spolin, understood the inherent power of play. Johnstone based much of his pedagogy around games, remarking, "You can teach anything if it's a game."[10] Much as he found education in Britain stifling creativity, he became equally frustrated by the theatre. Working with The Royal Court Theatre, Johnstone was observing rehearsal, and his main takeaway was boredom – "until the actors broke for coffee or stagehands began moving sets around the stage. It was only at these times that there seemed to be moments of truth on the stage."[11] Johnstone quickly realized that spontaneity was far more engaging than rote memorization (both in the classroom and onstage) and set about developing his improvisation system. His philosophy would manifest itself in the hugely popular and influential form of improv he developed called Theatresports, which inspired

ComedySportz and *Whose Line Is It Anyway?* and continues to be one of the most popular styles of improvisation performed around the world.

Johnstone would shape his game-play philosophy around various iterations of the mantra "dare to be ordinary." He based his classes around his list "Things My Teachers Stopped Me From Doing," creating games and exercises focused on the skills his formal education had tried to stamp out. Like Spolin, Johnstone was less interested in the comedic aspects of improv (not that he ignored them) and created games to help players get better. Patti Stiles said, "He invented impro games to solve problems."[12] Again, like Spolin, Johnstone believed anyone could act and improvise, and the key was allowing performers to be their authentic selves without fear of failure or of doing it correctly. Like Spolin's, his training was less about developing "talent" and more about removing self-or-societally-imposed barriers. Johnstone famously told his students and performers to "Be more boring," "Be more ordinary," "Don't concentrate," and "Please, don't do your best." Johnstone understood that improvisation required the performer to be present in the here and now, not looking to the future or worrying about the past. His adages of ordinariness unlocked performers by giving them the freedom to be themselves and stop worrying about "doing it right."

Undoubtedly influenced by the negative experiences in his own top-down sage-on-the-stage educational experience, he regularly downplayed his own success, lowered his status, and minimized his role in his students' success. So much so that he created a game called "Fuck off, Keith," that he used with students who seemed intimidated by him or consistently looked to him for approval – like, literally looked at him during scenes and games. During a scene or exercise, anytime a player caught themselves looking at Johnstone or seeking his approval, they would have to turn, look Johnstone in the eye, and yell, "Fuck off, Keith." The exercise helped unlock improvisers, freeing them from doing it right and allowing them to take ownership of their improv journey. Status is one of the key concepts in Johnstone's pedagogy. He writes about it extensively in *Impro* – the various ways performers can use status in scenes to develop characters, deepen connections, or advance the plot. By applying his pedagogy of status to himself in such a simple and direct way, his students freed themselves from the pressure of "doing it right" by Johnstone lowering his status and allowing the students to elevate their own.

Johnstone had a barrier Spolin did not – technically, improvisation was illegal on British stages. Before the Theatres Act of 1968, all performances and scripts had to be pre-approved by The Lord Chamberlain. Performing without a script presented a problem since there was no script to be approved. So, Johnstone called many of his earliest performances "demonstrations" or "classes" to avoid censorship. Thea-tresports predecessor, The Theatre Machine, grew out of these demon-strations, with the core four of Ben Benison, Roddy Maude-Roxby, Richard Morgan, and Tony Trent forming the backbone of Britain's first improvisational theatre company. The Theatre Machine toured Europe from 1968–1971, spreading Johnstone's improv theories and practice. Johnstone would move to Canada in 1972 to teach at the University of Calgary and later formed The Loose Moose Theatre Company in Cal-gary in 1977 (see #14).

It was in Canada at Loose Moose that Johnstone created Theatresports. Establishing a decades-long connection between sports and improv, The-atresports was partially inspired by professional wrestling. Writing about the origins of Theatresports, Johnstone said, "Wrestling was the only working-class theatre that I'd ever seen."[13] Theatresports attempted to emulate the more populous atmosphere of professional wrestling and bor-row the competitive structure. The basic format involves two teams of improvisers competing in a series of improv games, with judges scoring the play and, perhaps most importantly of all, the audience cheering, laughing, yelling, sometimes joining the players on stage, and having a great time. Johnstone wrote about the atmosphere,

> If the performance has gone well, you'll feel that you've been watching a bunch of good-natured people who are wonderfully cooperative, and who aren't afraid to fail. It's therapeutic to be in such company, and to yell and cheer, and perhaps even volunteer to improvise with them. With luck, you'll feel as if you've been at a wonderful party; great parties don't depend on the amount of alcohol, but on positive interactions.[14]

This more populist atmosphere evokes many of improv's earliest influ-ences and has become one of contemporary improv's most attractive qualities.

The rest of this book does not exist without Viola Spolin and Keith Johnstone. Their philosophies, games, and exercises form the bedrock of contemporary improvisational performance. They are arguably two of the most essential theatre theorist-practitioners of the last one hun-dred years, have profoundly changed the way we produce, consume, and understand comedy, and yet are not widely known outside the world of improvisation. Their works are required readings, as is Theresa Robbins Dudeck's *Keith Johnstone: A Critical Biography*. As of this writing, there is no full-length biography of Viola Spolin. Perhaps one of you reading this book will remedy this most egregious omission.

3. DAVID SHEPHERD, PAUL SILLS, AND TED FLICKER

David Shepherd wanted to change the world through the theatre. Like Johnstone, he wanted an immediate theatre that spoke directly to the audience's wants, needs, and dreams. Shepherd didn't want what he saw as the stuck-up and out-of-touch New York theatre that catered to the upper classes; he wanted a workers' theatre that was timely and intimate and was a genuine conversation between the audience and the players (see #0). His only teeny-tiny problem was that he didn't know how to do that. Luckily for him, Spolin's teachings were beginning to spread, and he just so happened to cross paths with a brilliant young theatremaker who just so happened to be Viola Spolin's son – Paul Sills. While the two men would butt heads over the tension between artistic aesthetic and political messaging, they would go on to create the first professional theatre to put Spolin's teachings into practice – The Compass Players (see #9). In so doing, they transformed contemporary American comedy.

Spolin and Johnstone were first and foremost teachers. David Shepherd did a bit of everything in his time, but he was, first and foremost, a producer and innovator. Shepherd was the creator or co-creator of numerous improvisational theatres and formats, including the Playwrights Theatre Club (Chicago, 1953), The Compass Players (Chicago, 1955), Community Makers (New York, 1971), and ImprovOlympics. Shepherd had the original idea for the ImprovOlympics format in the 1970s, and with Charna Halpern, it would form the beginning structure for iO in 1981, though that structure would soon give way to the Harold (see #16). While he did not create The Second City (see #11), in their own words, "Simply put, there would be no Second City without David Shepherd."[15]

Shepherd studied English at Harvard, served in World War II, and received a Master of Arts in Theater History from Columbia University. He would use that background and his interest in the theories of Bertolt Brecht (see #0) and other European Avant-Garde artists, combined with the practices of commedia dell'arte, to revolutionize the American theatre. He came to the Midwest and Chicago in 1952, believing that his vision for a workers' theatre was more likely to be realized in the heartland than on the East Coast. He quickly immersed himself with a group of University of Chicago students – including Paul Sills – who would form the core for the Playwrights Theatre Club and The Compass Players. As we'll see, however, Shepherd never truly realized his vision for a politically charged theatre for the ordinary person.

Paul Sills was, at heart, a director. While he shared Shepherd's political intent, the two would find themselves conflicted about the artistic direction of The Compass Players. Like Shepherd, Sills would spend most of his life bringing improvisation to people by creating new theaters, companies, communities, and styles. Of the many contributions he made, some include The Game Theater, which he opened with his mother, Viola Spolin, and the creation of Story Theatre (not to mention a little comedy place called The Second City). We'll delve deeper into The Compass (#9) and The Second City (#11) later, so let's look at some of Sills' other contributions and his work as improv's first director.

Based on folk tales and an oral storytelling tradition, Story Theater harkened back to traditional storytelling. Inspired by an improvised set based on Snow White at Game Theater, Sills created the new form that would take both classic fairy tales and the turmoil of the 1960s as its foundation. One of Story Theater's first public performances took place during the tumultuous 1968 Democratic National Convention in Chicago, a week that saw violence pour into the streets of Chicago. Sills had rented the old Second City space (the theatre had recently moved due to its popularity), and he set about creating theatre that could speak to the times. According to Sills:

> We charged no admission, but asked for a donation at the end. When Convention Week started and 'the whole world was watching,' the police chased demonstrators out of Lincoln Park right into our gate but did not enter. Like the churches of the neighborhood, the theater was somehow a sanctuary, off-limits to police. Convention Week has been called a 'turning point in American History' and when our audiences saw an old soldier defeat all authority in *The Blue Light*, the ones most deeply touched by the spirit of liberty shouted 'Right on!'[16]

As Viola Spolin's son, it should be no surprise that Sills was a politically aware master improviser. However, his time as a student at the University of Chicago cemented his artistic and political vision. We'll further explore the role the University of Chicago played when discussing The Compass Players (#9), so for now, let's focus a bit more on Sills, the director. It might seem incompatible to think of a spontaneous art form as having a director. Still, within sketch comedy (which is scripted and therefore absolutely needs a director) and traditionally improvised performance, there is almost always someone acting as director or coach. With sketch comedy, the director works much like a traditional stage director – they work with the actors, set the artistic vision, create the blocking and stage movement, etc. In an improvised performance, the director often works with the ensemble to create the piece's structure, gives actors notes, and sets the artistic vision. Again, Spolin and Johnstone did their fair share of directing, but they were teachers (as is every director), and Sills truly acted as the first improv director.

Sills' directorial results speak for themselves. From acting as The Second City's first director to his earlier work with The Playwrights Theatre Club and his later work with Story Theater, Sills was a master at his craft. His style would also influence a generation of improv directors, though his style was not quite as gentle and positive as his mother's or Johnstone's. Sheldon Patinkin, a Sills collaborator and later theatre historian, wrote of Sills in *The Second City: Backstage at the World's Greatest Comedy Theatre*:

> Paul's genius was transmitted as often as not with grunts, groans, mumbles, and hollering, accompanied by various kinds of body language and an occasional thrown chair ... He got more out of people than they knew was in them. He insisted improvisers had to stay in the moment, never going into their heads to find what to say and do, but, by bypassing the intellect, keeping themselves free to react to just what's happening between them there and then ... He was the first, and he was the best.[17]

Sills is often credited with taking his mother's games and philosophy and putting them into practice. But that description is unfair to both of them. Spolin had been producing improvised performances before her son did, and he and Shepherd relied on her immensely in training the ensemble that would be The Compass Players. It also reduces Sills' contributions to simply being Viola Spolin's son. Obviously, he was hugely influenced by Spolin. He spent his life teaching her games and philosophies. Still, he was also immeasurably important to the future of improv, creating numerous styles and theatres of his own and laying the blueprint for how someone directs improvisation and sketch comedy.

Ted Flicker is often left out of improv's origin story. Spolin, Johnstone, Shepherd, and Sills are worthy of their elevated status, but Flicker's influence on improv's style in performance is evident on stages worldwide. Flicker was instrumental with The St. Louis Compass Players, which opened after the Chicago branch closed. Flicker went on to have a multi-faceted career as a writer, producer, director, and sculptor, but he was also instrumental in creating improvisational performance. As we'll see,

The Compass Players in Chicago closed relatively quickly, and a branch would open in St. Louis at the Crystal Palace. Flicker would act as the "Ringmaster" of the St. Louis branch and change the trajectory of improvisational theatre in two significant ways.

The first was all about style and presentation. Flicker wanted to make improv itself the main attraction, rather than scenario plays or scripted scenes (as had been the case in Chicago), and he wanted improv presented as an actual show in every sense. As Janet Coleman explains:

> If David Shepherd had seized upon improvisation as a tool for developing new plays that reflected the lives of the audience, it was indeed Ted Flicker's un-Violan contribution to present improvisation as "an unusual feat," a cross between a cocktail party and a carnival act. Flicker's gimmick would become so successful and so widely imitated as to obscure his more significant innovation in St. Louis in finally throwing the spotlight on improvisation as process by escalating the degree of audience involvement and framing the show around each evening's audience-suggested scenes.[18]

Flicker advocated a faster, funnier, and more polished approach than the Chicago Compass. He had his actors in more formal attire, banned smoking onstage, and focused more on presentation. For instance, Flicker was a massive advocate of blacking out scenes on a big laugh, giving the scenes a more defined structure and a more solidified ending to benefit the performers and help guide the audience. When Shepherd finally saw a St. Louis performance, he remarked, "You've turned it into entertainment. You've ruined my dream."[19]

Flicker's other massive contribution is the so-called Westminster Place Kitchen Rules, developed by Flicker and Elaine May (see #4), with help from a young Del Close (see #7). At heart, Spolin's game system was a teaching tool, a series of exercises meant to teach acting, creativity, and social skills. She would transform it into a performance blueprint, but that hadn't fully happened yet in 1958. Johnstone hadn't yet developed his philosophy or Theatresports, nor had Sills created Story Theater or The Second City. While there were games, exercises, and systems, there was no manual for improvisational *performance*. So, Flicker and May (and Close) made one. They would gather after shows or during the day to discuss what made improvised scenes work. The rules were not prescriptive – "you must do these three things" – but rather descriptive, "we have observed that when improvisers employ these three tactics, their odds of success increase dramatically."

The three rules they devised still form the basis for most improv rules, at least for those who follow them. The first rule deals with agreeing to the reality created onstage and not negating what your scene partner offers. The second involves making active rather than passive choices. The third rule is less a description of actions or tactics and more a philosophical description of what it means to be an improviser: in "an improvisation, where there are no lines, or given actions, or dramaturgical 'spine' to set a character in motion, *you* are your character ... All characterization or 'acting' comes from an exaggerated or intensified rendition of yourself called by another name."[20] As improv developed, the third rule has morphed a bit into some version of "support your partner." Regardless, these three (plus one) rules are still being taught or, in some cases, rebelled against today.

Shepherd, Sills, and Flicker founded and established the beginnings of improvisational performance. They would go on to found numerous theatres and styles (as well as work beyond the improv stage). Their contributions to the development of improvisational theatre are immeasurable, and while they would all take the stage, none were first and foremost performers.

4. MIKE NICHOLS AND ELAINE MAY

We've made it to #4 on the list in this book about improv performers, and we finally have reached our first set of performers, though both Nichols and May would go on to successful careers off-stage behind the camera. I have grouped them not just because they were a comedy duo but also because improvisation is so dependent on collaboration that it can be challenging to isolate individuals. This intentional framing device is used throughout the book to reflect the reality of improvisational performance as a collaborative art. As such, there aren't 50 performers listed in this book – there are performers, teachers, duos, groups, television shows, and theatres/groups. Nichols and May are the first such inseparable performers, who were the first public faces of improvisational theatre, becoming comedy stars and paving the way for future improvisers to use improvisation as both a system of training/performance and as a springboard to comedy stardom. As individuals and as a duo, Nichols's and May's fingerprints are all over the origins of contemporary improvisational theatre. They are arguably the most important improv performers in theatre history.

Nichols and May were part of the original Compass ensemble in Chicago. May was perhaps the most skilled improviser in the group, capable of working with and flourishing with the entire company. Nichols ... less so. However, working with May seemed to unlock his potential. The two began working together, and their scenes quickly became legendary. As was the practice at Compass and later The Second City, the group began writing and honing successful improvised scenes into scripted sketch comedy. One of their earliest "hits" was a scene called Teenagers. The scene is pretty much what you think it is – two young teenagers navigating their desires within the cultural and social confines of the 1950s. Their rapport and connection, however, made the scene shine. They found humor in reality and then infused that reality with their immense comedic talents. The scene was also an excellent example of the improv revolution – the scenes were about real life, sex, drugs, relationships, and social/cultural expectations. It wasn't the Brechtian workers' theatre Shepherd had imagined, but it was speaking to the realities of the audience in a way that contemporary scripted theatre did not. It just so happened that the audience at The Compass was a white, middle-class, highly educated audience rather than the working-class audience Shepherd wanted. Nichols and May were reflecting – in a hilarious way – the reality of life for young, liberal, middle-class white people.

Nichols and May were instrumental in the success of Compass, both in Chicago and then in St. Louis (May more so in St. Louis as Nichols got fired). They built on that success and became America's premiere comedy duo when they went to Broadway with their show *An Evening With Nichols and May*. The album recording of the performance would go on to win a Grammy Award for Best Comedy Album in 1962, introducing both them and their new improvisational style to a national audience. While not improvised, they used the Compass/Second City model. They would use either literal improv or an improvisational aesthetic (following Spolin's philosophy and guidelines) to develop scenes, then take those scenes and hone them as written sketches.

The duo was also ideally suited to the technology of the time. Their scenes were not highly physical or nonverbal, which was one of the hallmarks of Spolin's teachings and Sills's directorial style. Instead, they were full of wit and wordplay. The comedy was intelligent, yet it remained highly accessible. They often riffed on current events but did so in a simultaneously innocuous and cutting way. Their scenes were uncommonly still, tailor-made for radio and television. Their scenes were auditory delights, and their physical comedy was more subtle, conveyed through facial expressions or small gestures in a way easily captured on television. For instance, the aforementioned "Teenagers" sketch was revolutionary in that it presented young people talking about sex – which simply did not happen. The scene was hardly explicit. They let the topic be taboo rather than filling it with explicit content. The subtext – we all know what they're talking about even if they aren't being overtly sexual – made the scene exhilarating. They also mined vast amounts of comedy from tiny physical bits. When the two characters kiss, an immense amount of laughter is elicited not from the kiss but from the two teens' hands – both have a cigarette in one hand and cannot figure out what exactly to do with the other. It was provocative and acceptable at the same time. When May's character is reluctant to break the social taboo of having sex and worries Nichols's character won't respect her, he replies, "I'd respect you like crazy!" Their comedy was perfect for television. The sketch involves the two sitting together – ostensibly in his father's car, though we only see two chairs. The sketch features hilarious dialogue and physical comedy that a camera easily captures and conveys. They understood comedy for television, and in return, television made them national stars. They arguably understood how to make improvisationally based comedy work better on television than anyone else before or since.

Nichols and May disbanded, like Compass, after a very short time. By 1962, they were working independently. Nicholas would become a film director, while May became a screenwriter. Their influence is immeasurable, and more importantly, their comedy still resonates. "Teenagers" works as well in the 2020s as it did in 1960; "Mother and Son" is a phone call between a busy son and his "very nervous" mother guilting her son for not calling home more. It sounds like it was recorded yesterday. Spolin and Johnstone are the philosophical/theoretical/teaching icons, Shepherd and Flicker are the producers, Sills is the director, and Nichols and May are the foundational improvisational performers. American improvisation, in many ways, replicates the rhythms and relationships formed in Nichols and May's sketches.

5. PAULO FREIRE AND AUGUSTO BOAL

While improvisation is deeply rooted in Chicago (and Calgary), it was developed and used in other places, often with different goals. The philosophical roots of improvisation are deeply invested in using improvisation as a force for social change. While many of the entries in this book are performers in the realm of comedic performance, improv has been used far and wide for many other purposes (see #37), including as a catalyst for social change – including by the Brazilian duo Paulo Freire and Augusto Boal. Freire and Boal had a similar relationship to Neva Boyd and Viola Spolin, with Freire's philosophical approach providing the foundation

Boal would use to create the Theatre of the Oppressed. Like David Shepherd, the Brazilian pair were less concerned with improvisation's performative and comedic potential than its inherent power to catalyze change. Freire's theoretical framework and Boal's implementation (and quite a bit of his own theoretical work) would demonstrate – even more so than Spolin's work – that improvisation was more than just a comedic tool: improvisation could change peoples' lives.

Freire grew up poor in Brazil during the global Great Depression, an experience that would shape his political and social views that came to be defined by social and economic classes. He was already an influential teacher and theorist in 1964 when a military coup forced him into exile (after briefly imprisoning him). During his exile, he wrote several books, including the hugely influential *Pedagogy of the Oppressed* (1968). One of the threads throughout this book is the tight interconnectedness between improvisation and education. Freire was not a performer. He was, at heart, like Spolin and Johnstone, an educator. Freire's work examines the relationship between the oppressed and their oppressor, placing education at the center of the social construction of oppression, meaning it is both the key to maintaining oppression and the key for the oppressed to regain their agency and humanity. As Spolin and Johnstone argued, Freire saw educational models where students were empty vessels waiting to be filled with knowledge as a terrible educational model, what he called "the banking model of education." This educational method is passive and, as such, not that effective. More importantly, it becomes a tool for oppressors as it discourages critical thinking and creativity. Instead, Freire advocates for students to be seen and treated as co-creators of knowledge, thus giving them the tools and agency to overcome and dismantle oppression.

A well-accomplished theorist in his own right, Augusto Boal built upon Freire's philosophy to create the Theatre of the Oppressed. Like Freire, Boal was imprisoned and later exiled (Boal to Argentina, Freire to Chile) after the 1964 military coup in Brazil, which saw the men and their theories as extremely dangerous. Again, like Freire, who published the *Pedagogy of the Oppressed* while in exile, Boal would publish *Theatre of the Oppressed* (1974) in exile. Like Shepherd and Sills, Boal was also heavily influenced by the work and theories of Bertolt Brecht and avidly believed that theatre could bring about social change. Combining the theories of Brecht and Freire with his own brilliance, Boal created a system of theatre designed to give regular people – whom Boal would call spect-actors – the tools they needed to overcome political, social, and cultural injustices. Like everyone else discussed thus far, Boal saw contemporary theatre practice (and education) as problematic in its approach, echoing the critiques in Freire's "The Banking Model." Instead, Boal wanted active participants in the classroom and the theatre. For Boal, that meant not just the actors were active participants but also the audience members.

Boal introduced three types of theatre in *Theatre of the Oppressed*: Forum Theatre, Image Theatre, and Invisible Theatre. He would later introduce a fourth, the Rainbow of Desire. Each type centers the spect-actor. The most widespread of these is Forum Theatre. In a forum theatre piece, a set of actors will perform a short scene involving some sort of oppression relevant to the audience. The players then replay the scene, but the audience is encouraged to stop the action, step into the situation, and actively propose a solution. The audience cannot merely suggest things from their seats – they must actively participate in the action. The concept is that the spect-actor will not only face the challenges of overcoming the oppression but that, with the experience, they will be more likely to take action in their real lives. Forum Theatre has become a large part of Applied Improvisation (see #37). It is one of the main tools in many improv-based Diversity, Equity, and Inclusion (DEI) workshops across corporate America.

Image Theatre is a technique where one person becomes the sculptor and molds one or more actors/players into statues or images onstage. The sculptor ideally avoids using language and instead uses touch to create the images. The idea is to remove language to get to the true meaning of a word through physical expression. For instance, "love" can mean many things, but an image will give all present a concrete expression. Invisible Theatre moves outside the traditional theatrical space and into the streets (or stores or restaurants or train stations ... you get the idea). The players never give away that they are performing and instead attempt to present the performance as an actual event. Onlookers may or may not intervene.[21]

Freire and Boal demonstrated that improvisational performance did not have to be comedic, though comedy is a tool used in Theatre of the Oppressed. As we will see (#37), improvisation outside the theatre has become hugely popular and influential. Freire's and Boal's work has provided a theoretical and practical framework for using improvisation in several ways, and their theories have been applied in numerous fields, including sociology, psychology, therapy, and, as noted, in recent DEI initiatives. Along with the theories of Brecht, their work also ties improvisation at a philosophical level to social change. Even though many people associate improvisation with silliness or frivolity, the philosophical roots of improvisation are deeply invested in using improvisation as a force for social change.

6. JOSEPHINE FORSBERG AND MARTIN DE MAAT

Look, more teachers ... who are related ... and connected to Spolin. The success of The Compass Players, The Second City, and Nicholas and May meant that many young performers wanted to study improvisation. The slight problem was that there were very few opportunities or places for students to study, that is, until Josephine Forsberg opened The Players Workshop in 1970. Not officially affiliated with The Second City, it acted as its de facto training center for many years.

Forsberg had worked with many of the early titans of improvisation in the 1950s with The Playwrights Theatre Club and throughout Chicago. A Shakespearean actress, she was invited to join the original Second City cast but was pregnant and joined the next year as the company's female understudy. After training with Spolin, Forsberg became Spolin's teaching assistant and, by the mid-1960s, was teaching most of the center's classes and leading her "Children's Theatre of The Second City." While formalized improv classes and training centers are now standard, that was not the case in the 1960s. There were workshops and the like, but there was no formal means for a student to take classes until Forsberg created the framework of what would become Players Workshop. Second City's success meant that many aspiring comedians wanted to work there, and Forsberg became many future stars' first improv teacher. She would likewise create and direct the first Second City Touring Company, which spread the theatre's work and style across the country and provided additional training and performing opportunities for aspiring performers.

In 1970, she opened Players Workshop in a different space from Second City, which allowed her to expand her teaching roster and classes (and performance opportunities) but would slowly lead to her divorce from Second City. Between founding the Touring Company and Players Workshop, she had spent a brief sojourn in Colorado, during which other teachers had begun to put their stamp on Second City's training, namely Del Close (see #7). Despite her move, Players Workshop was still seen as the premiere improv training school and retained its informal affiliation with Second City. Countless performers who would adorn Second City's stage trained at Players, as did many others who would teach and perform across the country, including Charna Halpern (see #7). David Shepherd also taught briefly at Players, first rolling out his idea for a new competitive games theatre that would become ImprovOlympic/iO (see #16). Players also trained countless "regular people" in improvisation, who maybe did not aspire to comedy careers but still wanted to learn and perform improvisation. When Andrew Alexander bought The Second City in 1985, the informal arrangement between Forsberg's Players Workshop and the theatre went south, leading to the creation of The Second City Training Center, which hired one of the Players' teachers to lead the new school, Forsberg's nephew Martin de Maat.

Players Workshop would continue for another decade-plus, finally closing in 2003. Still, it had been supplanted by both iO's new training center and Second City's Training Center, in no small part because of the brilliance of Martin de Maat. Because of his connection with his aunt, de Maat had been involved with Second City since he was 18, moving from dishwasher to Artistic Director of The Second City Training Center. He honed his teaching chops working for his aunt (and taking classes with Spolin) teaching workshops at Second City and Players Workshop. However, his work with the Second City Training Center would transform improvisational education. Building on Forsberg's work, he would create a giant scaffolded model of classes in improvisation, acting, and writing that became the bedrock for Second City's training. After a brief stint in New York, where he established himself as a successful theatre and film director, de Maat returned to Chicago to teach improvisation, leading the Second City Training Center from 1985–2000. During that time, de Maat led the center's transformation into the largest improv training center in the world, often called the "Harvard of Improv."

Martin de Maat is one of improv's most beloved teachers, bringing passion and kindness to his classes. His former students speak of him reverently, evoking how he worked to bring out their best and unlock the full potential of improvisation. Jimmy Carrane wrote of de Maat:

> What was amazing about Martin was that you always did your best work in his classes. I can't explain how he did it. It seemed magical … He created a space that wasn't about competition, but about collaboration. He removed the pressure of being funny so you felt you couldn't make a mistake, which of course encouraged everyone to take more risks. He did this with Spolin's games. His classes were part improv, part philosophy. He believed that improv was bigger than just being funny. Though I was young at the time, he was the first person I met that believed improv was bigger than just making people laugh. He was passionate that improv could change the world with concepts like 'yes, and' and 'making your partner look good.' That is what he gave to his students.[22]

De Maat was relentlessly positive, bringing acceptance and positivity to Second City, which worked to counter the negativity that often arises in highly competitive places.

Forsberg and de Maat are often overshadowed by the third storied improv teacher of the last twenty-five years of the 20th century – Del Close. *Chicago Reader* theatre critic Jack Helbig assessed the two teachers, saying, "They used opposite techniques to arrive at the same end." As we'll see, Close was much harsher than de Maat. He "embraced the dark side, dabbling in the occult and reveling in his wild druggy bohemian past. He ripped his students to shreds, interrupting improvisations with bitter criticism." Close even unleashed that negativity on a young de Maat after a Second City show when Close responded to his young audience fan's praise with a wry "I hate children." Contrasting Close's negativity was de Maat's positivity, with Amy Seeley referring to him as "our Yoda." According to Helbig,

> De Maat's strengths were empathetic and emotional. He was a great listener, and he could read a person quicker than anyone I've known. This made him an extraordinary teacher of improvisation. He always seemed to know exactly what to say to break through a student's block or what game to prescribe to change the temperature of a class. He was a born teacher and his students recognized it.[23]

Yet it would not be de Maat who would live on in improv lore as "The Guru." That honor went to his teaching contemporary, Del Close.

7. DEL CLOSE AND CHARNA HALPERN

While Forsberg and de Maat are the forgotten duo of the 1980s and 1990s, Charna Halpern and Del Close are the most celebrated duo of the era, in no small measure because of their work at ImprovOlympic/ iO and the publication of their book, co-written with Kim "Howard" Johnson, *Truth in Comedy* (1994). Close and Halpern have ties to many other icons and serve as a bridge between what Seham describes as the First and Second Waves of improv, marking a shift in performance style and philosophy that morphs improv from a process (sketch comedy) into the product. Their creation and popularization of the Harold transformed what improv could be in performance and largely created what is known today as long form improv (for more info on long form and the Harold, see #16).

Del Close symbolizes much improv history – he's a mixture of myth, legend, lore, and mystique. He's inspirational and problematic. He was a brilliant teacher who could be cruel and deeply misogynistic. He began his career with the St. Louis Compass Players and helped establish the first set of rules or guidelines for improvisational performance, along with Ted Flicker and Elaine May. He spent much of the 1960s between San Francisco and Chicago, sampling the drugs the two cities offered and their respective comedy scenes. He performed, directed, and taught in Chicago with Second City, though he often clashed with Second City producer Bernie Sahlins. The two had the great philosophical debate about improvisation – was it merely a tool or process, as Sahlins argued, or was it a performative end in its own right? They also clashed over Close's erratic behavior. He was a substance abuser and often would miss or skip rehearsals, leaving Sahlins to pick up the pieces. Sahlins fired Close numerous times from Second City, and after one such parting, Close made his way to San Francisco to join The Committee (see #10) and work with The Grateful Dead. As we'll see, The Committee was the first group to perform the Harold. As would become part of Close's legend and lore, many attributed the form directly to him, a claim that he would not fully accept but never refuted despite the contributions made by The Committee and later by Charna Halpern (and the many early students and performers who first worked on the form).

In 1972, he returned from California to Chicago and spent the rest of the decade as Second City's resident director. During this time, he became a celebrated teacher, working with Forsberg, often refusing to teach new students and only working with more advanced students, and continuing his pattern of substance abuse and employment tension with Sahlins. They were both tough teachers, but Close was a notoriously difficult teacher, a misogynist, and quick to hurl negative comments toward his students. However, his work with Improv Olympic would cement his legacy as "the guru." Close would become arguably the most consequential figure within improvisational theatre in the 1980s and 1990s, with his students going on to great success in film, television, and other forms of comedy.

Charna Halpern began her improvisational career like many Chicagoans in the 1970s – she took classes with Forsberg at Players Workshop. Like many other icons, Halpern worked in education, teaching at a juvenile delinquency center. When the grant money for the program dried up, she helped her father hold interviews for the new McDonald's opening in her small hometown of Dixon, IL. That experience helped her land a radio gig and pushed her onto the path of an entertainment career.

When she moved to Chicago, she studied improv at Players Workshop and eventually created ImprovOlympic based on David Shepherd's Canadian version. It was her partnership with Close, however, that would change improvisational theatre forever.

Like anyone working in improv in Chicago in the 1970s, Halpern knew the stories and legends about Del Close. As we'll see, Halpern had become a bit bored with the ImprovOlympic format and knew there was more within improv to unlock. She approached Close, hoping he would come to teach some workshops for her, as he had once again been fired from Second City, but he was skeptical of Halpern and her company. The two had met once before, during an invocation Close held the previous Halloween. They had differing views on the experience, and it seemed they were not destined to work together. A few months later, Close was having coffee at CrossCurrents, which just so happened to be where ImprovOlympic was then performing. Halpern took one more shot, allegedly offering Close $200 and some pot to teach a workshop, promising him total artistic freedom. Referencing their earlier contentious meeting, he replied, "Can I invoke demons?" And their partnership was born. After the first workshop, Halpern knew they had something special and that she had finally found the keys to improv – "I took a year at Players Workshop and thought I knew everything. Then when I got to [Del], I thought, 'Oh my God! I know nothing!'"[24] With the promise that she'd close her "little game theater," Close agreed to work with Halpern. The result would be a brand new ImprovOlympic, which performed long form improvisation and specialized in the Harold.

Close and Halpern were the perfect odd couple, complementing and contrasting one another. Achy Obejas described them in the *Chicago Tribune*, noting that Halpern "is frequently peppy, always tastefully put together." At the same time, Close is "iconoclastic, sloppy, devastatingly dry, and—at least when they met—completely alienated from normalcy to the point that he refused to have a phone for fear of threatening public officials in a moment of rage. He was, frankly, nuts."[25] Close gave Halpern's theatre credibility, while Halpern gave Close the structure and administrative skills he sorely lacked. While Close is often credited with much of iO's creative success, Halpern was the theatre's guiding force, building the company from a rag-tag group that performed in bars into one of the world's most prominent and most influential comedy theatres. The duo spearheaded the philosophical shift from improv as a tool to improv as a performative end in and of itself. They are also responsible for creating long-form performance improvisation, moving from a games-based style (short form based in Spolin's games) to a long form style based on scenes, relationships, and connections. Halpern and Close did have their detractors, and the pair have faced criticism for Close's misogynistic teaching and leadership style, for Halpern's handling of complaints of sexism and racism, as well as iO's sudden closure during the pandemic amidst accusations of institutional racism (see #47).

Close and Halpern helped create long form improv and set the business model for running an improv theatre. While Close was the theatre's artistic leader, Halpern took iO from a nomadic group performing in bars to one of the most influential comedy institutions, one that performs in a multi-million-dollar multi-stage performance complex. Based on *lots* of free labor, that business model likewise came under scrutiny during the pandemic (see #47/48). It also created a true comedy and entertainment titan. The iO model – both in terms of content and administrative structure (both the good and the problematic) – has been copied by lots of theatre and helped launch improvisational theatre into another stratosphere.

8. MICK NAPIER

Last but certainly not least, Mick Napier would reshape improv's rules and what improv could look like on stage. Napier is a performer, teacher, and director, often directing at Second City, but is best known as the founder and artistic director of The Annoyance (see #19). Napier's theories combine Spolin, Johnstone, Close-Halpern, and fuck-off, by which I mean anti-authority. Napier is a disrupter of complacency. He questions authority and how things are done, especially those things that have "always been done that way." His style and that of The Annoyance are often described as punk rock – pushing back against authority and making your own rules. He would be the first major figure to push back on the rules, guidelines, and philosophies that shaped early improvisation.

In the same way that Close and others pushed back on Second City's use of improv as a tool, Napier would push back on the strict adherence to Close's rules and guidelines, mainly via the Harold. It isn't even that he disagreed with them. More so, he was bothered by their strict adherence, feeling that the rules were more harmful than helpful. Ironically, he would use many of the same arguments Johnstone and others used in creating their philosophies to push back on those philosophies – that the "rules" of improv were creating too much order and rote responses and fear of "doing it wrong," and not enough creativity and freedom.

Napier lays out his philosophy in both *Improvise: Scene from the Inside Out* (2004) and *Behind the Scenes: Improvising Long Form* (2015), two must-read texts for any improviser. Napier felt that strict adherence to rules made players worry more about following the rules than being good improvisers. Instead of living by "yes, and," which Napier felt created passive, polite improvisers, he argued for a "take care of yourself first"[26] approach. He argues that to be a good improviser, you must be a good improviser – you cannot solely focus on your partner and what they want/need. You need to give your partner plenty of gifts by being a strong improviser in your own right rather than always passively reacting and worrying about breaking a rule. Instead, Napier argues the most important thing for any improviser is to simply do something – "*That* you do something is far more important than *what* you do ... The audience is waiting. They don't care about your support. They care about what you do. What you do now."[27] This philosophy would anchor The Annoyance and redefine the possibilities of improvisational performance in the 1990s and beyond – forming the philosophical backbone of what Seham defines as The Third Wave of Improv.

In many ways, Napier became the face of improv's blending in the 1990s. The fierce debates of the 1980s between Second City's Bernie Sahlins and iO's Del Close about the role of improv – Sahlins arguing it was best served as a tool, Close arguing it was an art form in its own right – created a dynamic that pitted theatres and improvisers against one another. It was common for an improviser in the 1980s and early 1990s to identify themselves with a particular theatre – "I'm an iO improviser" – and each theatre carried a specific style. Those individual styles are still present, but the walls between institutions began to come down largely because of Napier. That might seem odd given that The Annoyance and many of Napier's theories seem like reactions against iO, but they are alternative paths. Napier's core improv beliefs are similar to those of Johnstone, Spolin, and even Close – he simply disagrees with the almost cult-like devotion to a particular teacher, style, or rule(s). They all want authenticity, truth, and originality in improvisation – Napier simply argues there are many ways to reach those goals. Most importantly, Napier worked across the big three Chicago theatres and helped revitalize Second City. The co-creator and director of many of The Annoyance's biggest hits, including *Co-ed Prison Sluts,* Napier's no-BS approach allows him to navigate between the different needs of the theatres without getting caught in the drama.

As we'll see, by the early 1990s, Second City began to be viewed by some as stagnant or merely a place for tourists. Their sketch comedy revues stayed true to their original format, which led to criticism that the satirical theatre was no longer cutting edge. Meanwhile, The Annoyance was taking the Chicago comedy and improv world by storm with shows like *Co-Ed Prison Sluts, Miss Vagina Pageant*, and *That Darned Antichrist*. Firmly established as Chicago's "alternative theatre," The Annoyance was everything Second City was not: bold, brash, and fearless. So, Second City hired Napier to help revitalize the theatre. Building on the success of *Piñata Full of Bees* in 1995, Napier directed a series of revues at Second City that gave the theatre new life. Starting with 1996's *Citizen Gates*, the first Second City show with a gender-neutral cast (three men and three women, the tradition had always been four men and two women). The "extra" woman he cast? Tina Fey. He followed that in 1997 with *Paradigm Lost*, which deepened the connections between Second City revues and long form improvisation, bringing a greater sense of narrative connectivity and the voice of a new generation to the Second City stage. Napier has since become an artistic associate at Second City, regularly helps with auditions, and continues to direct mainstage revues.

Napier has always made The Annoyance his home. Still, he is so well respected in the improv world that he directed Second City's 50th-anniversary sketch revue and was tasked along with his long-time Annoyance partner (and life partner) Jennifer Estlin to oversee iO's post-pandemic post-racial-reckoning re-birth (see #48). As Second City's Kelly Leonard says, "he's one of the most respected, if not the most respected, living improv minds in the country, no question."[28]

These improv icons created contemporary improvisation. They built the theoretical framework and developed the games, exercises, and forms. They trailblazed how to teach, perform, and direct improvisation. They disagreed with one another and built upon each other's work. To understand their impact, the following section looks at many of the theatres and groups these icons created and inspired.

Notes

1 Sam Wasson, *Improv Nation: How We Made A Great American Art* (New York: Houghton Mifflin Harcourt, 2017), xi.
2 Qtd. in "Free to Experience: Viola Spolin and the Invention of Improvisation," *Inventing Improv*, Chicago Stories, WTTW. https://interactive.wttw.com/chicago-stories/inventing-improv/free-to-experience-viola-spolin-and-the-invention-of-improvisation

3 W. Paul Simon, "Neva Leona Boyd (1876–1963) – Social Group Worker, Professor of Sociology, and Proponent of the Modern Play Movement," VCU Libraries Social Welfare History Project, 2011. https://socialwelfare.library.vcu.edu/people/boyd-neva-leona/

4 Aretha Sills with Carol Sills, "Biography: Viola Spolin," ViolaSpolin.org. https://www.violaspolin.org/bio

5 Qtd. in "Biography: Viola Spolin."

6 Qtd. in Dan Friedman, *Performance Activism: Precursors and Contemporary Pioneers* (New York: Palgrave Macmillan, 2021), 39.

7 Qtd. in "Biography: Viola Spolin."

8 Viola Spolin, Improvisation for the Theater: A Handbook of Teaching and Directing Techniques (Evanston: Northwestern University Press, 1963), 3.

9 Spolin, Improvisation for the Theater, 4.

10 Theresa Robbins Dudeck, "The Man Who Tickled the Great Intelligent Beast." *American Theatre Magazine*, 25 April 2023. https://www.americantheatre.org/2023/04/25/the-man-who-tickled-the-great-intelligent-beast/

11 Qtd. in Neil Genzlinger, "Keith Johnstone, Champion of Improvisational Theater, Dies at 90." *The New York Times*, 14 April 2023. https://www.nytimes.com/2023/04/14/theater/keith-johnstone-dead.html

12 Patti Stiles, "Keith," *Status*, Year 12, Issue 143, May 2023, 10.

13 Keith Johnstone, *Impro for Storytellers* (New York: Routledge, 1999), 1.

14 Qtd. in Neil Genzlinger.

15 "Remembering David Shepherd." The Second City. 18 December 2018. https://www.secondcity.com/remembering-david-shepherd

16 Paul Sills, *Paul Sills' Story Theater: Four Shows* (New York: Applause Books, 2000), Preface.

17 Sheldon Patinkin, *The Second City: Backstage at the World's Greatest Comedy Theatre* (Naperville, IL: Sourcebooks, 2000).

18 Janet Coleman, *The Compass: The Improvisational Theatre that Revolutionized American Comedy* (Hyde Park: University of Chicago Press, 1990), 215.

19 Qtd. in Coleman, 220.

20 Coleman, 225–226.

21 Matt Fotis and Siobhan O'Hara, *The Comedy Improv Handbook: A Comprehensive Guide to University Improvisational Comedy in Theatre and Performance* (New York: Focal Press, 2016), 29–30.

22 Jimmy Carrane, "Remembering Martin de Maat," ImprovNerdBlog, 22 January 2022. https://jimmycarrane.com/remembering-martin-de-maat/

23 Jack Helbig, "The Mysterious Martin de Maat," Chicago Reader, 22 February 2001. https://chicagoreader.com/news-politics/the-mysterious-martin-de-maat/

24 Qtd. in Matt Fotis, *Long Form Improvisation and American Comedy: The Harold* (New York: Palgrave Macmillan, 2014), 55.

25 Achy Obejas, "Comedy Guru Charna Halpern Carries On," *Chicago Tribune*, April 3, 2001. https://www.chicagotribune.com/news/ct-xpm-2001-04-03-0104030038-story.html

26 Mick Napier, *Improvise: Scene from the Inside Out* (Porstmouth, NH: Heine-mann, 2004), 16.

27 Napier, 16.

28 Qtd. in Mark Caro, "Chicago's Mick Napier: Master of Annoyance," *The Chicago Tribune.* 16 May 2014. https://www.chicagotribune.com/entertainment/theater/ct-mick-napier-annoyance-theater-20140516-column.html

PART 3

THE FIRST GROUPS

The luminaries were not working in a vacuum. Many of them worked very closely with (and often founded) some of the first improvisational theatres in the world. Some of these early companies lasted for an incredibly short time, while others are still in operation today. Regardless of how long their doors were open, each group profoundly impacted how improvisational performance developed. This section's first set of entries (#9–15) comprise what Amy Seham has deemed The First Wave of Improv. Even though many of these companies are still active, they were the first theatres to produce improvisational theatre and, for better or worse, set many of the guidelines and traditions of improvisational performance. The next set of entries (#16–17) comprises The Second Wave of Improv. These theatres, established in the 1980s, while directly influenced by First Wave theatres, often rejected or challenged their predecessors' philosophy or working model, most notably in positioning improvisation as the main attraction rather than a creative tool. The last two entries (#19 and #20) mark the beginning of The Third Wave, which emerged in the 1990s and began to reject the theories, philosophy, and structure of The Second Wave.

DOI: 10.4324/9781003359692-3

9. THE COMPASS PLAYERS

Documented extensively in Janet Coleman's *The Compass* and Jeffrey Sweet's *Something Wonderful Right Away*, The Compass Players was the first improvisational theatre in the world. In the July heat of 1955, in a storefront next to a bar in Chicago's Hyde Park, in the shadows of the University of Chicago (and heavily influenced by the institution), The Compass Players opened and fundamentally changed American comedy.

Originally intended as the Brechtian-cabaret-workers' theatre of David Shepherd's dreams, The Compass used improvisation to speak to its audiences. Shepherd wanted a theatre that could speak immediately to the audience's world and knew that the traditional theatrical model was both too slow and too dull (in his opinion) to achieve his goals. Just two years prior, in 1953, he had co-founded The Playwrights Theatre Club with former University of Chicago students Paul Sills and Eugene Troobnick. While the company produced cutting-edge and avant-garde work, including by Bertolt Brecht, Shepherd again grew dissatisfied with the product. In May 1954, he wrote in his journal that he had "helped build a miserable self-centered arts club which talks over the heads of its bourgeois members at the same time it licks their feet for support."[1] Playwrights closed over artistic differences, the grueling production schedule, and political reasons (they had a tough time obtaining and keeping the proper permits, and many felt it was due to the company's left-leaning ideology).

Shepherd tried again to create his ideal theatre with Compass, hoping to "remove the glass curtain that's formed between the actors and the audience."[2] Rather than relying on the words of European playwrights, this time, Shepherd turned instead to the commedia dell'arte for inspiration. Commedia plays were structured around a series of plot points, but it was up to the performers to move the action from point to point – in other words, they improvised. Shepherd wanted to use the same format, scenario plays, with Compass. Shepherd and others in the company would write the outline for a play but leave it to the actors to fill in the dialogue. With the scenario play format in place, the company turned to Viola Spolin and Paul Sills to train the company in improvisation. The company debuted with Roger Bowen's scenario *Enterprise*, about a dubious used-car salesman meant to show the dangers of American enterprise. Rather quickly, Compass was performing sold-out shows six nights a week.

In addition to a brand-new scenario play every week, they performed "Living Newspapers," harkening back to the form popularized during the Federal Theater Project in the 1930s. Compass actors would read newspaper articles aloud onstage and then act out and expand upon the articles, attempting to show both the humor within the stories and the "real" story behind the story. After the semi-scripted scenario play, the evening usually ended with scenes inspired by audience suggestions. Legend has it that the owner of the Compass Tavern, where they performed, wanted the shows to be longer so he could sell more drinks, and thus the audience suggestion scenes were born. Much to Shepherd's chagrin, the improvised scenes grew in popularity, while the scenario plays became increasingly laborious. Rather than reflecting the working class, many Compass scenarios instead reflected their actual audience, so scenes were more about the white middle-class anxieties of the 1950s than class oppression. That's not to say they weren't political or early forms of social and cultural satire that would come to form Second City's identity. It just wasn't what Shepherd wanted.

The actors also preferred the improvised bits and soon began writing, rehearsing, and polishing the improvised scenes into scripted sketches that were subsequently performed (see Nichols and May). Compass performers were becoming stars, with Nichols and May at the forefront. Folks like Severn Darden, Shelley Berman, Barbara Harris, Alan Alda, Valerie Harper, and many more started with Compass. Despite their immediate success, the group disbanded in 1957. In part due to their grueling production schedule (a new scenario every week on top of writing and rehearsing their bits), plus an ill-fated move to a more traditional theatre space on the North Side of Chicago that transformed their audience from intellectual University of Chicago types to more well-to-do North Siders contributed to Compass's demise. The driving factor was the competing aesthetic visions for the group. Shepherd desperately wanted that politically charged workers' theatre.

A second Compass branch was opened in St. Louis under the direction of Ted Flicker. Shepherd was again involved, but less so than in Chicago, where he was integral to the company's operations. While the Chicago Compass created improvisational performance, the St. Louis branch sought to consider the performative aspects of the genre more fully – including the audience experience. The Chicago Compass had a specific audience – white, liberal, and highly educated. The St. Louis branch led by Flicker wanted to expand the audience, and their primary vehicle to do that was standardization. That's not to say that they stripped improv of its spontaneity, far from it. Instead, Flicker and the St. Louis branch – mostly Elaine May – worked to help create systems and structures that would more often lead to successful improvisation. The most notable of these are the Kitchen Rules (see #3). Flicker also instituted a dress code and constantly drilled the company in a louder, faster, funnier approach. Flicker sought to highlight the process and magic of improvisation by creating a more carnivalesque atmosphere than the bohemian hipster vibe of the Chicago branch.

Like its Chicago predecessor, the St. Louis branch had a short life. But both branches were immeasurably crucial to the development of improvisational theatre. The Chicago branch would directly lead to Second City, while the St. Louis branch laid the foundation for iO and other improv-as-the-product style theatres. It is also a bit obvious, but there was no improvisational theatre before The Compass Players. Improv had been used in performance, including by Spolin and her Young Actors Company. But nobody had used improvisation as the driving creative force to talk about the social, cultural, and political world around them. Given the "quest for normalcy" that marked much of American life in the 1950s, The Compass is even more revolutionary – getting onstage every night with little more than an outline and a newspaper and then performing without a script about the world around them was a genuinely revolutionary act that transformed American performance.

10. THE COMMITTEE

The Compass Players and The Second City get most of the attention when it comes to early improvisational theatres. Still, San Francisco's The Committee is integral to developing long form improvisational theatre, becoming the first theatre that performed what would become the Harold and long form improv. The Committee was likewise the most overtly political improv-based theatre in the 1960s. Hired by The Second City in 1961, Alan Myerson quickly grew dissatisfied because, in his opinion, there was "no real solid political stance in the theatrical culture there."[3] Echoing Shepherd's critiques of New York theatre in the 1950s, Myerson felt Second City was more interested in a mass popular audience and less interested in biting political satire. Much as Del Close and Second City had a rocky relationship, so did Myerson and the famed comedy theatre, as Myerson reportedly picketed the theatre during the Cuban Missile Crisis. As with most disputes, there was some truth to both sides. Second City was catering more and more to a popular audience, but they were also still the hub of performance-based political satire.

So, Myerson and his wife Latifah Taormina, headed west to San Francisco, a place they felt more accurately reflected their political points of view. They quickly formed The Committee, named after the 1950s House Un-American Activities Committee made famous by Senator Joe McCarthy. Like Shepherd, Myerson's "main mission was to afflict the comfortable," yet like The Compass, their audience was mainly made up of the comfortable, what Art Peterson described as the "hangers out, college kids, old beatniks and liberal dentists."[4] The Committee performed sketch comedy and improvisation, including the Harold. The staple of long form improvisation and the signature style of iO, the Harold was first developed by The Committee. Del Close had joined the group after another parting with Second City, though he was hardly the exclusive father of the form as is often attributed. The Committee had been experimenting with longer improvised scenes, and several group members had been tinkering with ways to give those longer pieces some structure (not too much, after all, this is San Francisco in the 1960s).

Three members of the group made significant contributions to the creation of the form, and of course, all members helped to develop and shape the early Harold. According to Myerson, the first Harold "was simultaneously developed by a class he was teaching at San Francisco State, a Committee workshop in games taught by Del, and a third class, a musical workshop with selected members of the company headed by pianist Allaudin (Bill) Mathieu."[5] The three men had all come to the same idea – a collage of interconnected scenes that allowed for callbacks and connections, "an interweaving of scenes that returned, made references to one another, and sometimes directly crossed over. The games served to heighten and crystalize previously introduced ideas, playing in counterpoint to the other characters."[6] Through workshops and performances, they continued to hone the form, though it would not be until Close and Halpern teamed up at iO that it would take its current state (more fully explored in #16). When The Committee finally settled on their Harold structure of interweaving scenes, Close declared, "We've invented a new form of theatre! This is amazing! This is the future! We've got to have a name for it." Mathieu sarcastically suggested, "Well, Harold's a nice name." The group all laughed, adopted the moniker, and eventually, it just stuck, a fact that would bother Close for the next three decades.[7] The Committee performed the first Harold in 1967, but it would take another 17 years before the form crystalized at iO. The Committee established that improvisation could be performed by the entire company rather than limited to a set number of players in a sketch, scenario play, or game. Everyone could contribute in real-time.

11. THE SECOND CITY

There is little debate regarding the most influential comedy theatre: The Second City. It is the most influential American theatre of the past 50 years – I said what I said. *The New York Times* critic Clive Barnes summed up the company's influence in a 1969 review, stating, "The entire recent tradition of American theatrical satire can be summed up in three words: 'The Second City.'"[8] Since its founding in 1959 by Paul Sills, Bernard Sahlins, and Howard Alk, The Second City has been the dominant force in improv-based comedy. Ironically, Second City was also at the forefront of placing improvisation into the process rather than the product category, using improv to create scripted sketch comedy.

The Second City followed in The Compass's footsteps, using the process/practice of improvising audience-suggested scenes, refining those through a script-writing process, and then presenting the polished versions as sketch comedy. Rather than create scenario plays, The Second City produces sketch comedy revues, which, according to Sahlins, is "a stage presentation that uses short scenes of varying lengths. Add music and songs and think of it as generally comical and topical by nature."[9] Each revue is built around a particular topic, say artificial intelligence, and contains a variety of scenes – blackouts, parodies, songs, relating scenes, character scenes, and improvised games. Much like the early Harold, which was a collage of interweaving scenes, a sketch comedy revue makes its satiric point through the way ideas combine and interconnect rather than through a traditional narrative arc.

The Second City was immediately successful, and the company quickly moved to its current home on Wells Street, where it expanded into a comedy complex. As noted earlier, The Players Workshop served as the company's informal training center for many years until The Second City Training Center opened under the direction of Martin de Maat in 1985. The Second City Touring Company was established in 1967, which sent teams of performers around the country performing "best of" shows, spreading Second City's influence while also providing a valuable training ground for up-and-coming performers. Satellite campuses opened across North America, with Second City's opening in Detroit, Las Vegas, Los Angeles, and elsewhere. Some flourished, and some floundered, but none were more critical than the Toronto branch of Second City, which opened in 1973. Featuring among its cast Dan Aykroyd, Eugene Levy, John Candy, and Gilda Radner, the Toronto branch would become hugely influential. Of their many achievements, the Toronto branch launched *SCTV* in 1976 (on the heels of many of Second City's top talents joining the original 1975 cast of *Saturday Night Live*, a relationship that continues to this day with Second City being one of the primary talent sources for *SNL*). With the Toronto branch's success, the new Touring Company, and the theatre's ties to *SNL* and *SCTV*, Second City had become a comedy powerhouse by the mid-1970s. The company would expand in 1983, adding a second stage – Second City e.t.c., with their first revue, *Cows on Ice*.

The format for Second City revues has remained relatively stable during its sixty-plus-year history, which has been both a source of pride and criticism. In a review of 1988's *Kuwait Until Dark; or, Bright Lights, Night Baseball*, one reviewer summed up Second City at the time:

> In the end, my ambivalence persists. I don't know. I guess I'm hungry for something spicier. Even when it's good, this is cafeteria food. What happened to Second City's reputation for cut-and-slash satire? Are they consciously appealing to an upscale audience by hanging back and pulling their punches? Is this the gentrification of Second City? Have they become, God forbid, an institution?[10]

Longtime Chicago theatre critic Jack Helbig likewise commented on Second City of the 1980s, saying, "the Second City of the 80s perfected the corporate comedy revue, absolutely free of satire and controversy, capable of entertaining the most philistine of audiences without a single challenge to their values or wit."[11] Those criticisms would disappear with *Piñata Full of Bees* (1995). Directed by Tom Gianas and featuring Adam McKay, Rachel Dratch, Scott Adsit, Scott Allman, Jon Glaser, and Jenna Jolovitz, the revue suddenly made Second City hip and relevant again. They replaced the traditional live piano/keyboard with rock music, the sketches were much more interconnected with virtually no blackouts, and all the costume changes happened in full view of the audience. The real revolution was the darker tone rather than the style, with Helbig calling this show "easily the funniest and most intelligent, surprising, and creative stuff Second City has done in a long time."[12]

The Second City would spend the next several decades facing similar criticism of being too stodgy and responding by making new stylistic/tonal revisions. Like many other improv and comedy theatres, Second City was reshaped (maybe?) during the pandemic and the racial reckoning of American comedy, more fully explored in #47/48, where the theatre attempted to reshape its future to be more inclusive. Despite its limitations, The Second City reshaped American comedy in the late 20th century. It continues to be a powerful force in 21st-century comedy, remaining at the pinnacle of live improv-based performance for over sixty years.

12. THE GROUNDLINGS

The Groundlings began in Los Angeles in 1972 as The Gary Austin Workshop, named after its founder and former member of The Committee, wait for it, Gary Austin. The company was initially a workshop space where folks could come and work together. It became so popular with performers that they began doing shows. In 1974, they officially became The Groundlings (with 50 company member co-founders), an homage to the working-class audiences that stood at the foot of the stage to watch Shakespearean theatre (and yet another example of a company founded on the philosophy of creating art for "regular" people). Like many contemporary comedy theatres, they perform a variety of styles, with sketch comedy as the primary offering. Again, like their predecessors, The Groundlings started in a small space, found success rather quickly, and moved to a larger and more permanent space (they secured the space in 1975 but did not officially move in until 1979). Being in Los Angeles didn't hurt either, as the company quickly became a training ground for comics looking for careers in film and television. Lily Tomlin hired several original members to write for *The Lily Tomlin Show* and Lorne Michaels hired Laraine Newman to be part of the original cast of *Saturday Night Live*, the start of a pipeline that would include Will Ferrell, Phil Hartman, Jon Lovitz, Julia Sweeney, Cheri Oteri, Chris Kattan, Ana Gasteyer, Chris Parnell, Maya Rudolph, Will Forte, Kristen Wiig, Taran Killam, Mikey Day, Heidi Gardner, and Chloe Fineman.

The Groundlings opened a training school in 1979, and Suzanne Kent founded The Sunday Company in 1982 as a vehicle for talented students to continue training and performing. Performers would have to join The Sunday Company before becoming eligible to join the Main Company. Several notable performers came through The Sunday Company, including Conan O'Brien, Jimmy Fallon, Rita Wilson, Darryl Hannah, and Nasim Pedrad. The Groundlings remained committed to a committee approach, with the Main Company collectively becoming the artistic director in 1989. Each new sketch comedy revue was directed by either a current or former Main Company member. In addition to the Main Company shows, The Groundlings began producing alternative shows, including Paul Rubens *The Pee Wee Herman Show* and Melanie Graham's *Cooking With Gas*, a short form improv show that quickly became a staple for the company (and often features celebrity guests).

The Groundlings style is rooted in Spolin's work but heavily emphasizes developing specific characters. Many alumni who have made it to *SNL* and beyond, like Melissa McCarthy, Lisa Kudrow, Kristen Wiig, Will Ferrell, Maya Rudolph, and Phil Hartman, are well-known for playing strong and specific characters. They tend to shy away from the "game of the scene" style of improv that is so fundamental to The Upright Citizens Brigade style of improv (see #20). Given The Groundling's immense success and the career paths of so many alums, it has become the premiere improv and sketch comedy theatre in Los Angeles.

13. THE BRAVE NEW WORKSHOP

Dudley Riggs was born in Arkansas but spent most of his youth and early adulthood traveling. An aerialist and circus performer with roots in vaudeville, he had been bantering with and using audience suggestions in performance for decades. When the physical demands of being an aerialist became too great, he transferred his improvisation to the stage, creating a touring comedy company called the Instant Theatre Company (1954–58). They had a space in New York but mainly performed on the road, often asking the audience for suggestions to inspire their performances. Riggs didn't exactly call it improvisation, which he associated with jazz, preferring instead to call it instant theatre. Whatever he called it, he was tapping into the same spirit as The Compass Players and Second City. Despite touring in the winter, Riggs relocated to Minneapolis in 1958, establishing a more permanent home for Instant Theatre at the Dudley Riggs' Café Espresso, which was ostensibly a coffee shop but was really a comedy theatre. According to Riggs, "The espresso was really only kind of a front for having a subversive theater."[13]

The early performances included all sorts of stuff – music, poetry, comedy – and weren't always well attended.[14] Located near the University of Minnesota, the coffee shop theatre began pulling in students and professors, like the original Compass crowd near the University of Chicago. Word began to spread, high schoolers began to show up, and the theatre went from unsure if there would be a show tomorrow to an underground sensation. They began to settle into political and cultural satire, ditching the more eclectic approach to performance. The group moved (or was evicted) a few times. In 1965, they eventually settled into the uptown neighborhood of Minneapolis at 2605 Hennepin Ave, where they would stay (with one brief move) until relocating downtown in 2014. They changed the name to Dudley Riggs' Brave New Workshop in 1961, taking the name from Aldous Huxley's dystopic novel.

Aside from a COVID hiatus, the company has produced satiric sketch comedy revues for decades, often with a stronger bite than one might expect from an area known for "Minnesota Nice." Like Compass and Second City, Brave New Workshop is interested in social, cultural, and political satire. Their revue *The Future Lies Ahead* took on Nixon and his "lies," opening before the Watergate scandal broke. According to Riggs, the local major paper "*The Star Tribune* said it was about meaningless events and a waste of the audience's time. But it was about Watergate. Six months later, people came back and said, gee, you sure had that one right."[15] It also got them a brick thrown through their window. So goes the life of a political satire theatre.

While they don't boast the sheer numbers of commercially successful alums as Second City or The Groundlings (nobody does), BNW has produced many successful comics (and a senator) who have worked in live comedy, television, and film (and the US Senate), like Al Franken, Tom Davis, Louie Anderson, Mo Collins, Pat Proft (wrote *Naked Gun*), and *Daily Show* co-founder Lizz Winstead. The Brave New Workshop continues to this day, though they have left the more trendy and younger uptown neighborhood for the more commercially lucrative downtown (for various reasons). As with all comedy, folks seem to lament "the good old days," but that's probably more mythology than reality. More importantly, like Second City, BNW has lasted over half a century. According to Riggs, who was used to an itinerant life where one gig led to the next, "Nobody that I know of ever thought that this would last that long, and I certainly didn't. I was a suitcase act, and always figured I'd go back on the road again. I always think there's another engagement coming up. You can't ever completely unpack."[16] While Riggs was fundamental to BNW, John Sweeney and Jenni Lilledahl bought the theatre from him in 1997, vowing to continue his legacy (Riggs was associated with the theatre until his death in 2020), which they have now done for over a quarter-century.

14. THE LOOSE MOOSE THEATRE COMPANY

When Keith Johnstone left England for a position at the University of Calgary in 1972, he set up one of the most important improv companies in the world – The Loose Moose Theatre Company. Co-founded by Johnstone and Mel Tonken in 1977, the company has become the home of Theatresports, created new forms such as Maestro, Gorilla Theatre, and Life Game, and has become one of the most essential companies in developing performers and improv teachers.

Johnstone taught at the University of Calgary and heavily incorporated improvisation into his acting classes. The students gravitated to the work, and rather quickly, Johnstone began the Secret Impro Show on campus during lunchtime. According to Clem Martini, "Fifteen minutes before we were going to stage it, someone would write the place on a scrap of paper and pin it to the board. We'd perform for whoever showed up."[17] After several years of developing improvisers at university, many of them wanted a professional place to perform. Led by Tonken, a veterinarian and former student, Johnstone put his enormous brilliance into what would become Loose Moose. Based on Johnstone's philosophy and teachings, Loose Moose adopted the Theatresports style – two teams competing in improvised games. Wanting to create a space where the audience felt free to interact with the show, Johnstone kept ticket prices low and the audience engagement high by treating the shows like a sporting event, complete with winners and losers, trading cards, and a commentator. Like many other improv-based theatres, Loose Moose wanted a different kind of theatre with a different type of audience than traditional theatre.

In 1982, Bruce McCulloch, Mark McKinney, Garry Campbell, Norm Hiscock, and Frank van Keeken asked Johnstone about adding a late-night sketch show, and true to Johnstone's ethos, he agreed. Johnstone gave them both literal space to do the show and creative space, knowing that the best way to get better at something was to do it. He also stayed true to the idea that the audience is most important. Speaking about the foray into sketch comedy, Johnstone reflected:

> Anybody could do a late-night show on evenings when we weren't occupied as long as they could get an audience. I wouldn't let them just f— about. So I saw their show, which was totally chaotic, and I refused to give them any notes. I said, "I'm an old guy"—I was about 45 or something—"and you had this fantastic teenaged audience." What may look like s—to me, may be the very thing that has value.[18]

The show – *Late Nite Comedy* – was a hit with young audiences. Buoyed by Johnstone's support, the group left Loose Moose to try their luck in Canada, with McCulloch and McKinney becoming half of the famed group *Kids in the Hall*, while Campbell, Hiscock, and van Keeken became writers for the group.

While comedy was Loose Moose's calling card, they continued to produce traditional theatre until 1989. Theatresports was booming, and the company entered a very fertile period. In 1995, though, Johnstone handed over Artistic Director duties to longtime company member Dennis Cahill, who oversaw the company's move from its longtime home at an old cattle auction pavilion to the Garry Theatre in Inglewood, until they moved again in 2005 to the Crossroads Market. In 1998, the company began the Loose Moose International Improvisation Summer School, a destination learning opportunity for Theatresports players and teachers worldwide. It was so desirable partly because of Johnstone himself, of course, but it was also because Johnstone and Loose Moose had begun licensing their shows, allowing the formats to spread across the globe. Rather than try to open Loose Moose branches, they allowed other theatres to license and perform Theatresports. Eventually, in 1998, they created The International Theatresports Institute (ITI) to handle the licensing, transferring the ownership from Loose Moose to the Institute. The ITI created a global Theatresports empire, producing Theatresports shows in nearly 50 countries. Johnstone passed away in 2023, just over 50 years after he arrived in Calgary and transformed improvisational performance, in large part, via his work at Loose Moose.

15. THE MATCH – ROBERT GRAVEL AND YVON LEDUC

While Johnstone was building Loose Moose in Calgary with wrestling as an inspiration, in Montreal, Robert Gravel and Yvon Leduc – who one could argue should be in the Luminaries section – were creating one of the most Canadian things ever to exist – Le Théâtre de la Ligue Nationale d'Improvisation (The National League of Improvisation, or LNI). Debuting in October 1977, the LNI's signature performance format – The Match – has been exported to most of the Francophone world. One of the most widespread improv formats in the world, The Match is the dominant form of improv in France, Belgium, Switzerland, and most of the French-speaking world, as well as places where French improvisers had a significant influence, such as Argentina. The Match, along with Theatresports and Chicago-style long form improv, make up the world's three most widespread forms of improv, forming the base for nearly all comedic improv.

Originally members of the Experimental Theatre of Montreal, Gravel and Leduc wanted to create a form of theatre where the performer–audience relationship was more central and came up with the idea to mix hockey with improvisational theatre. There are similarities in structure with Theatresports, including the idea of making the theatrical experience more like attending a sporting event. Much like Johnstone, Gravel's initial concept was to further explore performance possibilities that centered the actor and more fully incorporated the audience into the performance. While hockey-based improv might seem silly and frivolous, as we've seen with The Compass and other groups, Gravel was attempting to restructure traditional theatrical performance to give performers more freedom and audiences a more interactive and visceral experience. While Theatresports used wrestling as its inspiration, The Match is based on hockey and pushes the sporting elements MUCH further. For starters, rather than a stage, The Match is performed in a miniature hockey rink (sans ice), with the audience on at least three sides (with the apparent limitations of certain theatres and spaces). The improvisers wear hockey sweaters to delineate their team, and each team has a coach. There is a referee (likewise dressed as a hockey ref, who often also has two assistants), an organist, and an emcee/announcer. The timing is slightly different, but The Match unfolds like a hockey game, with three 30-minute periods and two 10-minute intermissions.

Like Theatresports, The Match features two teams of six players (three men and three women) competing in a series of improvised games. An evident influence for ComedySportz, which would open in 1984 in Milwaukee, audience members are integrated into the performance from the second they enter the arena. Each audience member is given a voting card with the color of each team on either side and a noisemaker. Much like ComedySportz would later do, the athletic aspect of the show is front and center – they even have their own Hall of Fame.[19] The teams enter like athletic teams, led by their captain, as the audience cheers. They do warmups in full view of the audience, much like at a sporting event. They then sing a pseudo-national anthem, a Quebecois folk song edited to suit the occasion. After the anthem, the players head to their respective benches that mimic actual hockey benches.

At the same time, the emcee announces the ground rules before the referee selects the first game from a bowl that contains hundreds of game possibilities. As with some Theatresports and ComedySportz games, the teams either play comparatively – they each play a game and the audience decides who is better, or a mixed game, where there is only one game played, but it features members from both teams playing together. Either way, the audience decides who should win each game using their voting cards. Before each game begins, teams get twenty seconds to do a quick planning session. The format repeats for three 30-minute periods (mimicking hockey's format, albeit with longer periods), with the audience ultimately picking the winner of the match.[20]

The Match has quite strict rules for the games and the structure of the show, and those rules help to provide structure for the format, though they can cause frustration among players. The strict structure acts as a control mechanism for the uncertainty of improvisation – we might not know what will happen onstage, but we know precisely how the show's structure will unfold. The Match is a series of short form games. For each game, the referee draws the challenge from a bin, and as noted, the game is either played comparatively or mixed (the number of each type is usually set before the match). Each game usually has relatively strict rules – from the number of players, sometimes even the particular breakdown of genders (e.g., two women from the Blue team and one woman from the Red). Aside from the rules of each game, which are essentially the same as other short form improv games, the other particularity of The Match is that the referee will call out the scene's duration. So, before the scene starts, the players know that the scene must be two minutes and 30 seconds, or in rare cases, even upwards of 20 minutes. As noted, each period is 30 minutes long, and if a game or scene is not finished when the siren goes off, ending the period, the game begins again at the start of the next period – picking up *exactly* where it left off. For games that end during the period, the audience votes for the winning team, who wins a point. The team with the most points wins the match.

The referee patrols the playing area during the game and can call "faults" on the players. As in hockey, there are two categories: major and minor. Major faults are ones where the infraction ruins the game and are rare. A major fault costs two penalty points. Minor faults are more common, cost one penalty point, and include dragging (playing too slow), wrong number of players, violation of the theme, confusion, obstruction, and blocking. Specific gestures go along with each fault, which helps make the referee's role more performative (the audience receives a fault card that explains each fault). Faults are assigned to an individual player or the entire team. When a team has three faults, the other team receives a point. When an individual player receives three faults, they go to the penalty box for five to ten minutes. If a player gets two faults in one game, they are expelled from the game.

The audience can also call faults. Each audience member receives a slipper that can be thrown into the rink, meant to mimic the hockey tradition of fans throwing things onto the ice – hats when a player scores three goals (or a hat-trick). In Detroit during the playoffs, fans will throw octopi, while the Florida Panthers fans throw rubber rats onto the ice ... so, maybe slippers aren't so bad. The slippers are another way to link improv to hockey and mimic the atmosphere of a sporting event. Audience members can throw slippers onto the stage to celebrate a good scene or to show their disdain for a scene or particularly bad joke. What is more common, however, is audience members throwing their slippers at the referee after they make a call the audience doesn't like. Team captains can request an explanation for any fault called, though faults are rarely overturned. At the end of the third period, the team with the most points wins. The winning team gets two points, and at the end of the season, the top 4 teams play in a championship tournament (early incarnations often only had four or five teams).

The Match and the LNI became quite popular, with its matches often broadcast on Télé-Québec from 1982 to 1988. They also formalized their format, with the competitions building to the Charade Cup, an improvisational version of hockey's Stanley Cup. The 1980s also saw the expansion of LNI within Quebec and abroad. Thanks to television, the format was quickly copied throughout Quebec, with amateur teams and leagues popping up in schools and communities. The Match was introduced to France in 1982, which sparked an improv-extravaganza in the country based on The Match, which ultimately led to the creation of la Ligue d'improvisation française (LIF) in France (in 1987, LIF was joined by LIFI in France – Ligue d'Improvisation française d'Île-de-France). Thanks to The Match's popularity in France and the tours of LNI and LIF, the format quickly spread through the French-speaking world, with teams and leagues appearing in Belgium, Luxembourg, Switzerland, Morocco, Congo, and elsewhere. In 1985, on the back of their European tours, they created the first Improvisation World Cup, which brought teams from France, Belgium, and Switzerland to Montreal. In 1988, the first Spanish-speaking Match improv was founded in Argentina (see #45).

The Match is the foundation of contemporary improvisational theatre in the French-speaking world and is, to this day, still the dominant form of improv in most Francophone countries. The Match is so entrenched in places that other improv forms sometimes have had trouble emerging. Improv in Quebec has mainly remained based in The Match, while in France, other forms like Chicago-style long form and improvised musicals have begun to emerge, but only relatively recently. Improvisers across the globe tend to find comfort in strict forms like The Match, ComedySportz, and Theatresports, especially as beginning improvisers, because there are very clear guidelines. The strictness of the format can act as a safety for performers (and audience members), though often, as players become more experienced, they will find themselves wanting to try other less restrictive forms. That's not to say that The Match is bad or that as players gain experience, they abandon the form. Still, it is a typical trajectory – both for individual improvisers and the evolution of improv in any particular city or country. Even in places like France, where other styles and forms have emerged and gained popularity, The Match is still overwhelmingly popular. The Match's influence on contemporary improvisational theatre has been monumentally important.

The next set of entries is technically no longer in what Amy Seham defines as the First Wave of Improv. Primarily founded in the 1980s and 1990s, I have included them in this section because two decades after Seham's *Whose Improv is it Anyway?* created those categories, these theatres – iO, ComedySportz, Comedy Store Players, The Annoyance, and Upright Citizens Brigade – have become fundamental. Yes, many of them were reactions/responses to the earlier theatres (or, as we'll see, as reactions against one another), but they now form the bedrock of improvisational theatre.

16. IO

iO was created to settle the debate between Del Close and Second City producer Bernie Sahlins about the role of improvisation. Well, not literally, but it became a symbol for what improvisation could be and is often cited as the birthplace and home of long form improvisation, thanks to iO's (re)creation of the Harold. Sahlins thought improv was best suited as a tool, which is how Second City has used it, preferring to present scripted and rehearsed sketch comedy revues as the final product. Close thought improv should be the end product. As Travis Stern argues, "iO was the first to move away from humor solely as sketch comedy. Second City performers put on a sketch show, then let the audiences stay for free to see something unscripted."[21] It took Close a few years to make his way to iO, but when he did, Close and Charna Halpern would change how improvisation functioned by making improv the product audiences paid to come and see.

iO's story, however, starts with David Shepherd. His second attempt to create his populist theatre, ImprovOlympics[22] was founded in 1981 to make improv the product. "The problem with Compass," Shepherd said, "was I lost track of the fact that what I was trying to do was based on the audience, not the performers."[23] To remedy this problem, Shepherd created a competitive format not unlike Theatresports called The Improvisational Olympiad, which he had been workshopping in Canada.

In his second populist theatre, two teams of improvisers would compete in a series of ten improv games, with the audience picking the winner each night. It wouldn't only be "professional" improvisers performing. To build his populist theatre, he also wanted teams of amateurs performing, grouped almost like a medieval guild, such as The God Squad (a team of rabbis), The Freudian Slippers (a team of psychologists), or The Court Jesters (a team of lawyers). Performing at Forsberg's Players Workshop, the new group was successful and intrigued one of the students studying there – Charna Halpern. She wanted to join Shepherd in his new venture, and they eventually paired up to launch ImprovOlympics.

The new theatre had moderate success, but Halpern and Shepherd quickly grew dissatisfied. Once again, Shepherd felt like he had failed to create the workers' theatre of his dreams and left, while Halpern stayed on but found the format repetitive and began to tire of the game structure. As luck would have it, in 1983, Second City had once again fired its resident director, Del Close. Like everyone in Chicago's comedy scene, Halpern knew of Close and wanted him to teach a workshop for her. The legend goes Halpern offered Close $200 and some pot to teach a class on whatever he wanted. The two had a little back-and-forth about a previous encounter at a Close-led séance that Halpern was not thrilled with, and he agreed to teach a workshop. Close's workshop showed Halpern that there was more to improv than the games she was playing, and they agreed to close ImprovOlympics and rebrand it as the home of long form improv and a new form Close had been working on for more than a decade called the Harold. They re-opened the new ImprovOlympic on October 1, 1984, rebranded as Home of the Harold, the world's first exclusively long form improv theatre.

The basic Harold structure has underpinned most long form improv structures, relying on relationships, callbacks, and connections. As was The Committee's original intention, most Harolds are performed by the entire team or company (usually 6–12 players), putting everyone onstage together (though not everyone is in every scene). The traditional 9x9 Harold has loosened over the years, but the basic format is as follows:

```
Opening
1A      1B      1C (The First Beat)
Group Game
2A      2B      2C (The Second Beat)
Group Game
3A      3B      3C (The Third Beat)
Ending
```

The nuts and bolts of "how" can vary greatly, so I will briefly lay out the basic "what" of the structure. The opener provides ideas, generates group mind among the players, and allows the audience to be "in" on the process – they can see where all of the later ideas are generated. The First Beat is three separate scenes, usually with 2–4 players. The scenes each pull some idea, premise, or concept from the opener. The First Beat lays the foundation, and the A, B, and C scenes must be far apart regarding content/theme. The Group Games allow the entire ensemble to reconnect, revisit, and expand upon themes. The Second Beat is about heightening and expanding the previous scenes (2A will build and expand the world of 1A, 2B for 1B, and 2C for 1C). These can take any number of forms but generally either follow the plot of the original scene, expand the world, develop the game of the scene (see #19 for more info), or explore a theme. The second group game reconnects the entire ensemble and helps launch them into the Third Beat, where all the characters, themes, and ideas begin connecting between the beats. In a traditional Harold, we still have three scenes (3A, 3B, and 3C), but the Third Beat can vary from one big scene to a series of very short scenes. The Harold has become more flexible since its debut in 1984, and as noted, it does form the foundation of most other long form structures. Behind the Harold, ImprovOlympic became THE long form improv destination.

Over the next decade, ImprovOlympic transformed from a rag-tag group of improvisers performing at various bars and locales to the preeminent exclusively improv theatre in the world, complete with their very own permanent space a few steps from Wrigley Field. In 1994, Close, Halpern, and one of the first company members, Kim "Howard" Johnson, wrote *Truth in Comedy*, which lays out the Harold and explains the ImprovOlympic style and philosophy and gave the theatre a global reach. One of the key concepts in the book is Close's idea of Slow Comedy. While Johnstone argues players should respond with their first thought to avoid overthinking and to release their true spontaneity, Close argues that players should take more time and respond with their third thought. Close felt the first thought would be a knee-jerk reaction, the second would be a reaction to the first, but the third would bring more truth, honesty, and humor. It underpinned another key Close concept – play to the top of your intelligence. He wanted performers to be smart, to avoid playing to the lowest common denominator, and to respect the audience by presenting them with "smart" choices. Slow Comedy is a bit of a misnomer because the idea is that through training, improvisers can access that third thought quickly, so he wasn't advocating for prolonged scenes with lots and lots of pauses (though he was perfectly fine with silence onstage and encouraged it).

Despite Close's passing in 1999, ImprovOlympic thrived over the next several decades, changing its name to iO, opening iO West in Los Angeles (it technically opened in 1997 before Close's passing, but the theatre came into its own in the early 2000s), and publishing the book *Art by Committee* in 2005. With an impressive and ever-expanding roster of successful alumni, most notably Tina Fey and Amy Poehler, they eventually moved to what can only be described as an improvisational complex in 2014. Everything seemed to be going great … until it wasn't. Longstanding issues began to come to a head, starting at iO West, when the theatre's then artistic director was accused of sexual assault. He was ultimately fired in 2016, but Halpern denied knowing anything about the accusations. This denial led to a public back-and-forth between Halpern and current and former iO West performers. Then, in 2018, Halpern pulled the plug on iO West, stating the branch was no longer financially sustainable. Two years later, problems would come to a head in Chicago, forced to the forefront by the Black Lives Matter protests and the COVID-19 pandemic (both explored more fully later, see #47). iO was hardly alone in facing both financial problems and accusations of racism and misogyny, though iO's sudden closure in 2020 sent shockwaves through the improv community. While its future was unclear at the time, Halpern eventually sold the theatre in 2021 and it re-opened in 2022 with a new leadership structure (see #48).

17. COMEDYSPORTZ

Like iO, ComedySportz sought to make improv the end product rather than part of a process. Founded in 1984 in Milwaukee, Wisconsin, by Dick Chudnow, ComedySportz now has 25 locations across the United States and a branch in England. Based on the Theatresports model and with many similarities to The Match and LNI, ComedySportz features two teams competing in short form games, with a hefty emphasis on the sports model – the teams are dressed in uniforms and referred to as Actletes, there is a referee dressed in uniform, and there are winners and losers of each game and match decided by the audience. The ComedySportz format is similar to Theatresports and LNI but is a more family-friendly and purposefully commercialized version.

One of the ways ComedySportz maintains its very carefully constructed brand is through the Referee, another trait borrowed from LNI (though the ComedySportz ref doubles as emcee and has no assistants).

Overseen by the Referee, each match pits two teams against one another. They act as a sort of emcee, but more importantly, they award points and enforce fouls. As with The Match, these fouls keep the content clean and act as quality control. Short form games tend to have a higher floor than long form, meaning they have less chance to bomb because each game has a built-in structure and is relatively short. Again, like The Match, ComedySportz doubles down on this by having the Referee call fouls on both the players and the audience.

There are three main categories of fouls: Out of Bounds, Groaner, and miscellaneous. The foul that does the most heavy lifting in terms of maintaining the brand is the Out of Bounds foul, which is called when a player or audience member uses explicit language or otherwise does something that would not be appropriate (think TV censorship rules). Out of Bounds was called the Brown Bag Foul for a time, and the offending player or audience member wore a brown paper bag over their head. The Groaner Foul is a more playful foul, called when a player makes a bad pun or Dad joke. The offending player often apologizes to the audience when they commit a Groaner Foul. The last category of fouls gives the Referee leeway in managing the show's flow – and is one of the critical differences from The Match. They can call a foul simply to move the game along or for any reason they feel may benefit the show.[24] The fouls bridge Sahlins and Close – improv as process or product. The fouls are a safety valve or quality-control check that allows ComedySportz to present improv as the end product but does so with a safety net that maintains both quality and a family-friendly environment.

Much like Theatresports, which has become licensed through The International Theatresports Institute, ComedySportz is licensed via the World Comedy League Incorporated. The WCLI acts as a headquarters, with each ComedySportz existing as a franchise branch in a model not dissimilar from fast food, which is not a coincidence. In a 1997 interview, Chudnow said, "We'd like to be recognized as the McDonald's of entertainment." He foreshadowed another development, saying, "Sooner or later we will be like the NFL and call ourselves the Comedy League of America, with competition among cities on TV."[25] While it is not yet a must-see-TV event, ComedySportz did launch the ComedySportz National Tournament in 1988, which became the ComedySportz World Championship in 2004. Hosted by one of the ComedySportz affiliates (the host city almost always wins), the tournament brings together players from around the world (though primarily from around the United States) for competition, workshops, and organizational bonding. With branches currently in 25 US cities, ComedySportz is one of the most recognizable brands of live improv comedy in the United States.

18. THE COMEDY STORE PLAYERS

The Comedy Store Players is a London-based group founded in 1985, performing at London's The Comedy Store. A stand-up club founded in 1979 based on New York and Los Angeles stand-up clubs, The Comedy Store is one of the most well-known comedy theaters in the world. Featuring an original cast of Kit Hollerbach, Dave Cohen, Neil Mullarkey, and Mike Meyers, would become one of Europe's most influential groups, with its cast members regularly featured on the original British version of *Whose Line is it Anyway?*

The Comedy Store Players have a similar origin to many non-US or Canadian groups that we will see repeated throughout the book. Much as The Match format spread like wildfire through the Francophone world, in the Anglophone world, many non-North American groups were founded by improvisers who had studied in the US or Canada (usually in Chicago or with Johnstone) and brought that training and style with them to establish an improv group or theatre where none existed. In the case of The Comedy Store Players, the American Hollerbach and Canadian Meyers taught the other players improv based on their work in North American improv. Meyers was the primary teacher/influence, noting that "it was like I came from another planet with some Beatles tunes that nobody knew. I showed them how to do it. But they got the hang of it very quickly. Before long they were writing their own tunes that were better than The Beatles. I thought, 'Oh dear, they're very good.'"[26] Initially, an evening's performance featured stand-up comedy followed by a 20-minute improv set. Because improv was so new, they thought nobody would show up just to see improv – especially at a stand-up comedy club in a country without an established improvisational theatre. While they claim only 20 people came the first night in October 1985, they quickly became a hit, and the stand-up first act began to give way to complete performances of improvisational theatre every Sunday night (and eventually Wednesday night as well), though The Comedy Store venue has continued predominantly as a stand-up comedy club.

It is worth noting that we repeatedly see a similar story over improv's history. This is of course an oversimplification, but first, a North American improviser(s) brings their training and experience to create a group or theatre where none existed (in much the same way The Match came to France from Montreal in 1982). Second, we see a "testing-out" of improv's efficacy. Much as The Compass Players began with a more "stable" first act of semi-scripted work before performing more improvisational scenes in the second act (which became much more popular), The Comedy Store Players followed a similar pattern with the safety net of stand-up comedy to draw in audiences. Third, in terms of the Waves of Improvisation, we see a similar story play out over and over around the globe, albeit with different dates, as the First Wave original theatres are challenged in terms of style and format by Second Wave theatres and so on.

As we'll see, The Comedy Store Players have remained stable in terms of players and content, but improv in the UK has followed a familiar global evolution. Revolving around the short form epicenter of The Comedy Store Players and *Whose Line is it Anyway?*, improv in the UK has followed a similar Wave pattern, with new companies and groups emerging to challenge the style and structure of the First Wave. In the UK, the most notable company to emerge as a sort of combo Second/Third Wave theatre would be Hoopla Improv, created in 2006 as the UK's first improv-only theatre (akin to iO), which performs a wide variety of styles and places an emphasis on developing a more diverse roster of performers and performance types (akin to The Annoyance). The performers and students then trained at The Second Wave institution(s) and created and formed new groups and theatres with evolving styles and genres.

But back to the British First Wave. One of the most remarkable aspects of The Comedy Store Players is their relative stability and longevity. While many of the companies included in this section are older, none of them approach the personnel stability of The Comedy Store Players. Hollerbach and Meyers left relatively early; Meyers left the group in 1986 to return to Canada, then Chicago, then *Saturday Night Live*, and then to become a Hollywood star. However, the cast has remained relatively stable from the late 1980s. The core of Neil Mullarkey, Paul Merton, Josie Lawrence, Lee Simpson, Andy Smart, Jim Sweeney, and Richard Vranch have been working together for decades. In 2010, The Guinness Book of World Records recognized them as the longest-running comedy show with the same cast.[27] In addition to a stable cast, they have seen little format change – sticking to tried-and-true short form improv games. While they feature guest performers (Greg Proops, Phill Jupitus, Eddie Izzard, and Stephen Frost, to name a few), the core group has barely changed.

In a world where improv groups come and go in a manner of months (sometimes even less), their nearly 40-year run is likely never to be matched. In addition to stability, The Comedy Store Players are notable for their contributions to *Whose Line is it Anyway?* (see #27). The show's cast is not exclusively made up of The Comedy Store Players, but they have been a steady presence on the show from the start. *Whose Line* has arguably been the biggest factor in improv's worldwide popularity over the past 30 years. As such, because of their huge presence on *Whose Line*, The Comedy Store Players have had an outsized impact on global improvisational theatre's development, spread, and evolution.

19. THE ANNOYANCE

The Annoyance is technically in what Amy Seham describes as the Third Wave of Improv. A reaction to what some saw as the rigidity of Second Wave theatres (the glorification of the Harold at iO, for instance, or the strict rules of play at ComedySportz), the Third Wave emerged in the 1990s and was characterized by a growing diversity – in terms of style, performers, geography, and rules (or lack thereof). Much as the Second Wave was a reaction to the first by making improv the product rather than a process, the Third Wave was a reaction to the rules of the Second Wave. While there were many Third Wave theatres, the most important and long-lasting is The Annoyance Theatre, which came to be defined by their willingness to break every rule and throw the rule book out the window.

Mick Napier and David MacNerland were students at Indiana University in the early 1980s. They had seen a revue at Second City and wanted to do something similar at IU, so they formed the group Dubbletaque. They had no experience but set about creating a brand-new sketch comedy show every week. Napier moved to Chicago after graduation and began training and performing wherever possible. He was selected to join the ImprovOlympic Harold team Grime and Punishment, but he grew leery of iO's sacrosanct view of the Harold. Napier knew there was more to improv than just the Harold (much as, ironically, Charna Halpern knew there was more to improv than games), but more importantly, he began to feel as though strict adherence to improv's rules was hindering players rather than helping them. Instead, Napier felt that uncensored play was the key to improvisation (much like Johnstone) and set about creating a company based on the power of play.

Founded in 1987 as Metraform, The Annoyance became one of Chicago's stalwart improv theatres. About a month before Halloween, the group thought putting on their own horror show would be fun. So, they set to work on what became *Splatter Theatre*, a Hitchcock-esque parody/satire/really (really really) bloody horror live comedy show. Nobody knew the show would launch the country's most important subversive comedy theatre, but the show foreshadowed their working style. It was derived from improv but wasn't improvised. It was simultaneously scripted and tightly constructed and loose with room for play. It was silly and fun (and really, really ((really))) bloody, but it was also smart and subversive.

Behind their "screw the rules" philosophy, they quickly established themselves as the leading alternative improv comedy theatre in Chicago. Their training center became a hotbed for improvisers trained at Second City and iO looking to break all the rules they had just learned. Seeking to un-inhibit improvisers and unlock their sense of play (and empowerment), The Annoyance developed a style that Napier described as "Fuck it."[28] That mostly meant training and teaching without a strict adherence to the rules or "the right way" to improvise. While iO's training was structured around the Harold and Second City's ultimately around creating sketch comedy, The Annoyance had a more individualized approach without a structure or end product in mind.

At the same time, many of the end goals were the same, albeit with a slightly different pedagogical approach. Both iO and The Annoyance teach that being a good scene partner is key to being a good improviser – but they differ on their approach. iO preaches supporting your partner as one of its key tenets. Improvisers should always be looking to build upon the ideas of others and fostering group mind. The Annoyance does not necessarily disagree but argues that the best way to actually support your partner is to take care of yourself first. Instead of looking to build and support your partner's ideas, which can lead to passive play, you should be willing and able to provide them with ideas, which will create more active play. By taking care of yourself (and, let's be honest, doing so often means following many of the rules like making active choices and agreeing to the established reality) you are supporting your partner. The philosophy is not so much a complete 180 from Close/Halpern/iO; more so, it is a different approach to achieve similar goals.

As much (or as little) as they "screwed the rules," The Annoyance truly made its mark by eschewing the improv as process vs. product debate. They produced scripted shows, entirely improvised shows, and shows somewhere in between. They had a string of cult-classic hits in the early 1990s – *The Real Live Brady Bunch* (1990); *Manson: The Musical* (1990); *Tippi: Portrait of a Virgin* (1991); *Ayn Rand Gives Me a Boner* (1991); *What Every Girl Should Know—An Ode to Judy Blume* (1998); and their flagship show *Co-Ed Prison Sluts* (1989), one of the longest running shows in Chicago musical theater history. The theatre's calling card became subversion, whether it was rules, traditions, or good taste.

Like many of its counterparts, in recent years, The Annoyance has opened a new, much larger physical theatre space. They moved several times during their history, ultimately landing on Belmont Avenue in a multi-stage space that feels more corporate than subversive. Along with a huge training center, The Annoyance continues to create and produce its own original plays, musicals, and other improvised shows while also acting as a producer for other outside shows that fit into the theatre's aesthetic.

20. THE UPRIGHT CITIZENS BRIGADE

The Annoyance in many ways was an alternative theatre – positioned as different from Second City and iO. The Upright Citizens Brigade was a lovechild of iO and The Annoyance. One of the first improv theatres in New York City, UCB quickly entrenched itself as one of the most influential theatres in the comedy and entertainment world. UCB was initially formed in Chicago in 1991 by a group of iO improvisers. While they embraced Napier's more aggressive approach to improv, they also revered Del Close and the Harold. Their irreverent style got them noticed, and in 1996, they relocated to New York City under the leadership of the UCB Four – Amy Poehler, Matt Besser, Matt Walsh, and Ian Roberts.

New York comedy had been dominated by stand-up comedy for decades, so much so that even a venue called The Improv was actually a stand-up club. The Magnet Theatre, PIT, and other improv theatres would emerge in NYC, but in 1996, stand-up was dominant. Initially performing in what had been a strip club, they eventually opened their first permanent theatre in 1999. They relocated several times, opened a second NYC stage, opened a Los Angeles branch, and then closed everything down during the COVID-19 pandemic, and ultimately re-opened in the Fall of 2023.

Amidst all the changes, two things remained constant – their focus on the "game of the scene" and their flagship show, ASSSSCAT. Based on the iO show *The Armando Diaz Theatrical Experience and Hootenanny*, created in Chicago by Dave Koechner and Adam McKay. The show was built around Armando Diaz (who would go on to create the Magnet Theatre in NYC), who would improvise a monologue based on an audience suggestion, which would then inspire a series of improvised scenes. The show would then bounce between monologues by Diaz and scenes inspired by his monologues. ASSSSCAT is essentially the same format, though instead of Diaz acting as monologist, a guest usually performs the monologues. The name came from an early performance by UCB featuring McKay, Koechner, Besser, Roberts, and Horatio Sans, among others. They were doing a show for a tiny audience that was going very poorly. As the improv devolved, they took turns saying "asssscat" onstage, backstage, and wherever possible.[29] They applied the name to their version of a monologue-inspired show and turned it into a staple of the comedy community. Performed every Sunday night for decades, the show became UCB's signature piece, attracting lots of attention and audiences, and eventually, some rather heavy hitters to act as guest monologists. The show's relatively free-form structure mixed with the company's aesthetic to marry the style and aesthetic of iO and The Annoyance. This mixture isn't surprising, given that many early UCB members had trained and performed at both Chicago theatres.

In addition to ASSSSCAT, UCB's other gigantic contribution to contemporary improvisation was developing the playing style based on "the game of the scene." Meticulously explained in their 2013 *Upright Citizens Brigade Comedy Improvisation Manual*, the game of the scene approach asks improvisers to essentially "find the first unusual thing" in a scene and then exclusively build and heighten that reality/premise/situation. Using the simple formula "If X is true in this scene/world, then what else must be true?" the game of the scene approach emphasizes finding what's funny about a scene and then focusing exclusively on building and heightening that element. Monty Python's "Dead Parrott Sketch" is an excellent example of playing "the game." In the sketch, John Cleese's character attempts to return a dead parrot to the pet store. While that is a funny premise, the game is that the shopkeeper refuses to acknowledge that the dead parrot is dead – refusing to acknowledge reality then becomes the game. Using the game of the scene means that in the scene, the two actors only have to focus on that single element. They don't need to invent new events or plots; they simply need to heighten and play the game. In the same way that the structure of short form games, or those original rules of improv Elaine May helped create, provide a type of floor for success, the game of the scene increases the odds of performing a good scene. The game of the scene approach has become a prevalent playing style, especially on the East Coast.

In addition to their work onstage, UCB also produced a television show on Comedy Central that was the first introduction for many to the concepts of long form improvisation. It had a short run, was not improvised, but was structured like a Harold. Unlike *Saturday Night Live*, *Upright Citizens Brigade* episodes revolved around a theme, with different characters weaving in and out of sketches, with themes and worlds colliding in unexpected ways – much like a Harold (in this manner, it was more like *SCTV* than *SNL*). While the content was not improvised, a good deal of it was generated from improvisation – past ASSSSCAT shows and other improvised scenes. The influence of The Annoyance and their early Chicago years were also evident, as the concept was that the actors were "social terrorists" who sought to disrupt the status quo through sketch comedy, with Del Close providing the voice-over narration for their opening sequence. The show's stylistic similarities to the Harold and long form improv served as the perfect mass-media diffusion of the last 15 years of development in improvisational style.

This group of theatres and companies established improvisational theatre as a viable art form. They became the embodiment of the various theories and philosophies of Spolin, Johnstone, Close, Napier, and the other luminaries, turning improv from a series of acting games into one of the leading forms of comic performance. First, using it as a tool to create scripted theatre via sketch comedy, by the 1990s, improv was a well-established artistic genre and style of performance, becoming recognized as one of the most influential training models for comedians and performers worldwide.

Notes

1 Qtd. in Stephen E. Kercher, *Revel with a Cause: Liberal Satire in Postwar America* (Chicago: University of Chicago Press, 2006), 122.
2 Qtd. in Kercher, 122.
3 Qtd. in Kercher, 250.
4 Art Peterson, "North Beach History: How 1960s Troupe 'The Committee' Influenced American Comedy," *Hoodline*, 27 June 2016. https://hoodline.com/2016/06/north-beach-history-how-1960s-troupe-the-committee-influenced-american-comedy
5 Kim "Howard" Johnson, *The Funniest One in the Room* (Chicago: Chicago Review Press, 2008), 134.
6 Johnson, 134.
7 Johnson, 134.
8 Clive Barnes, "Revue in New Version of Eastside Playhouse," *New York Times*, 16 October 1969.
9 Bernard Sahlins, *Days and Nights at the Second City* (Chicago: Ivan R. Dee, 2001), 115.
10 Tom Boeker, "Kuwait Until Dark: Or, Bright Lights, Night Baseball," *Chicago Reader*, 9 June 1988. www.chicagoreader.com/chicago/kuwait-until-dark-or-bright-lights-night-baseball/Content?oid=872320
11 Jack Helbig, "The Gods Must Be Lazy, or, There's More to Life Than Death," *Chicago Reader*, 23 March 1989. www.chicagoreader.com/chicago/

the-gods-must-be-lazy-or-theres-more-to-life-than-death/Content?
oid=873566

12 Jack Helbig, "Pinata Full of Bees," *Chicago Reader*, 6 July 1995. www.
chicagoreader.com/chicago/pinata-full-of-bees/Content?oid=887869

13 Qtd. in Marianne Combs, "50 Years of Social Satire at Brave New
Workshop," MPR News, 26 February 2008. https://www.mprnews.org/
story/2008/02/25/bravenewworkshop

14 There is a debate about the oldest continuously running improv/sketch
comedy theatre between The Brave New Workshop and The Second City.
While BNW opened in 1958 and Second City in 1959, Second City performed sketch and improv exclusively from the start, while it took a few
years for BNW to fully become an improv and sketch comedy theatre.

15 Qtd. in Erin Peterson, "He Who Laughs, Lasts," *Minnesota Monthly*, 20
November 2008. https://www.minnesotamonthly.com/arts-entertainment/
he-who-laughs-lasts/

16 Qtd. in Peterson.

17 Qtd. in Jon Roe, "An oral history of Loose Moose Theatre: 40 years
of improv in front of and behind the scenes." *Calgary Herald*. 18 August
2017. https://calgaryherald.com/life/swerve/an-oral-history-of-loose-
moose-theatre-on-its-40th-anniversary

18 Qtd. in Roe.

19 "Hall of Fame," *Theatre LNI*. https://lni.ca/temple-de-la-renommee/

20 Feral, Josette. "LNI: Ligue Nationale d'Improvisation (Canada)." *The
Drama Review: TDR* 27, no. 1 (1983): 97–100. https://doi.org/10.2307/
1145479

21 Qtd. in Rachel Hatch, "*Makeshift Chicago Stages*: New book explores city's
unique innovation in theater." Illinois State University, 24 August 2021.
https://news.illinoisstate.edu/2021/08/makeshift-chicago-stages-new-
book-explores-citys-unique-innovation-in-theater/

22 Originally named ImprovOlympics, the theatre changed to ImprovOlympic in 1984 when it became a long form theater. In 2005, it became iO
because the U.S. Olympic Committee had sued the theater for fear that a
small comedy theater would be confused with perhaps the largest international sporting event in the world.

23 Qtd. in Jeffrey Sweet, *Something Wonderful Right Away: An Oral History of
The Second City and The Compass Players* (New York: Avon Books, 1978), 9.

24 "How We Keep It Fun For Everyone," *ComedySportz.com*. https://www.
comedysportz.com/

25 Qtd. in David Holmstrom, "By Their Wits Alone: Comedy as Team
Sport." *The Christian Science Monitor*, 26 August 1997. https://www.
csmonitor.com/1997/0826/082697.feat.feat.1.html

26 Qtd. in "History," Comedy Store Players. https://comedystoreplayers.
com/history

27 https://www.guinnessworldrecords.com/world-records/longest-
running-comedy-show-(same-cast)

28 Qtd. in Rob Kozlowski, *The Art of Chicago Improv* (Portsmouth, NH: Heinemann, 2002), 146.
29 Lara Zarum, "The Oral History of ASSSSCAT, the World's Longest-Running Improv Show." *The Village Voice*, 26 June 2018. https://www.villagevoice.com/the-oral-history-of-asssscat-the-worlds-longest-running-improv-show/

PART 4

THE SECOND WAVE LUMINARIES

The Icons and First Groups put improvisational theatre on the map. They developed the theories and practices that established improvisational theatre, then created the groups and theatres that transformed the ideas of Spolin and Johnstone into concrete realities. The following entries – The Second Wave Luminaries – took those initial forays and expanded them, building improv up and out from the late 1980s to the early 2000s. They experimented with new forms, developed existing structures, performed at the highest levels, and brought Chicago-style improv to the world. While many of these luminaries are still active today, they strengthened improv's foundation and added new layers for the next wave of improvisers to build upon and expand.

DOI: 10.4324/9781003359692-4   65

21. iO HOUSE TEAMS

Many improv theatres and companies have House Teams. These improv teams are formed from within the company through classes, auditions, or producer creation. House Teams usually form the bedrock for a theatre's performance offerings and often represent the pinnacle of the respective theatre. There have been thousands of House Teams across the theatres already mentioned, but I would like to focus on four of iO's most influential House Teams – Baron's Barracudas, Jane, The Family, and Baby Wants Candy. These four House Teams were instrumental in advancing the Harold, the staple structure of long form improv. They also expanded what long form improv could be – either through experimentation with the Harold, with the makeup of their team, or by creating new forms and performance styles.

Baron's Barracudas was the original House Team, and as such, Baron's Barracudas helped define what it meant to be a House Team. They also are the Harold heirs, picking up the mantle from The Committee and working to solidify how a Harold works in performance. While long form improv is happening all over the world now, in 1984, when they began performing, *they* were long form improv. Second City was doing sketch revues, and there was no Annoyance yet. Performing at Cross-Currents, they were doing a style of performance that, before them, did not exist. In theory, sure, some improv performances weren't short form games. The Committee had been doing long form style improv among their many performances, but nobody was doing the Harold or performing long form consistently until Baron's Barracudas.

Featuring some improv heavy-hitters and directed by Close, Baron's Barracudas featured David Pasquesi, Steve Burrows, Brian Crane, Bill Russell, John Judd, Honor Finnegan, Kim "Howard" Johnson, Mark Bellson, Chris Barnes, and Judy Nielsen. Working closely with Close, they are the team most responsible for solidifying the three-by-three traditional Harold structure. They also provided a model for future teams of what a Harold looked like on stage. It is a tricky concept, especially when looking at the structure on paper or listening to someone explain it. Seeing a Harold meant that future teams, like Blue Velveeta and others, could quickly grasp the form and begin perfecting and expanding it. They also provided a non-Harold model, showing that House Teams could do more than Harolds. They performed in the Close written and directed *Honor Finnegan vs. The Brain of the Galaxy*. Close built the 1987 sci-fi fantasy piece around the team's talents, including the titular Honor Finnegan. The piece has reached cult status in the improv world and survived an ill-fated 2000 revival that Mick Napier described as "fucking weird."[1] Regardless, the Harold and long form improv owe much of their future success and influence to Baron's Barracudas.

While many successful and significant teams existed, The Family is perhaps the most important iO House Team. Baron's Barracudas established the Harold structure, but The Family unlocked it. Working in the early-to-mid 1990s, they were the first team to make Close's concept of slow comedy truly hum by performing slow comedy really, really fast. Halpern called them "the breaking point ... The Family broke the [Harold] structure."[2] Still regarded as one of the best improv teams ever assembled, The Family featured Matt Besser, Ian Roberts, Ali Farahnakian, Miles Stroth, Neil Flynn, and Adam McKay. Rather than stick to the Harold structure, they began playing to their strengths, focusing more on character, narrative, and game of the scene. They followed narrative threads, did tag-out edits (first introduced by Jazz Freddy), and scenic runs. While they still performed Harolds in the sense that everything was interconnected and there were three beats, they didn't care about the structure/order of scenes. As a result, their Harolds were much faster than other teams, included more scenes, and had a more distinctive style. After nearly a decade in performance, The Family demonstrated that the Harold was a skeleton to build upon, not a rulebook to follow to a T. In addition to unlocking the Harold and making slow comedy fast, they also introduced other new forms, namely the Deconstruction and the Movie. In addition to their structural innovations, the members of The Family have gone on to successful careers in entertainment and comedy. McKay became a successful film director, Stroth became a leading improv teacher/performer across the country, Farahnakian founded the People's Improv Theater in NYC, Flynn became a commercially successful actor, and Besser and Roberts helped found UCB in New York.

If it hasn't been apparent yet, the history of improvisational theatre is dominated by white men. So much so that it is only now becoming widely known in popular culture that Viola Spolin created much of contemporary improvisational theatre. iO was no different, and as The Family shows, its House Teams were mostly, if not all, men. The typical House Team had seven or eight men and one or two women – and virtually no performers of color. iO was hardly alone in its gender disparity. Second City revues were male-dominated, with four or five men and one or two women, and rarely included performers of color. Despite being invented by a woman (Spolin), its most talented and influential performer being a woman (Elaine May), and its signature company being run by a woman (Halpern), improv was hardly immune from the American comedic trope – women aren't funny. If you listen carefully, you can hear a man typing away *right now,* writing a think piece about how women aren't *really* funny. Women in improv are relegated to many of the same gender-specific roles that were defined in vaudeville – the ingenue, the soubrette, the nag, the sexually promiscuous, and the diva. Comedically and socially, these stereotypical roles put the women onstage in positions of subservience, becoming objects who set up their male counterparts for laughs. Male improvisers tend to be more aggressive onstage (in large part because they are socially conditioned to do so), and they often initiate scenes and actively place women in supporting roles or, as is all too common, into sexually suggestive or inappropriate scenarios.

Formed in 1996, Jane became iO's first all-female House Team. In addition to having an all-female cast, the group was notable because it was formed by Stephanie Weir and Katie Roberts, two iO performers, rather than by Charna Halpern or Del Close as was the custom (meaning most teams were selected and created from the top down). As is true with almost every group that non-majority members form, Jane was less about excluding men and more about including women. The cast consisted of Weir, Roberts, Tami Sagher, Abby Sher, Abby Schachner, Monica Payne, Bina Martin, Molly Cavanaugh, Sue Maxman, and Jennifer Bills, among others, as the cast members quickly became highly sought-after performers at places like Second City, and featured a number of new players during the group's three-year run. They wanted a different energy in the group and onstage, saying they wanted "to see what it was like to feel more fully supported in their choices and to explore performance options not open to them in their coed teams."[3] As noted above, women improvisers on overwhelmingly male teams found themselves playing wives, girlfriends, sisters, and mothers. They often were onstage in positions where they needed to support their partners' choices, even if the support didn't always flow both ways. They were constantly *reacting* to their male partners' offers. Being in a constant state of support and reaction means having power or agency onstage is difficult. With Jane, the women in the group always drove the scenes because they had to drive the scenes. The women in the group had power and agency over what kinds of roles, topics, and scenes they would perform. If they played a stereotype or a stereotypical scenario, they *chose* to, not because they were forced into the situation. Susan Messing described the scenes that would often emerge in her early 1990s women-only improv classes at The Annoyance: "People are coming offstage and saying, 'Wow, I've never done a character like that before.' I haven't gotten one PMS scene, one lesbian scene, one period scene, I haven't gotten anything like that, and I'm thrilled."[4] Jane demonstrated to themselves and the greater community that women could do more than play supporting roles.

Another critical aspect of House Teams became developing new structures. In 1997, iO anointed the musical improv group Baby Wants Candy as its first official resident company. The group is notable for several reasons. First, they became one of the first massively popular teams to perform at iO, drawing audiences that did not usually attend improv shows. A lot of improv can be "insider," improvisers performing for other improvisers. Baby Wants Candy helped broaden improv's appeal, bringing people to iO who had no idea what improv was and expanding improv's audience base. Second, they became the symbol for a group that took the basic tenets of the Harold and iO's improv philosophy and used them to create a wildly successful non-Harold form – an entirely improvised musical. Third, the group grew beyond iO, establishing itself as its own brand, with performing ensembles in Chicago, New York, and Los Angeles. Many early successful iO House Teams hit a kind of ceiling at iO, with their members then moving on to bigger and brighter stages and the team dissolving. Baby Wants Candy did the opposite. While the original cast went a thousand different directions, the team carried on and *expanded* rather than disappearing. Baby Wants Candy exists as its own entity, bigger than its cast, in part because so many of its alums have gone on to successful careers, like Chris Grace, Thomas Middleditch, Jack McBrayer, Aidy Bryant, Amber Ruffin, Tarik Davis, Craig Cackowski, and Peter Gwinn.

Baby Wants Candy is hardly the only group improvising musicals. The genre of musical improv has exploded. In New York, developed by Kat Koppett, Spontaneous Broadway debuted in 1995 at Freestyle Repertory Theatre and has gone on to be performed globally. Nearly every improv theatre has a musical format or team, and the podcast *Off Book: The Improvised Musical* with Jessica McKenna and Zach Reino, where the duo and a guest improvise a new musical each episode, has become extremely popular. Baby Wants Candy's positioning at iO gave them outsized influence in popularizing musical improv. Simultaneously, their expansion of what an iO House Team could be opened the creative gates to experimenting with performance improv. Musical improv is hugely popular worldwide, largely thanks to Baby Wants Candy.

Other important iO House Teams obviously existed, such as The Reckoning, which most improvisers know from the DVD of performances included in *Art by Committee*. Still, these four – Baron's Barracudas, The Family, Jane, and Baby Wants Candy helped shape the development of iO and of long form improvisation. One of the reasons iO's House Teams were experimenting with form and team composition is that outside of iO, there was a growing independent improv movement. Two independent teams in particular were pushing iO – Ed and Jazz Freddy. Directed by Jim Dennen, Ed grew out of the Piven Theatre Workshop in 1990. Perhaps the single most defining characteristic of Ed was their intense rehearsal schedule. While most improv teams rehearse once a week, Ed rehearsed six times a week. They rehearsed so much because Dennen wanted to push improvisation as an art form, to elevate it above the perception of improv as light cabaret performed in bars or back rooms. As such, Ed developed unique 90-minute, long form performances that were presented like traditional theatre, often in more conventional theatre spaces. Their style was two-person relationship-based scene work that revolved much more heavily around narrative than the Harold. They also introduced the tag-out edit, where an offstage player tags out one character from a scene while the remaining improviser plays the same character in the new scene/scenario. Ed was incredibly influential, though ultimately short-lived. Members of Ed and other Chicago groups and theatres, including iO and The Annoyance, banded together to form a sort of super team in 1992 – Jazz Freddy.

The original Jazz Freddy cast featured Susan MacLaughlin, Stephanie Howard, Meredith Zinner, Miriam Tolan, Chris Reed, Jimmy Carrane, Kevin Dorff, Noah Gregoropolous, David Koechner, Pat Finn, Rachel Dratch, Brian Stack, and Pete Gardner, who also served as the initial director but later gave way to Dennen during the group's second run in 1993. Like Ed, Jazz Freddy focused on patient relationship-based scene work worthy of a traditional play rather than gimmicky style improv. They performed in more traditional theatre venues, and they, too, caught the eye of Del Close and iO. In many ways, the innovations Close would make with The Family resulted from the work of Ed and Jazz Freddy and the buzz they were creating in the improv community. They also created a buzz with Chicago theatre critics. In *The Chicago Reader*, Jack Helbig said that while Close and others have urged players to work to the top of their intelligence, "Jazz Freddy is the first troupe I've seen that consistently heeds this often-given, seldom followed advice."[5] Tony Adler wrote in the *Chicago Tribune* that Ed and Jazz Freddy helped spark "an honest-to-God improv renaissance," saying, "they are taking what many continue to dismiss as nothing more than a set of workshop exercises, or a novel way to write jokes, and turning it into art ... Jazz Freddy offers work that is at once technically advanced and wonderfully funny."[6]

As the work of Ed and Jazz Freddy reverberated through iO and helped transform and free the Harold structure, the new independent spirit created a new home at The Playground Theatre, which was established in 1997 as an improv co-op. The theatre was partially inspired by what some saw as the draconian management at iO, where Halpern mainly formed and cut teams. The Playground sought to give power back to improvisers, so rather than the top-down administrative structure of iO and other improv theatres, The Playground was run by the teams and improvisers who made up the co-op. The Playground is a culmination of the growth and experimentation in 1990s Chicago improv. A decade before, iO was performing in bars and was relatively unknown. Thanks to iO House Teams and outside improvisers pushing the boundaries of improv's possibilities, improv flourished by the turn of the century. It was an undisputed art form and had become the premiere training for the world's most influential comedians.

22. TJ & DAVE

While Baby Wants Candy has been the most commercially successful former iO team, TJ Jagodowski and Dave Pasquesi – TJ & Dave – have become "the gold standard for group improv."[7] They are also part of a wave of "duo" performers that emerged in the 1990s and 2000s at various Chicago theatres, such as Stephanie Weir and Bob Dassie's "Weir-Dass" or Mark Sutton and Joe Bill's "Bassprov." TJ & Dave did not invent two-person long form improv, but they have become the international standard of improv excellence, continuing, as of this writing, to perform regularly in Chicago, New York, and across the country.

Jagodowski and Pasquesi had been improvising at iO and around Chicago. They established themselves independently as two of the best improvisers in town, but when they teamed up in 2002, they took improvisation to another level. Ryan Hubbard sums up the duo well in his review:

> T.J. Jagodowski and Dave Pasquesi, who have 30 years of stage time between them, are what most improvisers are not (liberally intelligent, extremely talented actors as well as comedians) and do what most improvisers do not (carefully listen to each other before responding). The result is an exhibition of verbal facility and pantomimic agility—they can do everything from multiple English accents to magic tricks—that anticipates and plays off the audience's reactions. During their hour of subtle character development, it's easy to forget that it's all made up.[8]

Based at iO, TJ & Dave have performed across the country, with a semi-regular residency in New York, and were the subjects of the 2009 documentary *Trust Us, This is all Made Up*.

In addition to their skill and dedication to slow comedy, the duo is unique in that they don't perform a set structure.[9] They don't do a Harold, an ASSSSCAT, or any of the many other long form structures – they just get onstage and perform together for about an hour. They don't even take an audience suggestion, hence the now signature catchphrase at the beginning of each show, "trust us, this is all made up." As Hubbard notes, sometimes it is hard to believe that it is all made up because there is a depth to their characters and a complexity to their improv that it is often difficult to imagine they made it all up on the spot. The intricacies of their performance are tied to the simplicity of their approach – listen, respond, and react to what is already in front of you.

Detailed in *Improvisation at the Speed of Life*, TJ & Dave's style and approach to improv has elevated the form, in part by bringing more traditional stage acting techniques and theories into improvisation. One of those key techniques they've brought into their style is "heat and weight." As in traditional scripted acting, what is said is often less important than *how* it is said. The "weight" in a scripted or improvised scene is not what your partner says but how they say it. Any line can be delivered in a thousand ways with a thousand different meanings, so rather than respond to what your partner is saying, an actor/improviser should react to how they are saying it – they should respond to the weight. The line, "How did you sleep last night?" can carry many weights. It can be light, informal, flirtatious, or heavy, laced with deep subtext. Responding to the weight is critical.

The "heat" is the intimacy or nature of the relationship between the two characters. They are meticulous in delineating the nature of the relationship from the *title* of the relationship. In improv, improvisers often rely too much on the relationship's title rather than the relationship's heat. Co-workers is a relationship title, but the nature of that relationship can vary wildly. Co-workers amid a torrid affair have a very different heat than two co-workers vying for a promotion or two co-workers who simply love exchanging gossip about the office. TJ & Dave advocate playing the *state* of the relationship rather than the title. A "hot" relationship is not always sexual. Those two co-workers vying for a promotion probably have a hot relationship. A cold relationship is not always loveless, as a loving couple might have a temporarily cold relationship the morning after a big fight. Playing the heat and the weight focuses the scene on the present. Responding to who is in the scene, the state of that relationship, and how they communicate (verbally and non-verbally) elevates their scene work and has helped them reach the pinnacle of improvisational performance.

23. MARK SUTTON AND JOE BILL

The other tour-de-force duo to emerge in the Second Wave is Bassprov, featuring Mark Sutton and Joe Bill. Sutton and Bill were part of the Indiana

University cohort with Mick Napier, Faith Soloway, and Dave MacNer-land, who became Dubbletaque and later formed the foundation for The Annoyance. Sutton and Bill quickly became fixtures in The Annoyance's early sketch and improv shows. Bill often played big, bold characters in the now famous "Annoyance style," while Sutton often found himself playing the straightman. As integral as the duo was to The Annoyance, they made a name for themselves by playing two laid-back characters fishing and having a chat. While The Annoyance became known for big, bold, brash punk rock style improv, Sutton's and Bill's duo Bassprov is the exact opposite. Launched in 2001, it is quiet and slow, and rather than punk rock, it features Donny Weaver (played by Sutton) and Earl Hinkle (played by Bill), two Indiana blue-collar guys who love fishing and talking about sports. Weaver and Hinkle are characters, but they do feature a good deal of autobiographical material. While TJ & Dave famously start without an audience suggestion, Bassprov begins by asking the audience the same thing each show: a current event and "something you can stick your fingers in." You can take the improviser away from The Annoyance, but you can't take The Annoyance away from the improviser.

From there, like TJ & Dave, they improvise what is best described as a one-act play. There isn't a narrative plot; instead, the show is a less nostalgic, more punk version of "Lake Woebegone." Sutton and Bill have created an intricate backstory of various invented friends and goings-on in their rural Indiana town. While Sutton and Bill always play Weaver and Hinkle, they have regular guests who join them, including Jagodowski, who plays the awkward teen Vaughn. The show's simplicity allows the virtuosic improvisational skill of Sutton and Bill to shine. *The New York Times* said Bassprov "refreshingly has the feel of a quiet character study. There are pregnant pauses, windy small talk and the kind of moseying banter that doesn't strain for laughs. The troupe gets them anyway. Jokes emerge organically, using wordplay, character quirks and quicksilver wit."[10] Like TJ & Dave, Bassprov proves that you don't need elaborate structures or gimmicks to make improv work – and that highly skilled improvisers can create vibrant and entertaining performances with little more than their collaborative skills.

Much like TJ & Dave survey the heat and weight to determine what's *really* going on in a scene, Sutton and Bill focus on discovering the scene at the very top and then just building on that discovery. Sutton describes it as:

> a matter of knowing what is enough. I find that improvisers spend so much time and energy at the top of scenes trying to figure out what it's about. When really all it's about is what you just did. Then

you build on that through listening and trust ... and discovery. That's improv.

The simplicity of the approach is rather difficult, especially for beginning improvisers or performers lacking confidence. Trusting what's there can be immensely difficult, but for Sutton, discovery and trust lead to good scenes: "You decide that this is what it is, and you follow that path. You don't search for another path that you like better. Now your energy is focused on doing and not on 'trying to do.'"[11]

Another overlooked factor in the success of Bassprov and TJ & Dave is experience. Both duos have tons of experience. Sutton and Bill have known each other for decades. That level of intimacy and trust is hard to replicate. Sutton explains,

> You can't manufacture that ... it just happens, and it informs the work. If we had done BASSPROV when we were 25 instead of 45, it would have been bullshit – made-up stories and attempts at reality – and it would have sucked. But now it's based in something grounded, and it works.[12]

Sutton's point that Bassprov works because they are 45 and not 25 speaks to another truth about improv. Because the improviser is the source material, everything one does and experiences *offstage* informs what happens onstage. The more life experiences a person has, the more they have to draw from onstage. Playing a complicated romantic relationship is easier after having been through one (or several). The more relationships one's had, romantic and otherwise, the easier it is to recognize and understand the heat and weight of a relationship. Experience onstage also matters. One thing that is difficult for non-improvisers to understand is that improv takes practice – people rehearse how to improvise. A large part of the rehearsal process is building a shared language and developing trust. The simplicity of TJ & Dave and Bassprov results from decades of work onstage and off. Making something look simple and easy usually results from very hard work.

Sutton and Bill are also notable as they are two of the most recognizable and sought-after teachers in the improv world. They have taught at almost every major improv theatre and have become major draws on the improv festival circuit. Like most great improv teachers, they preach honesty, truth, and playfulness over strict adherence to any set rules or structure. In an interview with People and Chairs, Bill explained his de-emphasizing right and wrong:

A big cornerstone of my teaching is, 'What's organic?' And it's just, 'Discoveries are instantaneous decisions we make that are unencumbered by the day-to-day self-judgmental bullshit that we walk around with in life.' I teach the idea that 'Obligation and inspiration are inversely proportional.' And I think people want to see inspiration in theatre, so the fixation on right or wrong puts you into a state of obligation, and you don't want to be obliged.[13]

Bill, as with many other improv teachers, sees himself as more of a guide than a guru, helping students to unlock their creativity and free themselves on stage rather than giving them a handbook of rules to follow. He also recognizes that different people bring different strengths and that we should celebrate them and work to highlight them rather than focus on deficiencies. For instance, when asked during an interview with *Status* to create an improviser using five different people, Bill responded, "The physicality of Felipe Ortiz, the studiousness of Omar Galván, the heart of Patti Stiles, the mind of Jill Bernard and the intensity/passion/whimsey of Inbal Lori."[14] In short, for Bill, improv should celebrate collaboration.

24. SUSAN MESSING AND JONATHAN PITTS

Susan Messing and Jonathan Pitts are not a duo like TJ & Dave or Sutton and Bill, nor are they affiliated with the same theatre. They are, however, equally responsible for improv's growth in the 1990s (and beyond). Messing came to symbolize Chicago-style improv and the cross-pollination of Chicago improv. At the same time, Pitts brought the world to Chicago through the Chicago Improv Festival, only to become a globe-trekking improviser, bringing Chicago to the world. An equally brilliant performer and teacher, Susan Messing has been a fundamental part of both The Annoyance and iO's ascension to the top of improvisational theatre and has become one of the most influential improv teachers in the world. Jonathan Pitts is perhaps the globe's biggest improvisational ambassador.

While not as celebrated as Close, Halpern, or Napier, Messing is one of the most important improvisers in Chicago, working and shaping the style and artistic aesthetic at all three big Chicago theatres (iO, Annoyance, Second City – less so than the other two). A founding member of The Annoyance Theatre, she became a foundational piece of their success. Like Elaine May anchored The Compass and Nichols and May, Messing became a cornerstone of the early Annoyance. A featured player in nearly all their early shows and big hits, she exemplified and illustrated The Annoyance's "screw the rule" punk-rock style better than anyone. Like

May, she also had to navigate being a woman in a predominantly male art form. In fact, "women in Chicago improv were such an anomaly that she was referred to as 'the girl.'"[15] Again, like May, Messing refused to be pigeonholed as "the girl" or only to play the girlfriend, the wife, and the mom. Instead, she became one of Chicago's most powerful and confident performers. Yet, as aggressive and assertive as she can be onstage, her confidence is mixed with boundless playfulness. The Annoyance's executive director Jennifer Estlin sums up Messing's style: "Her whole approach to it is, 'If you're not having fun, then you're the asshole.'"[16]

She has taken that approach to the stage and classroom. As mentioned, she was pivotal to the early Annoyance shows and a staple on iO's stages. In recent years, her two-person show "Messing with a Friend" has become one of the most celebrated improv shows in the country. Featuring Messing improvising with a new partner each show – often an improv big-wig in their own right (Aidy Bryant, T.J. Jagodowski, Rachel Mason, Andy Dick) – the show helped to foster community while also being a really, really good improv show. Messing described the show as a "joyful, uncensored, and improvised romp through hell."[17] Much like TJ & Dave, Messing with a Friend is an hour-long masterclass in improvisation – with Messing and her friend playing numerous characters and seamlessly jumping between scenes and worlds.

Messing is also essential to the cross-pollination of improvisation in the early-to-mid 1990s in Chicago, which then fanned out across the country. In the early days of iO and The Annoyance (as well as Second City), improvisers tended to align themselves and identify with a particular company. This siloing was mainly because each theatre emerged by identifying itself as *not* Second City (iO) and *not* iO (Annoyance). Messing was hardly the only improviser working, teaching, performing, or studying at more than one theatre. Still, she and Mick Napier were as instrumental as anyone in bridging the theatres while allowing them to maintain their core styles and philosophies. Rather than pitting themselves as rivals, Messing helped them become complementary.

As important as she is onstage as a performer, she is equally, if not more so, instrumental as a teacher. She has long taught at The Annoyance and was the driving force in developing and re-imagining iO's training curriculum. Messing, who claims to have developed the curriculum while getting stoned in her bathtub, created exercises based on movement, character, environment, and teamwork that ultimately became a fundamental cornerstone of iO's training curriculum by combining The Annoyance style of "take care of yourself" with iO's cornerstone of "support your partner." Her teaching style combines no-nonsense and pure joy that de-emphasizes rules and emphasizes bliss. She likens improv to sex, noting,

> Isn't the job to get off? Are there *suggestions* that I could offer as a teacher to support you in getting off sooner, and your partner as well? Sure, but the ultimate responsibility is to have more fun than anyone else; and if your partner's having fun that's even more of a turn-on in terms of this work. And then you win and the audience was in the moment with you, so they get off, too.[18]

Her introduction to a character-building exercise pretty much sums up her simultaneously aggressive and empowering approach: "What we're going to do now is two-minute scenes, followed by one-minute scenes. Do it. Live it. Love it. Let's go. Get up there, fuckers!"[19]

While Messing was building community (and hilarity) in Chicago, Jonathan Pitts was working on bringing Chicago-style improv to the world ... by bringing the world to Chicago. Founded in 1998 by Pitts and Frances Callier (see #25), the Chicago Improv Festival (CIT) cemented Chicago's place as the center of the improvisational world. Pitts and Callier co-produced the festival for three years, then when Callier moved to LA, Pitts took over as producer for the next seventeen years. Over its two-decade run, CIT featured a who's who of global improv and provided the blueprint for the explosion of improv festivals that now occur regularly worldwide, featuring performers from around the world and workshops taught by leading global players. In addition to the emergence of *Whose Line is it Anyway?* and the seminal texts of the field – *Impro, Truth in Comedy, Something Wonderful Right Away, Improvisation for the Theater* – the improv festival network has been the leading factor in growing improvisational theatre and performance. Pitts' role in creating the blueprint for improv festivals and being a teacher/performer at countless other improv festivals means that Pitts has had an outsized impact on developing and promulgating improvisational theatre. In addition to CIT, Pitts also founded and produced the College Improv Tournament for a decade. The College Improv Tournament brought college improv groups from around the country together to learn and perform, helping to build community at the collegiate level.

Being an improv pioneer is nothing new for Pitts, who has been starting improv groups since college. Enamored with the original cast of *SNL* and the work being done at Second City, he began taking classes at Second City before there was a traditional training center in the early days of The Players Workshop. He took that training back with him to college, where he founded and directed his college's improv troupe. Pitts said, "I produced, taught, performed, promoted, designed the set, and took the group photos. Doing all this gave me [the] starting point for the rest of my adult life."[20] Creating and connecting is part of Pitts' DNA. Before founding CIF, he worked with The International Theatre Festival of Chicago, which started his lifelong work with international performing artists. At CIF, Pitts ensured an international presence at the festival, which is no small feat given Chicago's geographic isolation relative to almost every non-North American country. As such, Pitts has spent decades reversing the flow and bringing Chicago and his improv style to the world. Borrowing the concept of a walkabout from Australian Aboriginal culture, where young men led a semi-nomadic life in the wilderness as they transitioned to adulthood, Pitts set out on a self-described "improv walkabout." For the three years prior to COVID, Pitts found himself teaching and performing in over 20 countries on three continents. While Pitts' vast improvisational knowledge makes him a sought-after teacher and collaborator, he gains as much from his travels as his students and collaborators:

> I remember sitting in the Vienna airport eating a Vienna pretzel when I had an 'ah-ha' moment! I realized that in Chicago, I made tables for others to sit at, but in Europe (and Asia and Oceania), I had a seat at the table.[21]

One of Pitts' staples on his walkabouts is teaching and performing Monoscenes, a very old long form style first introduced by Michael Gellman at Second City when he was trying to get players to improvise a one-act play. The structure takes away many of the trappings and gimmicks of long form improv and instead forces players to play only one character, with no time jumps, tag outs, or any other editing "magic," and instead follows the action in real time onstage. It is a true test for improvisers to sustain the action and relationships, which feeds into what he calls "the Chicago Way," which is both a joke about Al Capone bringing a gun to a knife fight, as well as the two-person relationship-based scene that is at the heart of Chicago-style long form improv that has roots in Spolin, Martin de Maat, and Del Close's teachings. By rooting his work in a staple of Chicago style improv, Pitts deepens Chicago's connection to the improv world.

25. FRANCES CALLIER, SHAUN LANDRY AND OUI BE NEGROES

It should be clear by now, but let me say once again: white men have historically dominated improvisational theatre. BIPOC performers and women have often found themselves on the outside of the system, denied performance opportunities, and reduced to playing stereotypes onstage.

Bob Curry was the first African American cast member at Second City, debuting in 1966's revue *Enter, From Above*. While they have a fellowship in his name to support aspiring Black comics, Second City and its improvisational brethren have been astonishingly white. Reflecting on his time at Second City in the 2010s, Dewayne Perkins (now a television writer for such shows as *Brooklyn 99*) reflected a common sentiment, "Second City is so heavily associated with whiteness ... I felt like it wasn't made for me, like I was a guest in a space, because they needed me to fill a box."[22] Second City was hardly alone in being a sometimes unwelcoming place, an issue that came to a head during the Black Lives Matter movement and the COVID-19 shutdown (see #47). The big improv institutions often stifled BIPOC performers, so they made their own opportunities.

One of the most important of these early independent groups was Oui Be Negroes. The group's origin stems from The Underground Theatre Conspiracy, which was founded in 1985 by Hans Summers and later added the hugely influential Shaun Landry in 1987. They incorporated multi-media into their work and worked as many independent teams did at the time – producing new work around Chicago. They relocated to Seattle in 1990, where they would produce *Tales from the Crib*, a two-person show featuring Summers and Landry at the Seattle Fringe Festival that laid the groundwork for what would become Oui Be Negroes. Landry and Summers, the only white cast member of the group, felt that it was long past time for an all-Black improv and sketch comedy troupe and relocated back to Chicago to make it happen.

Meanwhile, in 1992, Frances Callier, who, as noted, was co-founder of the Chicago Improv Festival with Jonathan Pitts, created The Second City Outreach Program to create more opportunities for marginalized performers. For Callier, "Black people improvising is one of the most natural things in the world ... All Black people do is make things out of nothing, create brilliance out of emptiness, create excellence from nothing."[23] On the heels of the Outreach Program, Callier spearheaded an effort to open a Second City training center in Bronzeville on the south side of Chicago, a predominantly African American part of the city, to provide more opportunities for Black performers. Despite Second City's institutional language calling the center a priority, the planned new center never materialized. This was all happening against the backdrop of Rodney King and the LA Riots, and Second City found themselves unable to properly comment and satirize the situation with an all-white cast.

Improv at Second City and beyond was also dominated by men, and Callier sought to address the gender imbalance via the Outreach Program. She commented on her earlier experiences in improv classes and performances, "At that time women were not equal parts in the work. My issue was, how can I begin to address how I can feel as an African-American person onstage without half of the genders being addressed?"[24] Callier tried to address issues of race and gender via the Outreach Program. However, when Second City ultimately failed to open the Bronzeville Center, she left and, along with co-founding the Chicago Improv Festival, went on to create the Black Comedy Underground.

Because of Callier's Outreach Program, there was a growing number of non-white-male improvisers being trained, and Landry went to the Outreach Program to recruit players for Oui Be Negroes, who mounted their first show at Café Voltaire in Chicago. They would continue producing original works, sketch comedy, and improv shows in Chicago from 1994–1999. With a predominantly Black cast (Summers is the only white cast member), the troupe could comment on issues and satirize topics that the majority white teams simply could not (or should not). For instance, during the O.J. Simpson trial, they performed a trial "who-done-it" sketch where the guilty person was always a Black man in a stocking cap. Yet, the idea was more than just being a "Black" group – the idea was that they were able to bring their whole selves to their work in a way that was nearly impossible in majority white groups. Rather than constantly being forced into stereotypical and often racist roles, the players could play whomever they wanted – and if they played a stereotypical character type, they could play it however they wanted without the imposition of an otherwise all-white cast.

Oui Be Negroes relocated to San Francisco in 2000, where they would become a staple of the improv and comedy community. They were even compared to The Committee in style and aesthetic. While in San Francisco, Landry co-founded the San Francisco Improv Festival in 2004 before relocating again in 2009 to Los Angeles (the troupe essentially followed Landry and Summers, who are married, as they relocated across the country). Their biting social and political satire became the group's signature, hence The Committee comparison. Yes, they were pioneers in terms of diversifying improv's landscape, and that is very important, but just as important is the fact that they are pretty damn funny too. Both Oui Be Negroes and Callier's Outreach Program provided blueprints for future groups and endeavors. One is The Black Improv Alliance, which aims to provide training and performer advocacy. Another group, Dark Side of the Room, is an Atlanta-based ensemble that performs "deleted scenes" from famous movies showing what the Black characters were doing during the film (see #42). There are many more similar groups, and they all are buoyed, supported, and made possible by the work of Landry and Callier.

More recently, Landry is the founder and CEO of The Ledge Theatre in Los Angeles. Many theatres shut down during the COVID-19 pandemic; unfortunately, many stayed closed. As the Black Lives Matter Movement rose in the national consciousness in the summer of 2020, Landry made a sort-of-serious sort-of-not-serious Facebook post asking if anyone wanted to give her money to start a theatre for people of color. Turns out a lot of people did. Ever since seeing her first show at The Second City, Landry always wanted a career in improv.

> I wanted to be as expressive on stage as Cab [Calloway] and Lena Horne. I wanted to create theatre with an ensemble like Elaine May and Mike Nichols and Gilda Radner. Be in the same creative world as Bill Murray and Dan Ackroyd.

She continued, however, saying, "I saw improvisational theatre as a very large disparaging cultural void as an African American female actor in a format everyone was saying was 'Just like jazz.' I found the irony pretty stifling. And I wanted to change that."[25] As we've seen, Landry has done a lot to change that, including her current work at The Ledge.

For all her vast accomplishments, before the pandemic, she still hadn't run a physical theatre space. "I knew somehow in the weirdness of the '90s, they were not going to give a 30-year-old Black woman a theater." But after a celebrated career and the attention the Black Lives Matter movement placed on the lack of diversity in the arts, she realized, "This was the time. I'm old enough. My reputation is good enough."[26] The Ledge was founded in the spring of 2021 – the culmination of a storied improv career and the right moment – as the first Black-owned-and-operated improv theatre in Los Angeles. While Landry is the driving force, the theatre is a community. The Ledge's Education Director, Stephen C. James, commented,

> We've basically – all of us that are on the board and are performers – all had the experience of being the one Black performer in a group of white improvisers or performers and feeling that onus of wondering why there weren't more people like us on the stage or in the seats.[27]

The Ledge aims to rectify that by providing space for BIPOC performers – onstage and off, in classrooms and in performance. While The Ledge is chronologically in the Fourth Wave (see #49), it is both literally and figuratively a part of Oui Be Negroes' legacy.

The above improvisers are some of the most essential and noteworthy improvisers in the art form's history. While they did not invent improv, they helped to refine, elevate, and disseminate it. They unlocked many possibilities of improv, performing and teaching at the highest levels. One irony of the Second Wave Luminaries is that nearly all focused on simplifying improv. As the Harold grew and new forms emerged, these folks discovered the key to good improv was excelling at fundamentals – trust, listening, collaborative building, and being present. Bringing your whole authentic self to the stage was likewise fundamental to good improv, and the Second Wave Luminaries worked to make that possible and accessible for more improvisers than ever before. Doing good scenes meant they could excel in any format, however simple or complicated. Their work in simplifying improv likewise made them all some of the best and most noteworthy teachers in the world. Long story short, they have become celebrated and inspirational figures in the improv community. As of this writing, they are all still performing and teaching. They also are still learning and evolving, setting the example that one doesn't ever stop learning in improv, even when you're TJ & Dave.

Notes

1 Qtd. in Jack Helbig, "Something Fishy," *Chicago Reader*, 19 October 2000. https://chicagoreader.com/arts-culture/something-fishy/
2 Charna Halpern, Personal Interview. May 21, 2011.
3 Qtd. in Amy Seham, *Whose Improv Is It Anyway? Beyond Second City* (Jackson: University Press of Mississippi, 2001), 71.
4 Qtd. in Neal Pollack, "Women in Improv," *Chicago Reader*, 28 October 1993. https://chicagoreader.com/news-politics/women-in-improv/
5 Jack Helbig, "Jazz Freddy/Every Speck of Dust That Falls to Earth Really Does Make the Whole Planet Heavier, #3," *Chicago Reader*. 6 August 6 1992. http:// www.chicagoreader.com/chicago/jazz-freddyevery-speck-of-dust-that-falls-to-earth-really-does-make-the-whole-planet-heavier-3/Content?oid=880211
6 Tony Adler, "Company Finds Art in Improv," *Chicago Tribune*, 11 May 1993. http://articles.chicagotribune.com/1993–05–11/news/9305110053_1_improv-deliveryman-teachers
7 Ryan Hubbard, "Best of Chicago 2008: Best Improv Group," *Chicago Reader*, 1 July 2008. https://chicagoreader.com/news-politics/best-of-chicago-2008-comedy/
8 Ryan Hubbard, "T.J. and Dave," *Chicago Reader*, 1 June 2006. https://chicagoreader.com/arts-culture/t-j-and-dave/
9 Lots of groups perform this way now … because of TJ & Dave.

10 Jason Zinoman, "Tightrope Comedy, On the Fly," *The New York Times*. 5 July 2012. https://www.nytimes.com/2012/07/06/arts/tightrope-comedy-on-the-fly.html

11 Qtd. in Pam Victor, "Geeking Out with ... Mark Sutton (Part One)," *My Nephew is a Poodle*, 20 November 2012. https://pamvictor.blogspot.com/2012/11/geeking-out-withmark-sutton-part-one.html

12 Qtd. in Victor.

13 Qtd. in "Wrong is the New Right," *PeopleandChairs.com*. 3 June 2016. https://peopleandchairs.com/2016/06/03/wrong-is-the-new-right/

14 Feña Ortalli, "Interview with Joe Bill," *Status*, Year 7, Issue 79. January 2018, 13.

15 Kevin Pang, "The dating lives of funny girls," *The Chicago Tribune*, 8 November 2009. https://www.chicagotribune.com/news/ct-xpm-2009-11-08-0911050428-story.html

16 Qtd. in Brianna Wellen, "Susan Messing has been Messing With a Friend for ten years." *The Chicago Reader*, 10 August 2016. https://chicagoreader.com/arts-culture/susan-messing-has-been-messing-with-a-friend-for-ten-years/

17 Qtd. in Wellen.

18 Qtd. in "Wrong is the New Right."

19 Neal Pollack, "Women in Improv," *Chicago Reader*, 28 October 1993. https://chicagoreader.com/news-politics/women-in-improv/

20 Feña Ortalli, "Interview: Jonathan Pitts," *Status*, Year 12, Issue 143, May 2023, 16.

21 Qtd. in Ortalli.

22 Qtd. in Melena Ryzik and Jake Malooley, "Second City Is Trying Not to Be Racist. Will It Work This Time?" *The New York Times*, 12 August 2020. https://www.nytimes.com/2020/08/12/movies/second-city-black-lives-matter.html

23 Qtd. in Ryzik and Maloonley.

24 Qtd. in Marie-Anne Hogarth, "Laughing Matters," *The Chicago Reader*, 8 April 1999. https://chicagoreader.com/news-politics/laughing-matters/

25 Qtd. in "Meet Shaun Landry: Actor, Writer. Teacher at The Pack Theatre. Improviser. Founder of the hopeful Ledge Theatre Los Angeles," *Shoutout LA*. 10 September 2021. https://shoutoutla.com/meet-shaun-landry-actor-writer-teacher-at-the-pack-theatre-improviser-founder-of-the-hopeful-ledge-theatre-los-angeles/

26 Qtd. in Jevon Phillips, "'A theater that is ours:' The Ledge opens a stage for L.A. improv actors of color," *The Los Angeles Times*. 5 August 2022. https://www.latimes.com/entertainment-arts/story/2022-08-05/la-et-comedy-issue-ledge-theater-improv-actors-of-color

27 Qtd. in Phillips.

PART 5

FILM AND TELEVISION

As improv continued to expand and evolve onstage, it became a more prevalent part of film and television. The sheer reach of film and television helped to usher in a new era of improvisation onstage. Improv and the screen have always had a tricky relationship, yet the presence of improv on screen spread improvisation beyond the hubs of live improv in places like Chicago, which led to the explosion of improvisation – both onstage and onscreen – at the turn of the 21st century. There's a reason there is so much more improv onstage than onscreen and so much more on television than on film – improvising on camera is problematic. From the cadence of speech to the cinematography to the editing room, improvising dialogue and action on camera (and making it look and sound good) is really, really hard. The evolution of improv onscreen mirrors the evolution onstage – from a tool to a product. As such, some entries in this section were not improv shows per se, like *SNL* and *SCTV*, but had a massive impact on the development of improvisational theatre. On the flip side, I have omitted important programs that are improv shows, like Australia's *Thank God You're Here* (see #46), or involve improvisation, like *Reno 911!*, *Murderville* (or the BBC series it is based on, *Murder in Successville*), *Jury Duty*, *The League*, *Outnumbered*, or *Impractical Jokers*. Most of the entries in this section represent American television, as those shows most directly influenced improv's style and tone.

DOI: 10.4324/9781003359692-5

26. SNL AND SCTV

It is impossible to talk about comedy on television without *Saturday Night Live* (*SNL*) and *Second City Television* (*SCTV*). *SNL* debuted in 1975, with *SCTV* right behind it in 1976, and comedy has never been the same. While there were comedy shows before them, these two shows had an outsized impact on improvisational comedy. Like Second City, *SNL* and *SCTV* do not present an improvised product. Instead, they use improvisation as a tool in creating their work. With multiple *SNL* cast members pulled from Second City and *SCTV* featuring the Second City Toronto, the original casts for both shows were steeped in improvisation. Both shows were rooted in Spolin's philosophy but had very different styles.

Tons of ink has been spilled about *SNL* already, so I will be brief and focus on two points: "liveness" and the casts' connection to improv. More concerned with popular culture and being a part of the zeitgeist than true social/cultural commentary, *SNL* has always presented itself as on the cutting edge of comedy. It prides itself on being a leader in political satire, celebrity impressions, pop culture parodies, and recurring characters. While *SNL* is not always concerned with social change or political satire, its *atmosphere* embodies Brecht's smokers' theatre. It's lively, it's fun, and it often sparks conversation. Contributing to the Brechtian cabaret is the show's structure, written and performed in less than a week, then presented live. The "live" of *Saturday Night Live* gives the show a similar energy to improvisational theatre. Part of *SNL's* appeal is the fact that *anything can happen*. Yes, it is scripted. Yes, it almost always follows that script (by and large). Yes, people still tune in because the show's liveness means "you never know." Its liveness and proximity to the present – i.e., it is making jokes about things that *just* happen – make the show exciting and (a little bit) dangerous. The "you never know" aesthetic is as much about seeing something taboo as anything. Live improv has the same energy, only heightened. For better or worse, because of its liveness, *SNL* has become the baseline for many audience members' expectations of what a live comedy show – sketch, improv, or otherwise – should look like.

The show's liveness also contributes to the background of a typical cast member. From the original cast to the present, improv experience and training are vital to being cast and succeeding on the show. Yes, there have been cast members who were stand-ups and excelled on the show, but the vast majority come from improvisation. Why? Two reasons. First, improvisers train how to create and work on very tight timelines. They can generate material quickly, adapt easily, perform at a high level with little to no rehearsal, and aren't afraid to fail. By casting a company of improvisers, *SNL* has an ensemble that all speak the same creative language.

Some problems are inherent, but it also means they know how to collaborate under intense pressure.

The second reason is a bit circular. Because *SNL* has always cast improvisers, they continue to cast improvisers. This circular casting loop has contributed to *SNL*'s diversity problem. Because improv is predominantly white, the talent pool created at places like Second City, iO, and The Groundlings is primarily white. *SNL*'s cast is predominantly white because the talent pool *SNL* usually pulls from is predominantly white. Because *SNL*'s cast is mostly white, it attracts future cast members who are mostly white, who go on to train at places like Second City, making them even more white. Because Second City's reputation is linked to its success in placing cast members on *SNL*, it prioritizes, consciously or not, training the type of performer who traditionally is cast on *SNL* (and attracts the kind of performer whom *SNL* usually casts). Because *SNL* has successfully cast improvisers from places like Second City and The Groundlings, they continue to cast from those theatres. The lack of representation on *SNL* creates an environment in improv theatres (and vice versa) that is difficult for BIPOC performers to succeed in. *SNL*'s extensive reach and popularity means this circular loop is particularly powerful.

SCTV was essentially the cast of Second City Toronto – Eugene Levy, Catherine O'Hara, Martin Short, Dave Thomas, Andrea Martin, and John Candy. Harold Ramis and Joe Flaherty joined them from Chicago's Second City, while Rick Moranis was the only non-Second City cast member. Even though they both were sketch comedy shows, *SCTV* was stylistically more understated than *SNL*. Whereas *SNL* is using pop culture and current events as its weekly source material and product, *SCTV*'s premise is that it is presenting the programming of a fictional television network. The sketches are in the form of a network's shows, commercials, behind-the-scenes drama, etc., rather than celebrity impressions or political satire. *SCTV* is much closer in presentation to long form improvisation, as the sketches often interweave and intertwine across an episode or season, and everything ties into the conceit of being part of the same television station.

Whereas *SNL* cast members go from improv to sketch (and then television and movies), many in *SCTV* would return to improv after the show, most notably Eugene Levy and Catherine O'Hara, who would become core members of Christopher Guest's iconic improvised films (see #30). *SCTV* is also representative of Close's concept of slow comedy. *SNL* is usually fast (except for that one sketch every episode that is excruciatingly slow). *SCTV* is notable in sketch comedy because many of its sketches and bits are a slow burn or don't rely on one big payout. The comedy runs the spectrum from understated to bizarre. *SCTV* trusts its audience more than *SNL* does, though the executives at ABC didn't trust *their* audience, turning down the show because they felt it was too intelligent.[1] *SCTV* eventually made its way onto NBC, though the new 90-minute format caused tension between the creators and the network, and the show ended after the 1984 season.

SCTV could be really weird … in a good way. In fact, even though it is known as *SCTV*, it was never officially titled *SCTV*. It had FIVE different titles, and none of them were actually *SCTV*. Go figure. Free from some of the pressures *SNL* faced – namely, time and money – *SCTV* delved into characters and storylines. The show's comedy had no direction – it wasn't directionless – instead, it went in every direction under the guise of it all happening at, or on, the same television station. *SCTV* was "a truly bizarre mishmash of pastiche and lyrical nonsense … based around the wily premise of a shitty, dysfunctional television network that aired everything from trivia shows, children's programs, and behind-the-scenes showbiz dramas."[2] Any given episode could have anything. Each episode was highlighted by the way it jumped from "show" to "show." While it would sometimes present a 30-second bit that would disappear forever, others would make their way back or tie together with other shows in odd and interesting ways.

The show also had its share of memorable characters, though it hardly had the same cultural recognition as *SNL*. The most recognizable are Rick Moranis and Dave Thomas's Doug and Bob McKenzie from "The Great White North." The pair originated as a gag about the Canadian Broadcasting Corporation's rule that each show needed a set amount of "Canadian-created" content and turned into the show's most popular bit, including the 1983 feature film *Strange Brew*. There are countless iconic characters and sketches that have been hugely influential. For example, Norm MacDonald's inspiration for writing the "Celebrity Jeopardy" sketches on *SNL*, which have become a decades-long recurring sketch, was Joe Flaherty's *SCTV* sketch "Half Wits." Flaherty also played the horny horror film host Count Floyd. There was John Candy as Harry, the guy with a snake on his face, doing commercials for Harry's Sex Shop. Then there was Martin Short's Ed Grimley. Even though it never reached the heights of *SNL* and has been somewhat forgotten, *SCTV* influenced pretty much everything, from *Mr. Show* to *The Eric Andre Show*.

Both shows boast a who's-who of comedy, many of them included in this book. As important as the people who worked on these shows, their presence in the homes of tens of millions of people profoundly reshaped the face of comedy. While improv was not the product of either show, its influence on the style of each show and the fact that so many of its cast members trained in improvisation ultimately lent legitimacy to improvisational theatre and gave it a national spotlight.

27. *WHOSE LINE IS IT ANYWAY?*

SNL and *SCTV* spotlighted Second City and improvisation. Still, there is perhaps no entry in this book with a more significant impact on improvisation than the television show *Whose Line Is It Anyway?* That is not meant to discount the work of others or suggest *Whose Line* presents the best improv in the world. Instead, it illustrates the power and reach of television. For many improvisers and audience members, *Whose Line* is their improv frame of reference. Rooted in Johnstone's philosophies and with talent initially often supplied by London's The Comedy Store Players, *Whose Line* debuted on Channel 4 in the UK in 1988. Created by Dan Patterson and Mark Leveson, with host Clive Anderson, the short form improv show ran until 1999. It spawned an American version hosted by Drew Carey that ran from 1998 to 2007, with a reboot launched in 2013 hosted by Aisha Tyler. Versions of the show (and imitations) have popped up around the globe, and its influence is undeniable on the form, style, and aesthetic of millions of improvisers and improv troupes.

The show's setup is relatively simple. Four improvisers ostensibly compete by playing a series of pre-determined short form improv games. The host emcees the show, runs the games, and gives suggestions for the players, often scripted beforehand (though the improvisers don't know them), and solicits suggestions and volunteers from the studio audience. The host also acts as a judge, awarding each player points "that don't matter" based on their performance in the games. The short form games work exceptionally well on television, as each is short and has reliably built-in laughs via each game's structural gimmick (e.g., the gimmick of any guessing game is that one player does not know a piece of information that everyone else – including the audience – already knows). Unlike long form improv or other performance styles, short form improv is easy for audiences to follow, making it ideal for television.

The format sets the show up to be successful, but the true success of the show relies on the improvisers. Across the show's many incarnations, three performers stand out for their impact on improvisational theatre – Colin Mochrie, Ryan Stiles, and Wayne Brady. Mochrie and Stiles became the show's most famous duo, and their improv roots together run deep. They both started with Vancouver Theatresports before moving on to Second City Toronto. They joined the show as guest performers in the first season, with Stiles joining as a main cast member in Season 2. Mochrie had a slightly rockier road, auditioning for the show three times before finally making it on as a regular in Season 3. Their chemistry, however, was undeniable, and the duo quickly became the show's anchors. The show's faux competitive structure allows Stiles and Mochrie to play together. Everyone knows the competition aspect "doesn't matter," so rather than pit them against one another, the show works to give them as many opportunities as possible to work together. Stiles and Mochrie were the faces of improvisational comedy for many audience members, especially those outside of the few major cities with an established improv community.

As the show moved across the Atlantic, so did Stiles and Mochrie, joining the cast of the American version of *Whose Line*. They were joined by another breakout star – Wayne Brady, who became well-known for his improvisational singing ability and vocal impressions. Brady began his improv journey at the SAK Comedy Lab in Orlando, FL, then as a cast member on the *Whose Line* imitation show *Kwik Witz*, which ran on syndication on some NBC affiliates in the slot after *Saturday Night Live*.[3] From there, Brady joined the tail end of the British *Whose Line* run, which, ironically enough, was filmed in America. On the American version hosted by Drew Carey, Brady became a core cast member and the show's breakout star. He would win an Emmy for his performance on *Whose Line*, leading to several television shows and appearances, including *The Wayne Brady Show*. Stiles, Mochrie, and Brady, formed the core of the American version, with a fourth guest performer rotating amongst improvisers like Brad Sherwood or Greg Proops or a celebrity guest like Robin Williams or Whoopie Goldberg. As with the British version, the show featured a small canon of repeated games, such as Scenes from a Hat, Hoedown, Questions Only, and Helping Hands. In addition to Stiles, Mochrie, and Brady, another performer had a considerable impact on the show – is pianist Laura Hall, who had worked previously as an accompanist for Second City. With Brady's immense singing talent, Hall became an ever more critical member of the company, with her music underscoring not just the signing games but many of the other games as well. Hall has the fourth most appearances on the show, trailing only Mochrie, Stiles, and Brady.

After the initial American version ended in 2007, a reboot was launched in 2013, hosted by Aisha Taylor and again featuring Mochrie, Stiles, and Brady. There was not much deviation from the format, though Taylor never played in games, whereas occasionally Drew Carey would join a game. To date, with all the various versions of the show, *Whose*

Line has run for twenty seasons. For the many people without a vibrant improv theatre in their hometown (and even for many who did), *Whose Line* became the defining version of improvisational comedy.

28. NICK CANNON AND *WILD 'N OUT*

Debuting in 2005, Nick Cannon's *Wild 'N Out* features short form improv-style games like *Whose Line* but embodies a different comedic aesthetic. The show mixes improv comedy and hip hop (both in aesthetic and via WildStyle literally), with Cannon saying he:

> created this show to be the desired destination for true fans of both comedy and hip hop ... Wild'n Out has all the elements of ground-breaking programming, in the same vein that In Living Color and Def Comedy Jam affected a generation.[4]

While the show doesn't quite have the influence of *In Living Color* or *Def Comedy Jam*, it has been a fundamental part of improv's growth over the past two decades, including players, voices, and styles that have often been excluded from improv.

While the show has some apparent similarities to *Whose Line*, it more closely resembles the structure of a ComedySportz or Match performance. Rather than four individual players, *Wild 'N Out* pits two teams of improvisers against one another, one captained by Cannon and the other usually captained by a celebrity guest, often a musician who will perform a song as part of the show. The guest captain helps bring variety to the show in terms of performers, and much like the host on *SNL,* part of the joy of each episode is watching the guest host doing something outside their usual comfort zone. Like ComedySportz or Match, the two teams battle via improv games and are awarded points by "winning" the round. After three rounds, the teams face off in the final round – WildStyle, where team members hurl insults at the other team via freestyle rap. Teams can score points for each "successful" punchline in this final round, meaning the team that wins WildStyle almost always wins the match.

The show has become a steppingstone for young comedians like Kevin Hart. The show likewise gave several future *SNL* stars their television start – Mikey Day, Taran Killam, Pete Davidson – as well as now fan-favorite regulars like DC Young Fly, Chico Bean, Justine, Emmanuel Hudson, DJ D-Wrek, Katt Williams, Affion Crockett, DeRay Davis, and many (many) more. One of the keys to the show's success is Cannon's willingness to keep putting young comics on the show (and his willing-ness to personally fund the pilot episode that convinced MTV to produce the show). The show's casting is quite different from *Whose Line*, which had relatively the same cast every single episode. While *Wild 'N Out* has regulars each season, it also continually turns over its cast and provides opportunities for performers to prove their comic chops and boost their profile. At the same time, Cannon continues to make room for more sea-soned performers and, in recent years, codified that by changing the team names to Old School and New School. Cannon preaches that the show is for everyone, saying, "Hey, you can be from the newer generation in hip hop, or you can be from the foundational space of hip hop because the show embodies all of that. So it truly is any age, any color, creed, class, Wild 'n Out, it has a space for you."[5]

29. ROBERT ALTMAN, JUDD APATOW, PAUL FEIG, AND ADAM MCKAY

Improv on film has been a bit trickier than improv on television. While *SNL* and *SCTV* introduced a new style of comedy on television with roots in improv and *Whose Line* and *Wild 'N Out* brought improv-as-the-product to the small screen, several directors/creators were experiment-ing with using improvisation on film and television. The very earliest films featured lots of improvisation, but as filmmaking evolved, scripts and camera shots became tighter and more structured to take advantage of the detail that film allows. While most directors eschew improvisation, several notable directors have embraced improvisation beyond allowing an actor to ad-lib a line or two. Four of the most influential directors using improvisation as part of their process are Robert Altman, Judd Ap-atow, Paul Feig, and Adam McKay.

To be clear, none of these directors rely solely on improvisation when making a film. They all use scripts and planned shots and the whole nine yards. They have embraced improvisation as a *part* of their filmmaking process. Robert Altman is not the first director to ever use improvisation, but he is one of the first contemporary directors to highlight improvisa-tion in his films, most notably in *Nashville* (1975). Again, it is worth stat-ing that Altman does not strictly use improvisation. Instead, he sees it as:

> a tool that the actors use and we use, just as the script is a tool … When you go and buy the Samuel French copy of the play, what you're really getting is the play as it was performed on the open-ing night. You back that up to when the rehearsals started and

> I'll guarantee you that much of the writing comes from the improvisation that occurs in the natural process of putting this thing together.[6]

Part of what makes improvisation work for Altman is that it truly is part of the process – not just for the actors but in how he shoots scenes. Rather than the traditional long shot, middle shot, and close-up takes, Altman tends to shoot scenes multiple times from a middle distance, keeping more actors in the frame than "normal" and allowing behavior and dialogue to emerge organically from the given circumstances of the scene. This style of keeping more actors in frame goes against the grain of American filmmaking, where carefully constructed shots and actor close-ups dominate. Altman did not make entirely improvised films – they weren't even close. But they did embrace improvisation as part of the creative process.

Judd Apatow, Paul Feig, and Adam McKay similarly embrace the process of improvisation in their filmmaking while, like Altman, making scripted films and television shows. This trio has also worked together on projects, such as *Bridesmaids*, where Apatow was producer and Feig director. The film is an excellent example of how they use improvisation in the process. In the writing process, they file every joke written or conceived. The jokes that don't make it into the script are kept in a separate document. More jokes are added to this document during the script revisions and rehearsals, so by the time the scene is shot, a vast trove of alternative takes is ready. You might be thinking, "That's not improv." You'd be correct. After they run the scene, the writers and director sit down and develop even more material. From this colossal trove, they select a dozen or so to film. After a few takes, they let the actors "go" and improvise more freely. Many of these moments make it into the film, but more importantly, it is an intentional choice to use improvisation as part of the process.

Like Altman, Feig and other improv-friendly directors will film scenes with cross shots. In addition to Altman's longer shots, cross shots involve filming the same scene simultaneously with multiple cameras from multiple perspectives. According to Feig, this is vital to capturing the magic of improvisation:

> You have these amazing moments that happen and if you've only got one side of it, it's impossible to re-create it again on the other side; you lose that first time magic. This type of comedy is never the same when you say it twice.[7]

McKay's process is similar, though McKay is the most experienced improviser in the group, having been part of Second City and anchoring several of their most essential revues, such as *Pinata Full of Bees*. When directing, like the others, McKay is working from a script, though he admits that he gets a "little itchy when everything was lining up *too* nicely. I want to make sure there are some mistakes flowing around ... So, I always throw improv in there to make sure that there's some collisions, and accidents."[8] McKay does not limit this technique to comedies, using it in more dramatic offerings like the television series *Succession*. He likewise changes his filming process to capture as much as possible. For instance, when describing how he shot a particular improvised scene in *Succession*, he said that they simply put the cameras on a dolly and moved it around the table as much as possible to capture as much as possible. Three takes later, and they had a wholly improvised scene.

As with *SNL* and *SCTV*, improvisation is part of the process for these directors, and their inclusion in this book stems from how their use of improv shines a light on improv's creative and artistic possibilities. These directors incorporate improv into the film's creative DNA, so it is much more than "an actor changed a line." Though not exclusively, their use of improvisation also means they hire improvisers or actors with a background in improvisation, further spotlighting improvisation. It is also worth noting that digital filmmaking has made improvisation much easier. Filming improvisation, let alone editing filmed improvisation, is not easy. Digital filmmaking makes it easier to shoot and one million percent easier to edit. While Altman was improvising on film before digital became the standard, it is not a coincidence that improv on film began to take off when technology made its implementation much more practical. Yes, improv on film's trajectory mirrors improv's ascendance in live performance and American comedy, but it also owes an enormous debt to technological advances.

30. MIKE LEIGH, CHRISTOPHER GUEST, LARRY DAVID, AND SACHA BARON COHEN

While the above directors use improv as part of the process (much like Second City uses improv to deliver a scripted product), Mike Leigh, Christopher Guest, Larry David, and Sacha Baron Cohen have made improv the central part of their processes *and* products (much like iO, ComedySportz, and other improv theatres). The four are not collaborators – one can dream – but do use improvisation more fully in their processes and products than the quartet of directors in #29. Leigh often begins a film with little more than a title and uses improvisation extensively to create everything. Guest and David harken back to The Compass Players' idea of scenario plays – using plot outlines but allowing the actors to fill in all the dialogue. Cohen embraces a more "improv is everywhere" role-playing style, where he improvises with real people who do not realize he is playing a part. While the above directors all use what's known as retro-scripting (having a script, allowing improvisation, and then incorporating the improvised dialogue into the final script), Leigh, Guest, David, and Cohen have little to no dialogue pre-scripted.

Mike Leigh began his career in the 1960s as a playwright working in Britain, before transitioning to film and television direction. He's been nominated for several Academy Awards as both a director and screenwriter, including for *Secrets & Lies* (1996), *Topsy-Turvy* (1999), *Vera Drake* (2004), *Happy-Go-Lucky* (2008), and *Another Year* (2010). His style relies heavily on improvisation, often beginning a project with little more than a concept. There's no script, no outline, no dialogue. Instead, Leigh spends weeks meeting with actors to develop characters and plot lines, then brings the actors together for rehearsals where the group improvises together and works out more details about the plot and characters. Leigh will often then create an outline from this extensive work, though often the actors still don't know exactly what's going to happen. When it comes time to shoot,

> Leigh and his actors improvise the scene they are going to shoot, and once they have decided the direction of the scene, they rehearse it over and over again to the point that their improvisation turns into a scripted scene they have all collaborated on. When the camera starts rolling, no one is improvising anymore.[9]

With painstaking care (and lots of rehearsal time), Leigh uses improvisation to go from a vague notion to a highly specific and scripted work. Technically, one could argue that Leigh does not use improv as the product, but it is so fundamental to his process – much more so than the directors in #29 – that it is also hard to argue improvisation is not part of the end product because it was so fundamental to the process.

There is no argument about improv as the product when it comes to Christopher Guest's films. Guest uses improvisation in his preparatory work, but rather than creating a scripted scene, he continues to use improvisation once the cameras are rolling. Guest popularized the mockumentary style film, using improvisation as the fundamental creative force to create a series of comic films that mix subtle humor with expert character development. Guest's first foray into improvised mockumentaries was 1984's cult classic *This Is Spinal Tap*. Guest had been working in improvisation for years before the film, most notably during his time with *The National Lampoon Radio Hour*, which was populated by many of the original *SNL* cast members. Most of Guest's contributions to the shows were improvised, often the ones he did with Bill Murray. When he began *This Is Spinal Tap*, the idea was to capture subtle rather than broad comedy, the latter of which is often what people associate with improv comedy (rightly or wrongly). For Guest, the difference comes down to the medium. Performing live often requires a broader style of comedy because you are performing in front of an audience. Performing for a camera allows (or even requires) more subtlety.[10] Guest's films are brilliant because they embrace the best parts of improv and film and marry them together rather than try to capture the largeness of live performance via a medium ill-suited to do so. In other words, improv was intentionally part of the process. "There's something about improvisation—the spontaneity of it," Guest said, "which sparks the actors that we work with here. There's a different feel. The comedy is different."[11] The documentary filming style allows for comic subtlety and for the product to be purposefully messy, circumnavigating some of the cinematographic issues that arise when trying to capture improvisation on film.

Another way that Guest intentionally uses improv is in the scripting, casting, and development of his films. While other directors might use improv to punch up a scene or explore a moment, Guest's films are almost entirely improvised from the start. That doesn't mean he just gathers a bunch of actors and yells, "Action!" Guest and Eugene Levy create a plot outline for their films (*Waiting for Guffman, Best in Show, A Mighty Wind*, etc.) with a script that is usually about fifteen pages as opposed to the traditional two-hour film with a script of about one hundred and twenty pages. Perhaps more importantly, Guest and Levy do extensive character development, which is then further explored by the actors. When it is time to film, the actors get a notecard with each scene's beginning and end points but nothing else. They rarely rehearse a scene before filming, capturing those initial discoveries and character interactions/collaborations on film. Guest also generally works with the same cast repeatedly, allowing them to deepen their skills and connections further. It doesn't hurt when that cast contains brilliant comedic actors like Levy, Catherine O'Hara, Jennifer Coolidge, Michael McKean, Harry Shearer, Parker Posey, Fred Willard, Jane Lynch, Bob Balaban, John Michael Higgins, and Michael Hitchcock.

Larry David has used a similar scenario play format for his television show *Curb Your Enthusiasm*. Much like Guest's films, *Curb Your*

Enthusiasm has an outline rather than a script. According to cast member Susie Essman,

> There's an outline, a 7-page-long outline and there's maybe a paragraph about what each scene is about. But there's no dialogue written. It will just say 'Larry and Jeff are eating at a Palestinian chicken restaurant talking about how great the chicken is.' The story is there, but there is no dialogue.[12]

Again, like Guest, the show relies on its acting cohort, which is relatively small and stable – David, Essman, Cheryl Hines, JB Smoove, and Jeff Garlin. The improvisation allows the actors to shine and highlights the show's central themes by emphasizing "real" reactions and emotions and the tensions between the mundane absurdities of life. In an interview, David spoke about why improv works (and why he can improvise), saying, "It's not really acting the way actors act, because it's just doing stuff that really anyone can do." David's invocation of Spolin's famous mantra, "Everyone can act. Everyone can improvise," speaks to the aesthetic tone of the show. In the same interview, David described how they needed a hotel clerk for a scene. So, rather than hire an actor, they simply hired a hotel clerk at the hotel where they were filming to be a hotel clerk. Rather than script the scene, they just had the hotel clerk respond and react as they normally would in their job as a hotel clerk. Commenting on the performance, David remarked that she was "terrific ... [but] if we had scripted that for her and had written it out, I'm sure she would have been terrible, as I would be if you scripted it."[13] Improv, for David, allows the actor a more natural and authentic response.

The hotel clerk is an excellent example because part of the reason improv works on the show is that the show does not have a complicated narrative plot, but instead, again, like Guest, is centered around more subtle or mundane things. The show is a character study rather than a plot-driven premise. That narrative structure, or eschewing of a narrative structure, plays to improv's strengths. Improvising and revealing character through dialogue and behavior is much easier than creating a spontaneous plot. It would be much more difficult to improvise a show that had a complicated narrative structure, so the lack of intricate plot details allows both David and Guest to make improvisation the central creative process because they embrace the strengths of improvisation rather than trying to cram it into a structure where improvisation simply is not the best choice.

Curb also works because of the tireless work of the editing team. Cutting together improvised takes is difficult and extremely time-consuming, which is one of the reasons using it on a network television sitcom would be next to impossible – it can take three weeks or more to edit an episode of *Curb*. The show is filmed with two opposing cameras capturing all the action, meaning each scene is often edited from a compilation of takes. So, while the scene might appear to be one free-flowing improvisation (as are many of the takes in Guest's films, particularly the "interview" sections), they are usually painstakingly cut together in post-production. David is often a part of that process, working with editors Steve Rasch and Jonathan Corn. The show's trademark dialogue flow, with overlapping dialogue and characters cutting one another off, makes editing particularly challenging. The show's "real" feel, much like Guest's mockumentary style, allows for some freedom in editing, but the show still maintains a high-quality visual and aural aesthetic. As noted above, digital tools play a central role in *Curb's* production and use of improvisation.

Sacha Baron Cohen has used improvisation in his most well-known works – *Da Ali G Show* and the *Borat* movies. What differentiates Cohen from Guest and David is that often, he is the only one in on the joke. Cohen's first major success, which would set up many of his subsequent projects, was *Da Ali G Show*, which first aired on the BBC in 2000 and had two more seasons in 2003–2004 on HBO. The show is a satirical news and entertainment interview-style show. Cohen played three characters in the show – the titular Ali G, a wannabe gangster influencer; Borat Sagdiyev, a Kazakh reporter; and Brüno Gehard, a gay Austrian fashion enthusiast. Cohen would interview celebrities, politicians, and other well-known figures as these three characters – though he never revealed to the interviewees that he was playing a character. He often asked them absurd questions or attempted to put them into awkward situations. He also asked probing and satirical questions to illuminate his interviewees' hypocrisy and politically incorrect opinions, usually by expressing his characters' politically incorrect opinions. The audience knows Cohen's opinion is a façade. Simultaneously, because the interactions are authentic, they view the interviewees' opinions as revelations of truth. One tactic Cohen relies upon is the element of surprise. His questioning style is one example – throwing out absurd or light questions, followed instantly by a deeply probing question. Cohen also used surprise to lull interviewees into a sense of ease, making them more likely to let their guard down and respond authentically. When playing Ali G, Cohen would enter the interview space already in character as Ali G, though he would often carry equipment and look more like a crew person than the interviewer. Another person would be dressed to look like an anchor, so when Ali G would sit down to ask the subject questions, they often thought it was simply a warmup or a test of the equipment before realizing that Ali G was, in fact, the interviewer and they were already five minutes (or more) into the interview.

Cohen would make feature films with both Brüno and Borat, with the latter much more commercially successful. Presented as documentaries, the premise of the two *Borat* films is that he's trying to learn about America. As such, only Cohen and a handful of other actors are scripted or "in on the joke," so the vast majority of the people who appear in the films are real people responding in reality to Borat. The films still have a script, though, a rather conventional one at that. In fact, both *Borat* films were Oscar-nominated for Best Adapted Screenplay. According to Anthony Hines, a writer on both Borat films:

> We get together in a writers room, we throw some ideas around, and we start to draw out an outline … Eventually, we get a conventional final draft script in which everybody in it, apart from Sacha and Maria Kakalova [who plays his daughter in the second Borat film], will be a real person. You write the script and sort of predict what you would like them to say in scenes – a sort of dream scenario for how you want the scenes to play out.[14]

In a way, the scripts become a kind of choose-your-own-adventure playbook. The actual actors are given scripts with multiple scenarios and dialogue based on how the real person might respond. They can't feasibly be ready for all possibilities, so the actors often rely on improvisation. Even if the script goes according to plan, the actors still must employ an improvisational mindset where they are ready to listen and respond truthfully in the moment. So, while the shooting relies heavily on improvisation, there is still a framework in place, much as in Guest's films or on David's *Curb*. Even though there is a script for much of Cohen's work and he has set lines, "his true achievement is to inhabit absurd characters believably over extended periods of time with people who are not in on the joke."[15] Aside from Cohen's comedic chops, the key to making it all work is that *the audience* is in on the joke. The humor relies on this knowledge gap, much like any short form improv guessing game. We know Borat is Cohen, even if the people he's interacting with do not.

Guest, David, and Cohen are important in improv's evolution for several reasons. For starters, they are all immensely talented comic performers, so their use of improv helps elevate the form. Much like Second Wave theatres did, they also prove that improv can be more than a tool – it can be the feature. Yes, they all have scripts, and they are not purely improvising in the way that TJ & Dave are, but they also highlight the role of improvisation. Whereas many film directors who use improv use it as a tool, it is front-and-center for Guest, David, and Cohen – albeit in three different ways. Those differences are also hugely important for showing how people can use improv beyond standard short form games and long form scenes.

30.1 The TV Shows I Said I Omitted but Then Changed My Mind About

In the introduction to this section, I said I was not going to include shows like Australia's *Thank God You're Here* or ones that involve improvisation, like *Reno 911!*, *Murderville* (or the BBC show it is based on, *Murder in Successville*), *Jury Duty*, *Outnumbered*, *Impractical Jokers*, or any number of others. Technically, I'm not including them, but let me briefly overview a few here in #30.1. I'm still not officially including some shows with improvised takes, where the improv is primarily a cast member riffing on a joke or subject, like *It's Always Sunny in Philadelphia* or *The League,* since those mirror some improv styles already included in this section. Since this entry isn't a full entry – it's a.1 entry – I will only briefly top-line each show.

Reno 911!, created by Thomas Lennon and Robert Ben Garant, weaves improvisation into the show's cop-style parody structure. Much like *Curb*, the show has an outline, which often includes lines or the scene's punchline, but little set-in-stone scripted dialogue. Much like *Curb* and Guest's films, the aesthetic appears freewheeling, but that results from massive preparation. Lennon discussed the use of improv on the show,

> I think what a lot of people don't know is, to make it look so loose and unprepared, a lot of planning went into it. We did write outlines for almost every single scene that ever happened, just so we had some sort of sense of what was going on. It was slightly more structured than it seemed.

Garant echoed those thoughts, saying, even though the show was shot more quickly than scripted shows, "to get about a minute and a half of material for *Reno*, we would shoot for about 40 minutes of improve … the show really did come together in the editing room."[16] For example, they'd take an entire day of shooting to get 15 minutes for the season's "morning briefing" scenes. They also had the cast wear the exact same clothes for most of each season's shooting so that they could edit together *anything* shot, even if they were from different scenes and not initially intended to go together.

In *Murderville*, cops and improvisation mix again as Will Arnett is Detective Terry Seattle. He is joined in each episode by a celebrity "cop-in-training" who must solve a murder. Everyone except the celebrity guest knows the scenario. The cast must work with and react to whatever the guest (it should always be Marshawn Lynch) says or does. Much like The Match, the show has a strict structure but allows improvisational freedom within each highly structured bit. In *Jury Duty*, James Marsden plays himself serving on a jury with ten other actors (and a fake judge and fake lawyers) and one real person, Ronald Gladden, who is entirely unaware that everything happening in the show is scripted. Unlike *Murderville*, where the celebrity guest knows everything is made up, on *Jury Duty,* Gladden *absolutely* thinks everything is real, and audiences are delighted in both structures. The British sitcom *Outnumbered* is a traditional family sitcom; only the parents (Hugh Dennis and Claire Skinner) have scripts, and the kids only get basic directions about a scene right before filming. This structure creates some hilarious moments, and the improvisation lets the show more realistically reflect family life. *Impractical Jokers* features members of the comedy group The Tenderloins competing against one another in hidden-camera style games, mainly meant to humiliate one another. They use improvisation in a similar vein to Sacha Baron Cohen, with much of the comedy coming from the hidden-camera quality of the show, where the group (and audience) know they are part of an improvised performance, but others do not.

One show that arguably should have its own entry is *Portlandia*. A quirky sketch comedy show that ran for eight seasons on the Independent Film Channel, the show features former *SNL* cast member Fred Armisen and former Sleater-Kinney guitarist and vocalist Carrie Brownstein. The show's creative structure is like other shows that prioritize improvisation. Armisen and Brownstein, along with director and co-executive producer Jonathan Krisel and a small team of writers, usually script out rough plots for sketches, but leave ample room for discovery and tangents in the filming process. Krisel says,

> The shooting becomes our rewriting ... because it's so heavily improvised. And that's kind of the secret of the show, that once you've got this simple premise and you've brainstormed it and you've written it, then on the day (of taping) you can just have fun with it.[17]

As with other shows that use improvisation, they lean into the "messiness" or reality-tv feel that comes from shooting improvised dialogue. Krisel described *Portlandia's* shooting style "like cable access nightmare was kind of the aesthetic."[18] That deliberate style allows the improv to flourish, rather than feel out of place (and is one of the reasons some cinematographers don't like improv because it is more capturing moments rather than crafting visuals). As with *Curb Your Enthusiasm*, much of the hardest work happens in the editing room where the creative team cobbles together the funniest bits, lines, and oddities from each sketches many takes and tangents.

This quick sidebar entry demonstrates that there is a lot of improv on television, even if it isn't always strictly improv a la *Whose Line*. The various ways each show uses improv are also interesting, as it reflects and influences how improv is evolving and used in live performance. They also demonstrate that improv on film *is a lot of work*. Most people assume doing improv means less work. Improv requires just as much preparation as any scripted scene, arguably more so since no one knows what's really going to happen, and you must prepare for multiple outcomes. Plus, it takes five times as much work on the back end in the editing room. Just as improvisers performing onstage practice regularly and don't just show up to a show and "go," improv on screen doesn't just happen.

Okay, back to the list. At number 31, I present ...

31. STEVE CARELL AND STEPHEN COLBERT

The following three entries are all duos (technically, so is the fourth), some official and some not. They all have a background in improvisation and have become some of the most notable and recognizable practitioners and alums of the various improv theatres/schools. They all became famous via television, so I have included them here.

The Steves – Carell and Colbert – started at Second City and came up together in the 1990s, working together at Second City, then *The Dana Carvey Show*, "The Ambiguously Gay Duo" on *SNL*, and as correspondents on *The Daily Show*. Colbert was actually Carell's understudy at Second City (when Lorne Michaels and *SNL* came scouting at Second City, they saw a performance where Colbert was filling in for Carell). The duo impressed almost everyone during their time at Second City, but they never seemed to be in the right place at the right time. Neither was cast on *SNL*, though Colbert did some short writing stints, and they voiced "The Ambiguously Gay Duo." Their casting on *The Dana Carvey Show* should have been their big break, but the "Show That Couldn't Fail" failed spectacularly and only lasted seven episodes. The duo eventually was hired by *The Daily Show*, where they began to make a name for themselves.

After *The Daily Show*, they went in separate directions. Carell would use his improv and comic training to create an impressive acting career. His comic improvisation in movies like *Anchorman* and the *Despicable Me* franchise have become iconic, but nothing matches his role as Michael Scott on *The Office*. The show is one of the most successful comic sitcoms of all time, and a lot of that success is due to Carell and the show's embrace of improvisation. *The Office* was a scripted show, but much like the films listed above that utilized improvisation, *The Office* incorporated improv into the show. The talking head interviews almost always featured improvised takes by the cast members, and they filmed many of the scripted scenes multiple times to allow for improvisation. Paul Feig was a frequent director of the series, so it should be no surprise that improv was a central part of the process. Similarly, the aesthetic of the show – a mockumentary – utilizes the same style as Guest's films, which creates a more "realistic" feel and allows improvisation to flourish.

Colbert, meanwhile, took off as a satiric news host, hosting the incredibly successful *The Colbert Report*, before eventually moving on to CBS' *The Late Show with Stephen Colbert*. While Carell uses improvisation as a performer, Colbert uses more of the structures and philosophies of improvisation in his political satire, most notably the theories of Bertolt Brecht. As discussed in #0, while Spolin's and Johnstone's theories are at the heart of improvisational comedy, Brecht's theories and philosophy underpin much of improv's aesthetic and style. As a refresher … working in the first half of the 20th century, Brecht wanted his own workers' theatre, what he called a smokers' theatre – a theatre of ideas presented in a cabaret style that was inviting and friendly for the audience and allowed them to engage with the performance intellectually (rather than emotionally). Brecht's smokers' theatre was hugely influential in the creation and execution of The Compass Players, and his style and techniques are evident throughout improvisational theatre, most notably through the performances and style of The Annoyance Theatre. To achieve his socially conscious theatre, Brecht wanted a deliberate acting style where the actor was always aware of the triangular relationship between the actor, the audience, and the character, what Ian Wilkie calls a "reflective practitioner."[19] Nearly all improvised performances use this actor-character detachment technique because improvisers inherently bring more of themselves to each character and role than a traditional actor, which brings us back to Colbert, who created one of the greatest Brechtian characters of all time on *The Colbert Report* – Stephen Colbert.

Colbert's construction of a right-wing narcissistic "news" anchor works to deconstruct both the news media, particularly Fox News, and comment upon the political issues of the day. The audience always knows that Colbert, the character, is being played by Colbert, the actor, who most often holds diametrically opposed views to the ones espoused by Colbert, the character. Segments like "The Word" further illustrate Colbert's use of Brecht. There is a split screen in the segment. On one side is Colbert pontificating, and on the other is text, which eventually undercuts what Colbert is saying. The character Colbert is also playing an elaborate "game of the scene," pushing his character's behavior to its logical extreme ends. Even though Colbert is not explicitly using improv or improvising per se, he is utilizing fundamental improvisational theories and concepts. Colbert's reach via *The Colbert Report* and *The Late Show* (which is less overtly based on improv principles) means his influence on comedy and satire is undeniable.

Both Steves have become pop culture symbols for improvisation. Carell's work on *The Office* and Colbert's on *The Colbert Report* is, for many, their access point for improvisation. The Steves also demonstrate the flexibility of improvisational training. Both came through Second City and used the skills developed there to carve out unique career paths. They've touched nearly every mediated form of improvisation, from sitcoms to feature films to late-night television. Their fingerprints and influence are all over improv on screen.

32. AMY POEHLER AND TINA FEY

Even though they are often placed together, Amy Poehler and Tina Fey are an official unofficial comedy duo. They have worked together for years, beginning as improvisers at iO, then as Weekend Update anchors at *SNL*, and then in a variety of ways on film and television – as co-hosts of awards shows, as movie co-stars, and via many television appearances. Even their respective sitcoms, *30 Rock* and *Parks and Recreation,* were seen less as competitors and more as complements.

Much like our next duo decided to support and complement one another rather than compete against one another, Fey and Poehler bucked the system by working together. Much of improv's history has been dominated by white men, and this was certainly the case when Fey and Poehler began their improv careers in Chicago in the 1990s. As we've seen, most ensembles were made up of mostly white men. The landscape often pitted non-white male performers against one another by having them compete for the limited spots available to non-white performers.

For example, it was not until 1996 that Second City had a show with an equal number of male and female cast members ("Citizen Gates," directed by Mick Napier and featuring Fey among its cast). Fey and Poehler, and Key and Peele, broke that trend by working together and supporting one another. Key and Peele, as we'll see, were very explicit about making themselves indispensable together by creating pieces for both of them. At the same time, Fey and Poehler worked to create an atmosphere of collaboration rather than competition that they would carry from Chicago's improv stages to *SNL*.

Like many aspiring comedians, Fey moved to Chicago after graduating from The University of Virginia. Poehler likewise moved to Chicago after graduating from Boston College. They both began taking classes at Second City and iO. They met in class in 1993 at iO and were teamed up on the group Inside Vladimir by Charna Halpern. Illustrating their cooperative approach, Fey said of the pairing, "We were put together like two beautiful baby lions in a cage who miraculously did not have the impulse to eat each other."[20] Fey and Poehler then auditioned together for the Second City Touring Company – shocker – they were both cast. From Second City, their paths diverged, though often reconnecting.

SNL hired Fey in 1997, and she eventually became the show's first female head writer. She was launched into stardom when she became a Weekend Update anchor, bringing a sharp wit and keen intellect to the anchor's desk. Poehler also went from Second City to New York, though she went as a founding member of the Upright Citizens Brigade. UCB was hugely popular and influential both onstage and via their television show (see #20). Poehler would eventually join the cast of *SNL* and soon found herself sharing the anchor desk with Fey, marking one of the high points in Weekend Update's history. They would be further linked via *SNL* through the 2008 presidential election, where Fey famously portrayed Sarah Palin, and Poehler played Hillary Clinton. Much like their exits from Second City, the pair again diverged when they left *SNL* – this time for a pair of successful sitcoms – Fey's *30 Rock* and Poehler's *Parks and Recreation*.

Both shows utilized improvisation in a variety of ways. *30 Rock* had less improvisation on camera than *Parks and Rec* but was heavily influenced structurally by the Harold. While the episodes are not intentionally meant to be Harolds, the structural similarities are undeniable. There is a chicken-or-the-egg argument about situational-comedy structure and the Harold, but *30 Rock* one hundred percent looks like a Harold. Each episode has three storylines that all start in entirely different places, and like a Harold, a lot of the comedy comes from how those storylines unexpectedly collide and interconnect. Thanks to the structural similarities to the Harold, the show became an invaluable reference point for many improvisers and audience members. When trying to explain (or understand) the Harold, it became common to say, "It's kind of like an episode of *30 Rock*." That shared shorthand was hugely impactful, as one of long form improv's biggest issues in becoming more popular has always been its opacity. If you don't know what the Harold is, seeing one on stage with little to no explanation can be confusing. *30 Rock* helped to clear up some of that confusion.

On the other hand, *Parks and Rec* uses improv like films such as *Bridesmaids* in that the show utilizes improvisation by the actors via multiple takes. Michael Schur, the show's creator whose credits include *The Office*, *The Good Place*, *Brooklyn 99*, and *Hacks*, built-in "fun runs." Like *The Office*, the show is scripted, but after each scene, they always film for an additional five minutes, where the cast can improvise anything they want. Many of these moments ended up in the show, including what Schur describes as "The funniest line ever spoken on the show [which] was improvised by Chris Pratt." In the season 3 episode "Flu Season," Pratt's character tries to help Poehler's Leslie Knope, who suffers from the flu: "Leslie, I typed your symptoms into the thing up here and it says you might have 'network connectivity problems'."[21]

These "fun runs" create an atmosphere of collaborative creativity. Most of the time, the written jokes are funnier than the improvised ones. But sometimes not, and more importantly, the spirit of collaboration these extra takes create gives the show an improvisational feel. The "fun runs" also mirror many safety-net style structures inherent in improv onstage. As we've seen, the Match has an incredibly rigid structure, but within that structure allows for spontaneity. The "fun runs" and every other entry in this section that works from an outline or has some relatively rigid safeguards in place is doing the same thing The Match and other structures are doing – providing stability and raising the odds of success. Limiting the "fun runs" to five minutes requires the actors to focus and heightens the importance of the improvised moments.

Fey and Poehler are two of improv's most prominent and recognizable improv ambassadors. They talk about improv and its influence on their careers and creative process ALL THE TIME. They each wrote a memoir-ish book chock-full of how they have used and been influenced by improv – Fey's *Bossypants* and Poehler's *Yes, Please!* Each also dedicated a chapter in their respective books to the other. Their success and openness about improv's role in that success have been monumental in increasing improv's prestige within the entertainment world. Similarly, Fey and Poehler have carved out a bigger space for women in comedy and improvisation.

33. JORDAN PEELE AND KEEGAN-MICHAEL KEY

Fey and Poehler are an unofficial comedy duo who sometimes officially work together. Jordan Peele and Keegan-Michael Key are an official comedy duo ... who don't work together as much anymore. Key and Peele formed their creative partnership through *MADtv*, though they first met via a comedy exchange between Second City (where Key was working) and BOOM Chicago (where Peele was working; see #40). They would go on to create one of the best sketch comedy shows of all time – *Key & Peele* – before venturing on to successful Hollywood and television careers. Like Fey and Poehler, Key and Peele were entering a landscape that was beginning to diversify – thanks to improv groups like Jane, Oui Be Negroes, and Stir Friday Night, and television shows like *In Living Color* – but still, more often than not, made non-white male performers compete against one another for performance opportunities. Rather than compete, Key and Peele decided to collaborate.

Keegan-Michael Key came to sketch and improv later than many folks in the book. He trained as a traditional actor, receiving an MFA in Acting from Penn State. Eventually, he decided to follow his impulses to pursue comedy and auditioned for the Second City in Detroit. His training in mime, commedia, and other forms of physical and classical theatre suited him perfectly at Second City, where he could marry his considerable performance skills to his considerable wit. Second City was also where he was first truly introduced to improvisation, becoming immersed in the Second City model of using improv to develop written sketches. In an interview with Sam Jones, Key describes his approach to improvisation, saying, "People think that improvisation is moving forward. What improvisation really is, it's walking backward ... it's backing up that gives you discovery."[22] The unearthing comes in pulling out and beginning to see all the things that are already there, that already exist, and taking those clues and building a world. It is a similar philosophy to TJ & Dave, who regularly talk about how the scene is already happening and they are merely stepping into it. Everything you need is already there; you simply must pan out to see it. At Second City, Key was becoming an inside comedy star.

Meanwhile, Jordan Peele improvised in Amsterdam with BOOM Chicago. Key and Peele first met via an exchange between the two companies, with everyone telling Key he needed to see Peele and Peele that he needed to see Key. While they weren't exactly performing together, the meeting set up a friendship and collaborative partnership that would see the duo rise to the top of sketch comedy. Before teaming up on their show, the duo auditioned for *MADtv*, ostensibly Fox's replacement for *In Living Color*. The show presented itself as an edgier, bolder, and brasher version of *SNL*, filled with many pop-culture parodies, recurring characters, and celebrity impressions. The audition was set up as a competition between the two to fill "the African American male" slot, but they worked so well together that they were both cast. Rather than compete, they collaborated. Peele suggested they write most of their material together to "become a valuable and inseparable unit."[23]

The duo quickly realized that they had a similar comedic sensibility and that their style was rooted in what Key calls *heavy game*. Like UCB's "Game of the Scene," it essentially means the bit in the sketch that escalates the premise. The more the characters play the game, the more the audience enjoys the sketch. Mr. Garvey, the inner-city substitute teacher, plays the game of mispronouncing the "normal" names of the suburban white students in his class. That's it – the more he mispronounces, the more we laugh. The scene has many layers, and it contains a commentary about names, "normality," and race in America, but the game is at the heart of the scene. This game philosophy became the base for *Key & Peele*, which, in Key's words, was less about "changing the world with comedy" and more about "making world-class comedy."[24] It's not surprising that game is such a fundamental part of their show because, in addition to their improv training, nearly everyone on the show's writing staff had an improv background. Their showrunner, Ian Roberts, was one of the co-founders of UCB. Even though very little improvisation made it into the final cuts of their sketches – they have an extremely rigorous writing, revising, and selection process – the influence of improvisation is at the heart of every single sketch.

In the same way *30 Rock* became a pop culture reference for the Harold, *Key & Peele* became a pop culture reference for "game of the scene." Teaching, learning, and performing long form improv became easier because of *Key & Peele* – not because the show featured improvisation, but because it was such a crystal-clear example of improv techniques in action. Like the other duos in this section, Key and Peele's background in improvisation informed their creative process. Once again, comedy stars pointed to their improv training – at Second City and Boom Chicago, respectively – as vital to their comedic success.

34. MIDDLEDITCH & SCHWARTZ

The last of our quartet of duos is Thomas Middleditch and Ben Schwartz, who star in the Netflix series of live long form improv shows *Middleditch & Schwartz*. The show is a kind of culmination of how improv has evolved on screen over the last forty years ... by showcasing improvisation via its theatrical simplicity. Both Middleditch and Schwartz trained in improvisation before landing a role on a television series that enhanced their profile. Middleditch trained in Chicago and cemented his comic legacy as Richard Hendricks on HBO's *Silicon Valley*, while Schwartz trained at UCB and rose to fame via his role as Jean-Ralphio Saperstein on *Parks & Rec*. The stature gained from these roles ended up being the main selling point to Netflix for allowing them to create three one-hour-long improvised "specials."

Before *Middleditch & Schwartz,* there was not much long form improv captured on film. *Whose Line* and *Wild 'N Out* feature short form games, and the various films utilizing improv, like Guest's work, still work from a set script or scenario. *30 Rock* is structured like a Harold, but it is not an improvised Harold. In 2005, Charna Halpern published *Art By Committee*, which included a DVD with several improv performances recorded at iO. Bravo aired a special with UCB performing ASSSSCAT in 2005, and then in 2009, *Trust Us, This Is All Made Up*, a documentary-style film recording of a TJ & Dave performance was released. In part due to technological limitations – in short, they all look like they were filmed in the early 2000s (you know, because they were) – and the fact that most of the improvised shows were not the very best performances of the respective groups, they didn't lead to a massive explosion in improv's popularity. They all are important and valuable resources, but none feature improv at its best ... which is one of the givens of improv; not every show will be a grand slam. The *Middleditch & Schwartz* Netflix special not only looks great (which is important in conveying to non-improv audiences that improv is important), but the three episodes (they are three different shows) feature some very high-quality improv. Perhaps most important in presenting improv to non-improv audiences is that Middleditch and Schwartz are recognizable comic actors performing pure improv. Audiences know them or at least recognize them, and that lends them credibility. As such, Jesse Fox and others have moved the special to the top of the recorded improv hierarchy, writing that the special "could have significant ramifications on improv's position in our culture."[25] Debuting in 2020, the duo also benefited, somewhat ironically, from *not* being the first long form improv on television, so they were not presenting a totally foreign product to audiences.

Another component of their success and the special's influence is that their show's structure is simple. A lot of long form improv can be complex to follow. Someone with little knowledge of long form will not necessarily follow the structure of a Harold, ASSSSCAT, or Deconstruction. TJ & Dave, Bassprov, and other straightforward shows have provided a blueprint for simple-structure-long form – not to say that their technique is simple – but the show's structure is relatively straightforward. The two ask the audience a few questions, have a conversation with an audience member to drill a little deeper, then take that information and create a roughly one-hour improvised long form show. Whereas TJ & Dave don't take a suggestion and ask the audience to "trust us, this is all made up," Middleditch & Schwartz pull back the curtain on the process. This distinction isn't to say one is right or wrong. Still, in terms of revealing the *process* of improvisation, Middleditch & Schwartz let the audience see how the sausage is made, which is important when considering that potentially millions of people will stream their Netflix show. Their pseudo-interview with an audience member provides them with the source material and allows the audience to be part of the creative process. The audience can link various characters or storylines to the original suggestions/conversation as the show unfolds. This interview technique reveals how improv works in a macro sense while allowing the audience to be part of the inside joke central to much of improv's appeal.

As with nearly every duo show, Middleditch and Schwartz play dozens of characters in each show, often playing multiple characters in one scene. This doubling technique is common in long form improv, but their skill at executing it – ON NETFLIX – allows a huge audience to see how long form improv works. They weave together plot points, callback ideas and characters, and make connections between plot, character, and theme. Those techniques are long form improv 101, but rarely have they been executed so clearly and simply for such a large and diverse audience. In the same way that *An Evening with Nichols & May* introduced audiences to a new style of sketch comedy, or how *Whose Line* showed millions of people short form improv games (and how to play them), *Middleditch & Schwartz* has become an example of what long form improv is when executed at a high level. Not to state the obvious, but the fact that the three shows in the special are hilarious is hugely important. Most people outside the improv community have very little reference for what long form improv is or should look like, so having this high-level example on a top-rated streaming platform is vital to improv's continued growth as an art form. It not only exposes audiences to long form improv, but it also provides a template for performers and teachers to use to learn and improve long form improv skills.

35. *IMPROV NERD*

Television and film (and streaming) have exposed improv to millions of viewers. The other technology that has exploded in the last decade has been podcasts. Everyone has a podcast about something – chances are you have a podcast. The following two entries highlight the two styles of podcasts that exist in improv – ones that talk about and analyze comedy and improv, and ones that produce comedy and improv. There are many great comedy podcasts, like *WTF with Marc Maron*, "the de facto godfather of comedy-interview podcasting."[26] Maron's show is an inside-comedy style show, where he interviews comedians and other folks like former President Barack Obama. Maron has interviewed improvisers on his show, but improv is not the focus of Maron's show. Jimmy Carrane's *Improv Nerd* is kind of *WTF*, but solely about improv. Carrane even saw himself as sort of the improv version of Maron, saying, "I really thought I was going to be Marc Maron, that popularity, so that's really what I was shooting for."[27]

Carrane trained and performed himself at ImprovOlympic, and like many improvisers in Chicago, he hit the ceiling of career advancement. While folks like Tina Fey and Steve Carrell did the tried-and-true career jump of Second City to *SNL* to Hollywood Star, countless other talented improvisers did not. One of Carrane's great gifts to the improv community is his open and frank discussions and writings about success, fame, and the lack thereof in a commercial sense. In addition to the podcast, Carrane writes a weekly blog and has written several highly accessible books – *Improvising Better: A Guide for the Working Improviser* (co-written with Liz Allen), *Improv Therapy: How to get out of your own way to become a better improviser,* and *The Inner Game of Improv: 5 Steps to Getting Bigger in Your Improv Career.* A celebrated teacher, he's worked with everyone from improv theatres to Fortune 500 companies. But what has cemented his place in the improv community is *Improv Nerd*.

Launched in 2011, Carrane's *Improv Nerd* has become an invaluable asset to the improv community. *Improv Nerd* features in-depth interviews with hundreds of improvisers. The biggest names in improv have appeared on the show, which would make the podcast hugely influential.

What makes it indispensable is Carrane's interviewing acumen. He asks probing questions, has honest conversations, and brings his own vulnerabilities to each interview. His kindness and generosity allow his guests to reciprocate – diving deeply into improv theory and their journeys. In addition to acting as pseudo masterclasses in improv, many episodes also highlight his guests' different paths. Many young improvisers struggle with "What do I do next?" or "Where do I go?" Carrane's self-obsession with fame and success (he's very open about his desires and struggles in that regard) allow his guests to talk about their struggles and paths. In an interview with Ilana Glazer and Abbi Jacobson, for example, they discuss how they did not make a Harold team at UCB, but rather than allow UCB to be a gatekeeper, turned around and made their own web series that turned into the Comedy Central series *Broad City*. Listening to the hundreds of interviews illuminates the MANY different paths various improvisers have taken, which helps to open doors and pathways for others. Carrane usually ends each episode by improvising with his guest(s) or conducting some exercises with them, though the meat of the podcast is the interview segment.

Dozens of improv podcasts have been launched, aspiring (intentionally or not) to reach *Improv Nerd*'s influence and stature. Many of them are quite good, such as *The Backline* with Rob Norman and Adam Cawley, *Improv Comedy Connection* with Whit Shiller, *The Improv Chronicle* with "Lloydie" James Lloyd, *The Improv Conspiracy* with Broni Lisle, *Improv Touchstones* from Improv Cincinnati, and many others. In the same way that all sketch and improv comedy kind of lives in the orbit of *SNL* and Second City, all improv podcasts revolve around *Improv Nerd*.

36. COMEDY BANG! BANG!, HELLO FROM THE MAGIC TAVERN, AND IMPROV4HUMANS

Many comedy podcasts, however, revolve around *Comedy Bang! Bang!* Debuting in 2009 as *Comedy Death-Ray Radio*, the podcast and spin-off television show have become staples of the comedy community. Hosted by Scott Aukerman, the show changed its name to *Comedy Bang! Bang!* in 2011. The podcast is a mixture of conversation and performance. Aukerman conducts interviews with his guests, but often, he and his guests play characters and perform elaborate and ongoing bits. The bits often have a structure or recurring theme/game, but they are mostly improvised, as is the final section of the show featuring Aukerman and his guests playing shorter games. Becca James called the podcast "a juggernaut … An incubator for absurd improv comedy that might not fly elsewhere, the show honors the form while simultaneously heightening its function, to reliably risible results."[28] *Comedy Bang! Bang!* bridges the gap between more serious podcasts about the art of comedy, like *WTF* and *Improv Nerd*, with podcasts that are more geared toward producing comedy. Much like *WTF*, it is the founding father of comedy-making podcasts.

It should come as no surprise that improvised podcasts have become so popular. After all, the early days of radio were filled with improv as vaudeville actors-turned-radio-stars transitioned their stage material to the airwaves. The bits on *Comedy Bang! Bang!* are more absurd than their vaudeville predecessors, but the concept of playing long-running characters and playing recurring bits is very vaudevillian. *Comedy Bang! Bang!* is hardly alone in using or featuring improv comedy, though it is arguably the genre's progenitor. While I will focus on two improvised podcasts here, there are hundreds – many of which are very good, like *Teacher's Lounge, With Special Guest Lauren Lapkus, Offbook, Sponteneanation ...* and a thousand others, like yours. The two highlighted below encapsulate the two main types of improv podcasts – world-building and one-off improvising. *Hello From The Magic Tavern* represents the world-building side of improv podcasts, as the players create an ongoing improvised fantasy universe, whereas *Improv4humans* features more traditional improvisation, with each episode being a stand-alone episode.

Launched in 2015, *Hello From the Magic Tavern* is in the genre of improvised narrative world-building. Featuring Arnie Niekamp, Matt Young, and Adal Rifai (and lots of guests over the hundreds of episodes), the premise is that Niekamp has fallen through a portal behind a Burger King and now finds himself in the magical realm of Foon, where he meets Usidore the Blue, a wizard played by Young, and Chunt, a shapeshifter usually in the form of a badger played by Rifai. Niekamp magically has a Wi-Fi signal, so he interviews the residents of Foon from The Vermillion Minotaur, a tavern in the town of Hogsface on the edge of the McShingleshane Forest. Like *Comedy Bang! Bang!*, the show relies on the hosts' skills and a plethora of recurring guests, many of whom are stalwarts in the Chicago improv community. Niekamp, Young, and Rifai likewise have an improv background, performing together as part of *Whirled News Tonight* and on various teams at iO and throughout Chicago.

The trio's chemistry drives the show, but what makes it unique is the intricate narrative and world-building they create improvisationally. The show is simultaneously incredibly simple – it's some guys and magical beings talking in a tavern – and immensely complicated (in a good way). The podcast can utilize narrative complexity because episodes are always accessible, and audiences can listen multiple times. The complex narrative and rich world-building highlight the hallmarks of long form improvisation, which relies on callbacks and connections. This style allows the players and the audience to fully immerse themselves in the improvised worlds and takes advantage of many of podcasting's inherent strengths. It can also be difficult to "drop in" to the podcast and listen to a random episode. So, while it rewards listener loyalty with a vibrant world, it will not likely be casually consumed. We see a similar double-edged sword in long form improv, where aficionados appreciate a complicated structure. However, audiences with little to no "insider" knowledge often feel confused and like they're missing the joke.

Hello From the Magic Tavern reflects another related use of improvisation rooted in fantasy and world-building:

36.1. Role Playing Games

RPGs, live-action (LARPing), and tabletop games – specifically Dungeons and Dragons (D&D) – rely heavily on improvisation. To be clear, RPGs are not *performances*, even though they can be *performative*. There is no audience in a traditional sense – the players are performing and playing for themselves and for one another. In case you've never played, RPGs involve players creating characters and worlds, acting spontaneously, and responding and adapting to ever-changing circumstances. One of the main draws of RPGs is their immersive quality, which allows players to create detailed and immersive fictional worlds (not unlike Foon) and nuanced characters. Improv is central to many RPGs. In D&D, for instance, Dungeon Masters with improv chops can create and adapt exciting campaigns, while players who can improvise have a distinct advantage over their peers in adapting to ever-changing circumstances.

I won't delve into the complicated world of D&D here since this is another ".1" entry, but anyone who has played knows that improvisation plays a prominent role in any successful campaign. Because RPGs often last for a long time, the characterizations and world-building can become highly detailed. Like improv comedy, RPGs have set rules and structures, which vary from game to game and style to style. The distinguishing difference between improvisational comedy and improv in RPGs is the audience. In improv comedy, the audience is a secondary group, usually there specifically to see an improv performance (plus one guy who thinks it's stupid and the significant other of an improviser who feels obligated to attend). Improvisers are ostensibly playing for the audience. RPGs involve a first-person audience, meaning the other players are the audience, so players play for themselves and one another (a criticism sometimes lobbed at improv comedy). RPGs are the most popular type of improvisation next to improv comedy and applied improvisation, and as such warrant inclusion.[29]

Okay, back to 36: Improv4humans

Matt Besser's *Improv4humans* is likewise dedicated to showcasing the craft of long form improvisation, but rather than building out extensive worlds, each episode is a self-contained performance. Besser, one of the UCB 4, hosts each episode and will bring on 2–4 guests for each episode, featuring some of improv's biggest names and up-and-coming talent. The improv is like something one might see at UCB or iO, with the obvious difference being that it is audio-only improv. There are live performance styles that mimic a radio play, namely The Bat, which is a long form style performed in the dark, but Besser's goal is to provide an example of improv at its best. Much like *Middleditch & Schwartz, Improv4humans* is trying to elevate long form improv by being good. The style of each episode is a cross between an ASSSSCAT and The Movie. Besser helped develop both forms, and their blending provides a window into the UCB style (ASSSSCAT) and helps transition improv from a visual to an audio form (The Movie). The Movie was developed by Del Close and The Family at iO in the 1990s, and it is pretty much exactly what you think – an improvised movie. One of the stylistic components The Movie introduced was scene painting, where an improviser describes in detail what is "onscreen" for the audience. This descriptive technique is prevalent in live improv, especially with UCB-trained improvisers. It also provides the perfect tool for making scenic-style long form improv work on a podcast.

Improv4humans and nearly all the entries in this section have helped to elevate improvisation. To state the obvious, many more people have watched *Whose Line, Wild 'N Out*, streamed *Middleditch & Schwartz*, or listened to an improv podcast than have seen a live improv show. Even for those who have seen live improv, the level of improv presented in many of these mediated forms is much higher than the average live improv show. As such, improv on film, television, and podcasts have exposed people to what improv can be at its best, which has worked to elevate all improvisation. That said, this section is important less for the specific content created than for the reach of that content and the profile of its creators. The average person has no idea who TJ & Dave are, but they know Tina Fey and Amy Poehler. They have no idea iO or The Annoyance exist, but they've seen *SNL* and *Whose Line*. Keith Johnstone is unknown to most people, but they know Steve Carrell and Stephen Colbert. Most people have never seen Adam McKay improvise at iO, UCB, or Second City, but they've seen *Anchorman* and *Succession*. When they discover his background (or anyone included in this section), that gives those institutions exposure, credence, and relevance. The average person hasn't been to a live improv show and has no idea what a Harold is, but they've seen *30 Rock*, so the show provides an instant frame of reference. As such, while many of the entries and examples in this section are not fully improvised (or even improvised at all), they have influenced the development, popularity, and spread of improv more so than their strictly improv counterparts among a general audience.

Notes

1   Mike Thomas, *The Second City Unscripted: Revolution and Revelation at the World-Famous Comedy Theatre* (Evanston, IL: Northwestern University Press, 2012), 100.

2   Dom Nero, "You Probably Didn't Watch *SCTV*, But It Shaped the Comedy You Love Today," *Esquire*. 12 April 2018. https://www.esquire.com/entertainment/tv/a19758092/sctv-reunion-netflix-martin-scorsese/

3   So, technically *Kwik Witz* came before the US version of *Whose Line*, so when I say rip-off, I mean it is a rip-off of the British version of *Whose Line*.

4   Qtd. in "MTV Announces Premiere of 'Nick Cannon Presents Wild'N Out'." *The Futon Critic*. 14 July 2005. http://www.thefutoncritic.com/news/2005/07/14/mtv-announces-premiere-of-nick-cannon-presents-wildn-out—18740/20050714mtv02/

5   Qtd. in Okla Jones, "Wild 'N Out's 20th Season: Nick Cannon On The Show's Talent, Impact, and Future." *Essence*. 12 June 2023. https://www.essence.com/entertainment/wild-n-out-20th-season-nick-cannon-on-the-shows-talent-impact-and-future/

6   Qtd. in Geoff Andrew, "Robert Altman Interview: 'If I Made A Film That Everybody Liked It Would Be Pretty Terrible.'" Chicago Movie Magazine, 24 January 2001. https://www.chicagomoviemagazine.com/post/robert-altman

7   Qtd. in Peter Caranicas, "'Bridesmaids' Caught Improv on Film," *Variety*. 17 May 2011. https://variety.com/2011/film/columns/bridesmaids-caught-improv-on-film-1118037164/

8   Qtd. in "Adam McKay on Using Improv in 'Succession' Family Dinner Scene, More – TV Director Roundtable." *The Hollywood Reporter*. https://www.hollywoodreporter.com/video/adam-mckay-using-improv-succession-watch-1217892/

9   Mike Shutt, "From Christopher Guest to Mike Leigh, How to Utilize Improv for Film." *Collider*. 21 September 2021. https://collider.com/mike-leigh-christopher-guest-improv-in-movies/

10 Keegan Michael Key and Elle Key, *The History of Sketch Comedy* (San Francisco: Chronicle Books, 2023), 249.

11 Qtd in Peter Canavese, "Christopher Guest & Eugene Levy—For Your Consideration." *GrouchoREviews.com*, 10 November 2006. http://grouchoreviews.com/interviews/191

12 Qtd. in Leila Kozma, "These Are the Tricks Larry David and the Creators of 'Curb Your Enthusiasm' Swear By." *Distractify.* 17 January 2020. https://www.distractify.com/p/is-curb-your-enthusiasm-improvised

13 "Curb Your Enthusiasm – Larry David on Unscripted Acting." *The Paley Center for Media.* 23 July 2009. https://youtu.be/m89BdatB12A?si=rkep UxoUejxjBGen

14 Qtd. in Tyler Coates, "'Borat Subsequent Moviefilm' Writer Reveals How to Craft a Screenplay for Improvisation," *The Hollywood Reporter.* 13 April 2021. https://www.hollywoodreporter.com/movies/movie-news/borat-subsequent-movie-writer-reveals-how-to-craft-a-screenplay-for-improvisation-4162129/

15 Dan Friedman, "The Improv King of America," *Forward.* 12 October 2018. https://forward.com/culture/film-tv/408962/exclusive-the-improv-king-of-america/

16 Qtd. in Samantha Highfill, "'Reno 911!' creators remember the show 5 years later, talk reunion," *Entertainment Weekly.* 8 July 2014. https://ew.com/article/2014/07/08/reno-911-thomas-lennon-ben-garant/

17 Qtd. in Lynn Elber, "Making 'Portlandia': Brainstorming, basketball, improv." *AP News.* 15 February 2017. https://apnews.com/television-arts-and-entertainment-a0768c0e6f064565ae43469ca05e1e91

18 Qtd. in Kathy Shwiff, "'Portlandia' Stars Say 95% of Dialogue Improvised." *The Wall Street Journal.* 29 January 2013. https://www.wsj.com/articles/BL-SEB-73328

19 Ian Angus Wilkie, *Performing in Comedy: A Student's Guide* (London: Routledge, 2016).

20 Qtd. in Brandon Voss, "The A-List Interview: Tina Fey," *The Advocate,* 12 November 2015. https://www.advocate.com/arts-entertainment/2015/11/12/list-interview-tina-fey

21 Emily Brown, "Parks and Rec creator says Chris Pratt improvised the funniest line on the show," *UNILAD.* 10 April 2023. https://www.unilad.com/celebrity/parks-and-rec-chris-pratt-improvised-funniest-line-603997-20230410

22 Qtd. in "Keegan-Michael Key Has the Perfect Metaphor for Improv," *offCAMERA with Sam Jones.* 25 May 2016. https://youtu.be/coZARWbdNls?si=rOk1jpWy6G-pt295

23 Key and Key, 176.

24 Key and Key, 196.

25 Jesse Fox, "What If Improv Were Good?" *Vulture.com.* 20 April 2020. https://www.vulture.com/2020/04/middleditch-schwartz-netflix-comedy-specials.html

26 Becca James, "The 10 Essential Comedy Podcasts That Shaped the Genre," *Vulture*. 3 October 2019. https://www.vulture.com/article/best-comedy-podcasts-all-time.html

27 Qtd. in "Jimmy Carrane on 5 Years of Improv Nerd, Battling The Fame Monster, And What He's Learned," *PeopleandChairs.com*. 4 November 2016. https://peopleandchairs.com/tag/improv-podcast/

28 Becca James, "The 10 Essential Comedy Podcasts That Shaped the Genre," *Vulture*. 3 October 2019. https://www.vulture.com/article/best-comedy-podcasts-all-time.html

29 For a more immersive (pun intended) analysis of improv and role-playing-games, see Sarah Lynne Bowman's "Live-Action Role-Playing Games: Connecting Role-Playing, Stage Acting, and Improvisation," *Analog Game Studies*. Vol. X, Issue II. 11 May 2015. https://analoggamestudies.org/2015/05/connecting-role-playing-stage-acting-and-improvisation/#note-2

PART 6

THE (FURTHER) EXPANSION OF IMPROV

Due to the success and exposure of improv-on-screen, mainly via *Whose Line Is It Anyway?*, improv's reach had expanded beyond the theatre. This reach reverberated in live performances with an expanded understanding of what improv could do and be. With the success of improv-as-product theatres like iO and ComedySportz, and behind improv-on-the-screen like *Whose Line Is It Anyway?*, improv at the turn of the century was expanding – in style, in medium (as seen in the previous section) and in performers. While the more rigid rules and structure of short form improv at ComedySportz or the Harold at iO helped create audience-worthy improv, some rules and structures became less important or necessary as the art form evolved. One of the key characteristics of the Third Wave of Improv, the loosening of rules at theatres like The Annoyance and UCB pushed improv's boundaries, while groups like Jane, Oui Be Negroes, and Stir Friday Night made performance opportunities for more diverse performers where the legacy institutions were not. As much as improv expanded in the 1990s, there was room for much more growth. The following groups and entities expanded improv beyond its Second and Third Wave borders.[1]

DOI: 10.4324/9781003359692-6

37. APPLIED IMPROVISATION

Even though this book focuses on improvisational comedic performance, one of the significant ways improvisation has expanded in recent years is via applied improvisation (AIM). Applied improvisation is everywhere, and nearly every major improv theatre does AIM training and workshops. The Applied Improvisation Network, founded in 2002 by Paul Z. Jackson, Michael Rosenburg, and Alain Rostain, is the hub of AIM for individual improvisers and trainers. Many theatres and improvisers support themselves financially via applied improvisation, and for many outside of the theatrical and comedy worlds, applied improvisation is their first exposure and experience with improv. Even though the technical field of applied improvisation is relatively new, the concepts are rooted in the same things Neva Boyd and Viola Spolin did in the 1920s, 30s, and 40s – using improv to teach.

Let's back up – what is applied improvisation. According to the Applied Improvisation Network, it is "the use of principles, tools, practices, skills and mindsets of improvisational theater in non-theatrical settings, that may result in personal development, team building, creativity, innovation, and/or meaning."[2] In short, applied improvisation takes the philosophy, skills, and mindset of improvisational theatre and applies it to other aspects of life. For instance, one of the key concepts in AIM training is creating and using a Yes And (or acceptance) mindset. The core of most AIM is transferring the skills of agreement, collaboration, and adaptability to non-theatrical settings. Most companies can significantly benefit from creating a more collaborative and creative work environment with agile and adaptive employees. As such, applied improvisational training has become hugely popular among Fortune 500 companies and business schools. Many leading MBA programs – UCLA's Anderson School of Management, Duke University's Fuqua School of Business, MIT's Sloan School of Management, and Columbia Business School, among many others – offer applied improv classes.

Applied improvisation goes beyond the corporate boardroom. In addition to MBA programs, medical schools incorporate improv training to help their students become better communicators and more empathetic with their patients. "Medical Improv" helps students become better listeners, more collaborative, more empathetic, and helps them think on their feet – all incredibly important things in healthcare. According to medical improv pioneer Katie Watson, an associate professor at Northwestern University's Feinberg School of Medicine, "the same paradox drives physicians and improvisers. They need to prepare for unpredictability."[3] A study in the *American Journal of Pharmaceutical Education* found that improv training can dramatically improve patient outcomes and communication skills.[4] Another study found that Medical Improv was a critical factor in building resilience, a massive factor for medical personnel during the COVID-19 pandemic. The report found that Medical Improv helped participants build core skills in resiliency, such as presence/mindfulness, self-awareness, tolerance of uncertainty, confidence, and divergent thinking, and helped build relationships through collaboration.[5] The benefits of Medical Improv are vast, and there has been a push by the Association of American Medical Colleges to integrate the arts, specifically improv, into medical education more fully.[6]

One of AIM's other most popular uses is to enhance and improve interpersonal communication skills. Applied improvisation can help people with social anxiety develop social and communication skills, improve empathy, and build confidence. Improv is used extensively to help people on the autism spectrum develop social skills and communication strategies. AIM techniques are at the heart of many experiential learning initiatives in education. AIM is integral in Drama Therapy and Psychotherapy to encourage and treat emotional and mental health. Much of the work of Augusto Boal, particularly his work with Forum Theatre and the Rainbow of Desire, can be classified as applied improvisation. Rainbow of Desire uses improv as a therapeutic tool to help participants realize and respond to internalized trauma and oppression.

The benefits of improvisation are real. It might sound like an infomercial, but several psychological studies have proven that improv actually changes the brain. Based on research using brain scans of people doing improvisation (both comedic and also via music), they discovered that improv activates parts of the brain associated with creativity and language while "quieting" the parts of the brain related to self-judgment and doubt.[7] Another study found that doing just 20 minutes of improv helped with brain wave coherence, an area of the brain that is "interrupted" by trauma, suggesting that improv (such as the Rainbow of Desire) can help treat trauma.[8] A marketing study by James Mourey found that students taking a ten-week improv course had higher levels of divergent thinking, collaboration, and self-efficacy.[9] On the surface, it seems odd that an art form that requires one to be onstage and perform without any idea what's about to happen would be beneficial for people with social anxiety. Yet, studies have found that even 20 minutes of improv can reduce social anxiety and uncertainty intolerance.[10]

Improv is beginning to become an incredibly useful tool for autistic and neurodiverse people. On the one hand, improv helps develop communication skills, lowers anxiety, builds confidence, and helps develop social skills. At the same time, using improv is not meant to make people more neurotypical. According to researchers Nathan Keates and Julie Beadle-Brown, improv empowers participants with "going full autistic." While improv builds social skills, it also allows participants to be their most authentic selves and helps them remove masks and barriers. Instead of pretending to be neurotypical, they can improvise as themselves.[11]

The benefits of improvisation go well beyond comedic performance, and there is extensive literature on applied improvisation. Anyone looking to dive deeper should start with Theresa Robins Dudeck and Caitlin McClure's two books – *Applied Improvisation: Leading, Collaborating, and Creating Beyond the Theatre* (2018) and *The Applied Improvisation Mindset* (2021) – which delve into the many ways applied improvisation is changing the way people live and work. There are dozens of books about applying improvisation lessons to your life, career, or business that have become essential reading. Bob Kulhan's *Getting to 'Yes And:' The Art of Business Improv*, Kelly Leonard's and Tom Yorton's *Yes, And: How Improvisation Reverses 'No, but' Thinking and Improves Creativity and Collaboration (Lessons from the Second City)*, Norm Laviolette's *The Art of Making Sh!t Up: Using the Principles of Improv to Become an Unstoppable Powerhouse*, and Patricia Ryan Madson's *Improv Wisdom: Don't Prepare, Just Show Up*.

38. THE IMPROV AMBASSADORS – JASON CHIN, PATTI STILES, AND JILL BERNARD

Some figures within improvisation are polarizing, either in their comedic sensibility or off-stage personality. Some figures within improvisation are universally beloved, like Jason Chin, Patti Styles, and Jill Bernard, who also happen to be three of the most influential improv teachers and ambassadors. Great teachers have always been the beating heart of improvisation, from Spolin and Johnstone to Martin de Maat, Del Close, Mick Napier, and Susan Messing. Chin, Stiles, and Bernard have carried on that legacy, though unfortunately, Chin passed away too soon at 46 in 2015. They have taught and influenced thousands of improvisers. Their respective books have become staples of most improvisers' libraries – Chin's *Long-Form Improvisation & The Art of Zen: A Manual for Advanced Performers*, Stiles' *Improvise Freely: Throw Away the Rulebook and Unleash Your Creativity*, and Bernard's *Jill Bernard's Small Cute Book of Improv*.

Like many aspiring comedians, Chin moved to Chicago in 1995 and began taking classes, though he was 30 when he began his improv journey. He quickly rose through the ranks of the Chicago improv scene, eventually becoming iO's associate artistic director and the first full-time director of its training center (he was responsible for creating both the permanent full-time position and restructuring the curriculum). Though Close trained him, he was in many ways the antithesis of Close – warm, uplifting, and deeply kind, always encouraging improvisers to find joy in what they were doing. In addition to teaching, he was a regular performer in the long-running "Armando Diaz Experience." He created numerous shows, including one of iO's signature non-Harold forms, "Whirled News Tonight." An improvised satiric news show that was a mixture of a Living Newspaper and *The Daily Show*, the form is one of iO's most successful non-Harold structures. Debuting in 2003, it helped pave the way for other non-Harold-based shows at iO, in addition to launching the careers of people like Jordan Klepper, who went from Whirled News to *The Daily Show*. There is now a scholarship in his name to support young comedians and one of the theatres in iO's latest home is named after him – The Jason Chin Harold Cabaret. His passing was also the impetus for "Say Day," which occurs every July 29th, a day in the improv world dedicated to telling others how much they mean to us and sharing our appreciation before it is too late.

If Jason Chin was carrying on iO's style, then Patti Stiles has been carrying on Keith Johnstone's impro/Theatresports style. Dubbed Canada's "Improv Queen," Stiles learned impro from Johnstone at The Loose Moose Theatre Company in 1983 before influencing improvisational theatre on three continents. While in Canada, Stiles first performed with Loose Moose before going on to found/lead several other companies in Toronto and Edmonton, including Rapid Fire Theatre and Dream Kitchen Theatre. She moved to London for a brief time and trained Deborah Frances-White and Tom Salinksy, founders of The Spontaneity Shop and authors of the hugely popular *The Improv Handbook* (2008), which includes a dedication to her. Stiles then moved to Australia to lead Impro Melbourne and appeared on the Australian soap opera *Neighbours*. She has become one of the most sought-after teachers on the international scene, with her book *Improvise Freely* cementing her status as one of improv's leading teachers.

Like many of the teachers in this book, Stiles de-emphasizes following the rules, arguing that the rules are more often a hindrance than a help. Much as Napier and Messing argue, Stiles argues that rules tend to build up anxiety and fear when the goal should be to help actors remove anxiety and fear to allow them to play freely and honestly. Stiles likens improvisation onstage to a tiger, and rules as a way to "put the tiger in the cage."[12] Rules discourage creativity and discovery, writing, "When the freedom of play is obstructed by the limitations of rules we restrict creativity and confine the imagination."[13] Stiles doesn't say all rules are bad. Instead, she questions the origin of each rule to illuminate the meaning of the rule because the rule's point has often become obscured by the rule itself. She argues that many of the rules Johnstone and Spolin used have been flipped on their head. While they used rules to help free performers – to remove fear or encourage collaboration – many rules now used in improvisation work to restrict play and "limit how to improvise."[14]

Her book refocuses many of the rules that have emerged in improvisation over the last 20 years, and none is more important than her reframing the improv maxim "Yes, And." Stiles argues acceptance is more important than immediately responding "Yes, And." The idea of "Yes, And" is about acceptance, not rotely responding "Yes" to any offer. As an exercise, saying yes can be helpful to teach agreement or help a student reframe their collaborative approach, but more important than saying yes is accepting offers and using the information. There are a thousand ways to accept an offer, so teaching students to respond only with yes limits them. An improviser can accept an offer by saying no or through indifference, just as they can with an enthusiastic YES! Stiles also argues that blind adherence to Yes And creates a dangerous environment where improvisers and students can trap themselves in bad situations – onstage or off – by always saying yes to offers, especially manipulative offers. And as we'll see, Stiles' warning proved prescient (see #47). Her philosophy is about uncovering what skill or philosophy is behind a rule and rediscovering that, rather than strictly adhering to the rule itself.

The third of the triumvirate is Jill Bernard. Based in the Twin Cities, Bernard is a founding member of Huge Improv Theater (see #49) and a regular performer with ComedySportz. She is perhaps most well-known for her one-woman show Drum Machine, which has taken her to dozens of improv festivals worldwide, where she is one of the most sought-after teachers on the festival circuit. The show begins with a brief interview with an audience member and the suggestion of a historical era. From there, Bernard's Drum Machine mixes music, multiple characters, monologues, and songs into a narrative accompanied by an electronic drum machine (or sometimes a live musician).

Dubbed "The Queen of Improv" by *Minnesota Women's Press*, Bernard began her improv career in 1993 by auditioning for ComedySportz while still a student at the University of Minnesota … and without ever having done improv before, but quickly realized "it felt like this is the thing I was built for."[15] By 2002, she had become a fixture of the Minneapolis improv scene and first performed Drum Machine at the Chicago Improv Festival. Her CIF performance led to invitations to perform at international festivals, which led to her traveling to dozens of countries to teach and perform. Like Spolin, Johnstone, and many other great improv teachers, Bernard approaches teaching improv from the starting point that everyone is innately good at improv. Unfortunately, formal education and the demands of being "a responsible adult" got in the way of our inherent sense of play.

In the same way Johnstone challenges students to "dare to be ordinary," Bernard's pedagogy is as much about removing obstacles and barriers as it is about teaching clever tricks or gimmicks. Her teaching approach has made her classes at improv festivals incredibly popular. She founded The Tiny Funny Women Fest in Minneapolis to create more space and opportunities for female comedians and improvisers. First published in 2011, her book *Jill Bernard's Small Cute Book of Improv* lives up to its name, coming in at roughly 20 pages. Despite its length, or more likely because of it, Bernard's book is arguably the most accessible improv book to date. Between Drum Machine, her classes at home and abroad, her other improv performances, and her book, Bernard is one of improv's most important figures – all the while doing it as one of the most genuine human beings ever to exist.

Chin, Stiles, and Bernard carved out a path in improvisation that celebrates kindness, empathy, and connection. Certainly, many, many improvisers fit this bill, but in an art form where sometimes the principles of improv have been exploited by teachers and performers for their own personal gain or, to take advantage of students, or simply against the backdrop of competition to get roles, or put on a house team, or to make it to *SNL* – these three have demonstrated that the core principles of improvisation should make you more kind, generous, and empathetic, and just as importantly, that those traits are the real key to success.

39. THE IMPROVISED SHAKESPEARE COMPANY

Founded in 2005 by Blaine Swen, The Improvised Shakespeare Company (ISC) has become emblematic of how improv has moved beyond the walls of its esteemed institutions and how a particular show can become a full-fledged worldwide entity. While most improv groups and forms are linked to a specific theatre, beginning in the 1990s, many teams, performers, and forms began working independently, such as Ed, Jazz Freddy, and Oui Be Negroes. While many of the ensemble members of ISC actively perform and teach at iO, Second City, and The Annoyance, the group itself has become its own institution. While it is now a worldwide entity, the origins date back to 2000 at iO West, where Swen's initial foray into

Shakespeare began with the Backstreet Bards. Performing a 20-minute set in Shakespearean style, the group won ten consecutive cage matches (after ten consecutive wins, a team can no longer compete). Audiences loved the format, and iO West offered the group, renamed the Spontaneous Shakespeare Company, a regular Friday night performance slot. This group was short-lived, as Swen left Los Angeles for Chicago, where he earned a graduate degree in Philosophy from Loyola University. In 2005, Swen brought back The Bard, performing at Donny's Skybox at Second City. They proved just as popular with Chicago audiences as those in Los Angeles, and Halpern offered the group a Friday night slot at iO in 2006, where they often performed two shows a night.

Aside from being in iambic pentameter, what is unique about this show is that it is heavily reliant on narrative. The group asks the audience for the title of a play that does not exist and then completely improvises a Shakespearean-inspired full-length play in Elizabethan style. Most long form improv forms and structures rely on non-narrative elements, often actively working to *avoid* narrative. Instead, the ISC actively works to create an original plot-driven narrative play. One of the ways they achieve this is through rigorous study. The group doesn't just play off tired Shakespearean tropes (though those do pop up). They seriously study The Bard, reading his plays and other Elizabethan drama, and discuss the work in ways that more closely resemble a graduate English seminar than an improv rehearsal. According to Swen,

> If you read Shakespeare and you put it down, you sort of start thinking with 'thees' and 'thous.' So in order to make sure we're staying true to the form, we constantly read Shakespeare and keep our noses in the text so that when we put it down it's fresh and we can jump up and just start speaking with a sort of Elizabethan language.[16]

The result is a playful mixture of comedy – not unlike Shakespeare's comedies – with both low-brow sexual innuendo and high-brow wordplay.

Initially an all-male ensemble meant to emulate Elizabethan theatre troupes, the group now includes women improvisers. As they've grown, the show has grown beyond iO and Chicago, with resident companies in Los Angeles and Chicago. The ISC also regularly travels, performing across the country, with the occasional European adventure. Their massive success demonstrates the growing popularity of improvisation and the growth of the improv world. While the group's early success came via iO – they still perform there regularly – they are an independent entity not exclusively tied to a single theatre. Like many Third Wave groups, they have expanded improv in terms of style, reach, location, and audience.

They have also inspired a cornucopia of other literary-genre-style improv, like Improvised Jane Austen. Founded in 2008 and featuring an all-female cast in period costume, Improvised Jane Austen creates an hour-long Austen-inspired story. The plots usually follow a young female protagonist searching for love who is navigating a patriarchal world. Like Austen's novels, the group aims to highlight the women's agency in her stories, creating three-dimensional characters against a backdrop of stereotypical prim and properness. The group seeks to pull out the humor in Austen's work and relies more heavily on her themes and style than on replicating her language than The Improvised Shakespeare Company. According to Kate Parker-Barrows, IJA artistic director and performer,

> We try very hard to tell a story that has heart and meaning and has real connection between characters. We don't just want our audience to laugh. We want to get them to put their hand to their hearts and say, 'Aw!'[17]

They also work very hard to demonstrate the struggles of 19th-century women in the present context. They say, "The audience can expect to laugh heartily, be wooed to tears, and be made to think on how much, *and how little*, has changed in two hundred plus years."[18]

40. BOOM CHICAGO

Few improv groups or institutions have the pop-culture worldwide recognition of Boom Chicago, which started off as a government sanctioned "bad idea" and continues to this day as one of the great improv talent incubators in the world. Moving from Chicago to Amsterdam in 1993, co-founders Andrew Moskos, Pep Rosenfeld, and Ken Schaefle created a comedy institution in a Dutch-speaking city with no real history of improvisational theatre or English-language comedy. They had taken classes in Chicago and performed at iO but were hardly on the verge of superstardom. So, they took a trip to Europe, got high in Amsterdam, and hatched a plan to open a Chicago-style improv comedy theatre. The idea seems ridiculous today, yet it has become a comedy icon. Even the Dutch Tourism Bureau thought it was a terrible idea, telling Rosenfeld and Moskos, "Your idea will not work. The Dutch don't want to see a show in English. Tourists don't want to see a show at all. Think twice about your plans."[19] Instead of giving up, they pushed ahead. Over the ensuing decades, Boom Chicago would become a staple of Amsterdam nightlife (which in itself is an accomplishment) and help launch the careers of some comedy heavy-hitters like Amber Ruffin, Seth Meyers, Jason Sudeikis, Jordan Peele, Ike Barinholtz, Brendan Hunt, and Kay Cannon (most of whom also trained and performed at other institutions). Boom performers have gone on to work on some of the most essential comedy projects of the past few decades, including *30 Rock, Community, Portlandia, The Office, Veep, Arrested Development, Eastbound & Down, Inside Amy Schumer, Brooklyn 99, Ted Lasso,* and various late night television shows, including *MADtv* and *SNL.* As noted above, Boom Chicago also played a vital role in bringing together Key and Peele.

They produce sketch-style revues similar to Second City and improv-based shows that mix ComedySportz style short form with iO style long form with The Annoyance's punk rock aesthetic. Their performance style is not as concerned with nuance and inner truth as it is with being big, bold, and funny. American pop culture references needed to be replaced with physical comedy, and because some of the audience spoke English as a second (or third) language, performers had to rely less on talking fast and more on being clear and precise with their language. Audiences were usually tourists or locals and usually had no idea what improv was, so Boom shows could not rely on the "insider knowledge" that was present in Chicago. An audience wouldn't appreciate a good game move because they wouldn't recognize it. So, instead, performers had to play more for and to the crowd. Liz Cackowski echoes many Boom performers when she says, "Boom helped us all become character actors ... Physical comedy, voices, big gags – that's what worked."[20]

One of the defining features of Boom Chicago, however, is not the content but the opportunity. While many improv and sketch performers work other jobs while performing "on the side," Boom Chicago, like Second City, is a full-time gig. What differentiates it from Second City is that there is a much more direct route to the main stage. Nearly all other big institutions require students to go through several levels of classes before earning stage time. While Boom does offer classes, the opportunity to get meaningful paid stage time has much fewer barriers. Boom also has the double-edged sword of being in Amsterdam, which is not quite the same as being in a comedy center like Chicago or New York. That allows the performers to be bold and adventurous – being in Amsterdam gives them more room to fail. One of the keys to a thriving institution seems to be its ability to celebrate failure. Tina Fey has talked at length about how Second City gave her room to fail and learn through failure. Keith Johnstone regularly celebrated failure at Loose Moose, and The Annoyance openly embraces risking failure. Because improv is an art form where failure is a certainty, the institutional allowance of failure is vital. Due to Boom's geographic location and the sheer number of performances each player does – they do anywhere from five to ten performances a week on average – most Boom players and alums point to the freedom to fail as a critical piece of their comedic development.

However, being removed from Chicago and other American comedy epicenters also means fewer immediate opportunities to climb the career ladder. The conventional wisdom in the first years of Boom was that leaving Chicago or New York to perform in Amsterdam was a bad career choice since it would remove you from the comedy networks of those cities. And that makes sense, yet the success of Boom alums suggests the conventional wisdom was wrong. When *SNL* hired Seth Meyers, it really changed the perception of Boom from an outlier to a legitimate career path. Boom's location also means that the type of person who will pick up and leave a comedy network and move to Amsterdam will be more un-conventional and bolder, which helped turn Boom into a fantastic comedy incubator and training ground. Jordan Peele commented about the opportunity of performing in Amsterdam at BOOM, saying,

> That experience—getting to improvise five, six nights a week, for three years in Amsterdam—was a grind that taught me a lot about showmanship ... That little audience voice in my head, that Boom Chicago gauge of whether something will work, feels like a skill I'll have with me forever.[21]

Boom also has become a symbol of improv's expansion beyond Chicago – both in the existence of improv hubs outside the city, but more importantly in terms of career – people can legitimately work in lots of places now outside of Chicago, and Boom was a big part of that expansion.

41. BARBIXAS

The trio of Daniel Nascimento, Anderson Bizzocchi, and Elidio Sanna make up Barbixas, one of the most popular improv groups in the world. Based in Brazil, the group has a wildly successful YouTube channel and regularly performs to sold-out multi-thousand-seat audiences. The trio has become bona-fide rockstars in Brazil. They began in 2004 by making short videos and sketches that became hugely popular on You-Tube.[22] They invested heavily in making high-quality videos at a time when YouTube was not quite the powerhouse it would become, and that investment paid off for the group as their video content – both scripted and of live shows – has helped them create one of the most popular You-Tube channels on the platform.

One of the reasons they filmed their shows was because they did their first show together after just one improv class with Màrcio Ballas, who requested the group film their show so that they could break down the show for their second class. In addition to watching *Whose Line Is It Anyway?*, Ballas introduced them to other performers in Latin America, and they began training and learning the craft of improvisation. They continued filming their shows to get better and quickly found that by increasing the technical quality, they could use the videos to get gigs. While submitting videos for festivals and other performances is now commonplace, in the early 2000s, very few companies were doing it. Part of what makes their filmed improv work so well is that they let it be – there isn't a ton of editing, and they don't try to "fix improv," which is often the case with televised improv. *Whose Line*, for instance, films nearly twice as much material as is needed for each episode, highlighting the games that work the best in the final product. There's nothing wrong with that – it is good television policy – but it is different than presenting everything. Barbixas borrows some methodology from *Whose Line* by keeping their filmed segments and shows shorter rather than longer. The big difference between the two is that *Whose Line* is a television show with a live audience, while Barbixas is doing a live improv show that is being recorded (intentionally and at a high level). Rather than trying to hide the rough edges or vulnerability – the very thing that many audience members love about improv – they let that be part of the show. It bears repeating that they also have high-quality audio and visual, so it is more than a live show taped from the back of the house.

They created the show *Improvável* (*Unlikely*) in 2007, their signature improv show, which is highly influenced by *Whose Line Is It Anyway?* and Johnstone's Theatresports. The show is a series of short form games inspired by audience suggestions, featuring the trio of Nascimento, Bizzocchi, and Sanna, along with rotating special guests. Their YouTube presence helped them generate a massive audience for their live improv shows. In 2009, they soon found themselves working on television, first as part of the cast of the improv show *Quinta Categoria*, then as part of the cast of É Tudo Improviso. They left television to return to live performances and to focus on their videos via their YouTube channel. Performing initially in São Paulo, the group regularly tours throughout Brazil and internationally. In addition to their stage shows, they regularly upload videos – either of games from their live shows or stand-alone sketches – to their YouTube channel, one of the world's most popular live comedy channels.

The trio went to Loose Moose in 2011 to take an intensive workshop with Johnstone that reframed their approach to their live shows. While Brazil has a long performance history and is the home of Augusto Boal, comedic improvisation is relatively new there. Their workshop with Johnstone reinforced many of Johnstone's fundamental theories. It also changed their audience–performer relationship by giving more attention to the emcee's role in their shows, something that has been a staple of improv from the very beginnings of The Compass, Loose Moose, and The Match. While there has been an emcee or host for quite some time, the importance of the role is an oft overlooked aspect of improvisational performance. A good host can elevate a game or show by maintaining flow, connecting with the audience, editing scenes, making suggestions or side-coaching, or simply adding what the scene is missing (or, perhaps most importantly, ending a bad scene quickly and moving on). That is doubly true for short form improv. The host/emcee has several duties in short form that play an outsized and underappreciated role in any game's success.

First and most obviously, they explain how the game works. This brief description allows the audience to be "in on the joke" but also works to relieve any nervousness or anxiety in the audience. Explaining the games is essential in any show, but especially ones in which the audience is not well versed in improvisation – the explanation allows them to settle in because they know what to expect. Laying out the structure of a game shines the "unexpected spotlight" on the improviser's choices rather than the entire experience. It is the same concept behind the rigidity of The Match's structure – remove unnecessary uncertainty to highlight expected uncertainty. The host/emcee also elicits and selects audience suggestions, an art form unto itself. A good suggestion gives players room to explore while allowing the audience to feel a sense of creative collaboration. Depending on the game, the host/emcee will often control the tempo or rhythm of a game and almost always oversees ending the game. Ending it at the right moment can elevate an average game to an excellent one, while conversely, ending it at the wrong time can take a great scene and make it feel less successful. In addition to re-emphasizing the emcee, the Johnstone workshop helped them learn how to play with status as a trio, constantly swapping, elevating, and losing status throughout their shows.

More so than their specific content, the group is an excellent example of improv's increasing global presence and how improv groups utilize media and technology. *Whose Line Is It Anyway?* is an apparent influence on Barbixas's style and show structure, demonstrating one of the ways that television has been vital to improvisational theatre's growth and evolution. Barbixas takes that evolution a step further by integrating their live shows into their digital content. While they also produce pre-written sketches, most of Barbixas's YouTube and online content is from their live shows. Viewed by millions, the online content creates an even larger audience for their live shows. The loop has helped them to reach audience levels that are often unattainable for American improv groups.

42. 3PEAT, THE BLACK VERSION, AND DARK SIDE OF THE ROOM

As much as improv has expanded and evolved, the following two entries demonstrate that sometimes, evolution has been awfully slow and has often come via the hard work and commitment of under-represented groups. During the late 1980s and 1990s, a swath of new groups emerged that sought to highlight and make space for non-white male performers. Groups like Oui Be Negroes, Jane, and Stir Friday Night in Chicago gave players opportunities to improvise without being relegated to minority status within a larger group (e.g., the lone African American in the group who is constantly put into stereotypical roles by the rest of the group). Following those groups' footsteps, a new wave of groups emerged in the 2000s and 2010s with similar missions. Many groups fall into this category, so while I am highlighting three all-Black ensembles here – 3Peat, The Black Version, and Dark Side of the Room – there are many more wonderful ensembles. Unlike previous groups like Oui Be Negroes, 3Peat, The Black Version, and Dark Side of the Room are linked to established improv theatres, iO, the Groundlings, and Dad's Garage, respectively. Though the groups also exist outside of their institutions, it is notable that they grew out of these institutions and received some institutional support (though there's always room for more).

Founded in 2012, the ten-member ensemble 3Peat came together the same way other groups have formed – they felt unsupported by the established improv institutions. In this case, the all-Black ensemble was "tired of each being the only minority in their shows."[23] Like Key & Peele, rather than compete with one another for roles, they decided to collaborate. So, they formed a team catering to their talents and strengths. They began performing at iO on Monday nights at 10pm, a slot so undesirable that it didn't even exist before 3Peat started performing in it. Despite the terrible slot, the group quickly took off. They became both wildly successful and hugely popular, quickly finding themselves headlining improv festivals, performing throughout the country, and grabbing the attention of Comedy Central.

The group performs improv and sketch; their improv sets are structurally open. They usually begin with a monologue inspired by an audience suggestion that leads to a set of freewheeling scenes that are fast and furious. Their style is self-described as "fun, fast, and educational."[24] The educational aspect comes from an all-Black group playing how they want. They turn stereotypes on their head and call out micro-aggressions onstage. In part, the "educational" aspect comes from playing with improvisers with shared experiences – and the freedom from navigating how non-Black improvisers might react/respond to an offer or suggestion. Quite simply, the freedom from being played into stereotypes, as Perkins said, simply "to normalize Blackness and shows that Blackness isn't monolithic."[25] The large ensemble all individually bring different strengths and styles, yet before 3Peat, they had historically found themselves constantly having to represent "the Black point-of-view." That said, the group does not improvise scenes exclusively about race – another aspect of the educational tag – that not everything a Black comedian does has to be related to race.

One of the unique things about 3Peat is that many of its members were already well-established in the improv and comedy communities – including Allison Blair, Chris Redd, Dewayne Perkins, John Thibodeaux, Lisa Beasley, Nnamid Ngwe, Patrick Rowland, Torian Miller, and Shantira Jackson. Rather than being a group made from classes or other means, they self-selected into the group and did so when they were already proficient improvisers. Their experience allows them to focus on their individual strengths as improvisers and lets them play with confidence and knowledge. While many of them were already known in Chicago improv, they would go on to success beyond Chicago in film, television, and stand-up – both individually and as a group, while continuing to perform improv and sketch comedy. 3Peat is also an excellent example of how improv and sketch have grown beyond live performance. Individuals have gone on to various projects, but Comedy Central commissioned them to create a series of short sketches. One sketch, *The Blackening*, was picked up and turned into a feature film released in 2022. The sketch's and film's premise centers around the pop culture stereotype that the Black cast member is always the first to die in a horror film – so what happens when the entire cast is Black? The group's live performance schedule has slowed in recent years primarily because of their immense success – the group has difficulty finding a time when most of them are available, which is a pretty great problem.

Dark Side of the Room also plays on Hollywood stereotypes. Based out of Dad's Garage in Atlanta, the group gets a suggestion of a well-known movie, play, TV show, or book and then improvises the deleted scenes of what the Black characters were doing during the movie. Though currently not performing, the group was founded in 2012 by company members of Dad's Garage, and its cast has included Jon Carr, Kirsten King, Jamie Alilaw, Ryan Jones, Chris Thomas Hayes, Ed Morgan, Ricky Boynton, and Mark Kendall among others. Like 3Peat and other groups, race is a part of their shows. It is not the sole or primary factor, but they purposefully attempt to weave social consciousness and racial awareness into their shows. According to the group,

> While we're making you laugh with our improv, we also use our show as a vessel to sprinkle in some cultural and systemic awareness about the state of racial injustices. So, we wrap some truth in a laugh and make you think not only about why you're laughing but then, hopefully, we are the catalyst for our audiences to then go out into the world and have the important conversations.[26]

For much of its early history, Dad's Garage was not unlike many other improv theatres – predominantly white. Founded in 1995 by a cohort of Florida State University graduates, the theatre produces comic plays, musicals, and improvisation. The group transitioned to producing mostly original plays and improv in the early 2000s and is the premiere improv comedy theatre in Atlanta. Yet, when Dark Side of the Room cast member Ed Morgan first took classes in 2007, it was "middle-aged white guys in Chuck Taylors and a couple of white women."[27] When Kevin Gillese took over as artistic director in 2009, he intentionally sought to make the theatre more diverse and accessible, especially so because the theatre is in Atlanta's Old Fourth Ward neighborhood, a gentrifying predominantly Black neighborhood. Dark Side of the Room is a direct result of these efforts to diversify – by creating more space and opportunities for BIPOC actors in their ensemble, Dark Side of the Room grew out of the ensemble. That said, like 3Peat and other groups, most group members initially had the same experience of being one of only a handful of BIPOC performers on a team or at a theatre. At Dad's Garage, thanks to its efforts to diversify, many performers found a sense of community lacking in other places. Rather than forming a group to showcase the existence of Black improvisers, they wanted to come together to showcase the talents of Black improvisers.

But they weren't quite sure what they wanted to do. On a trip to Los Angeles, they saw The Black Version at the Groundlings. Created by

Jordan Black at The Groundlings in 2010, the show has featured several prominent Black comedians, including Cedric Yarbrough, Gary Anthony Williams, Daniele Gaither, Phil Lamar, and Nyima Funk. One of the most well-known and long-running improv shows in the country, it begins by asking the audience to suggest a popular film title. In Act 1, the cast improvises the "Black version" of that film. Previous shows turned *Rocky IV* into *Pookie 4*, *Silence of the Lambs* into *Why You Eatin' People?*, *Pretty Woman* is *Hot Mess*, and *When Harry Met Sally* becomes *When Ray Ray Boned Keesha*. In *Black to the Future* (obviously from *Back to the Future*), when Black Marty McFly fixes the past and changes the future by saving his dad, he goes from bullied nerd to Barack Obama.

In Act 2, the group then improvises the movie's extras, which include a song or two from the soundtrack, deleted scenes, dance numbers, and audition reels. Inspired by The Black Version, rather than replaying the movie, Dark Side of the Room works from the premise that if Black people were in the movie, such as *It's A Wonderful Life*, what would they be doing? Both groups rely heavily on reframing white popular culture to ask questions about systemic inequality and racism. The groups can raise complex issues and spark conversation by making them laugh, all while asking audiences to look at something they already know from a different perspective.

3Peat, The Black Version, and Dark Side of the Room all represent how improv is diversifying and how there is still a long way to go. While there has been marked improvement since Oui Be Negroes, many of the same issues that Oui Be Negroes faced and sought to overcome are still present, and many of those issues would finally come to a head during the pandemic and the racial reckoning, more fully explored in #47.

43. ASIAN AF

Like 3Peat, The Black Version, and Dark Side of the Room (and many ((many)) (((many))) other groups), the members of Asian AF wanted to free themselves from the stereotypes that come from being a minority member in an otherwise all-white group. The group owes a debt to Stir Friday Night, an Asian American improv and sketch comedy group in Chicago. Formed in 1995, Stir Friday Night has performed at Second City, iO, and The Annoyance and was one of the very first Asian American comedy groups, providing both visibility and a platform for Asian American improvisers and comedians. Stir Friday Night has been hugely successful and important, featuring notable alums such as Danny Pudi, Mary Sohn, Christine Lin, Rasika Mathur, and Steven Yeun. Continuing the legacy of Stir Friday Night, which still exists and performs regularly in Chicago and across the country, Asian AF is a sketch comedy and improv collective. Asian AF is a variety style show featuring improv, stand-up, and sketch comedy, rather than solely an improv/sketch show, which debuted in 2016 and has quickly become one of the premiere comedy series in the US.

Asian AF is a series or collective rather than a singular group, making it slightly different from those highlighted, such as 3Peat or Stir Friday Night. Asian AF grew out of the UCB Los Angeles show "Scarlett Johansson Presents: Asian American & Pacific Islander Heritage Month," the first Asian American show at the theatre. The show was a response to the casting of Scarlett Johansson as an Asian character in the film *Ghost in the Shell* and the general practice of Hollywood whitewashing. Conceived by Will Choi, the show filled a glaring hole in UCB's programming and among Asian American performers. Choi remembers,

> I pitched it and got three improv teams to perform. Everyone responded within an hour ... I created a Facebook event for it and within a day or two it exploded. I think it ended up becoming the most attended show at UCB in that space. They had never seen the theater with that many people before.[28]

Asian AF grew out of the success of Scarlett Johansson Presents, with Will Choi, Mike Lane, and Connie Shin pitching the series to UCB, where it quickly became a mainstay, co-hosted by Choi and improvisor-comedian Keiko Agena. The original show featured Jenny Yang, Atsuko Okatsuka, Sheng Wang, Kevin Yee, Aparna Nancherla, and others. It featured Margaret Cho as their guest star (because the show is a variety style show, there have been hundreds of performers as part of Asian AF over the years, though Eugene Cordero, Lilan Bowden, Kim Cooper, Sarah Claspell, Zac Oyama, Dhruv Uday Singh, and Kathy Yamamoto are regular performers). Asian AF shows quickly sold out at UCB LA, so they took Asian AF to the UCB's New York branch, debuting in 2017 to similarly packed houses. In an incredibly short amount of time, Asian AF has reached headliner status. They have performed at the Off-Broadway Signature Theatre with special guest Ken Jeong and headlined multiple improv festivals, including San Francisco's Sketchfest, The Del Close Marathon in NYC, The Comedy Comedy Festival in LA,[29] Austin Sketchfest, Baltimore Comedy Festival, the SteelStacks Improv Comedy Festival, and were recently selected for the 2023–2024 Comedy Season at the Kennedy Center in Washington, DC.

Like 3Peat and other groups, race and ethnicity are common denominators among the ensemble but not the centerpiece of their comedy. They certainly do comedy about race, such as a sketch where the players "decode what your hard-to-please Asian mother means when she says things like 'Are you hungry?' The correct answer? 'I love you.'"[30] As with so many other groups, from Oui Be Negroes to Stir Friday Night to 3Peat, visibility is much more important. Simply having the show on the mainstage at UCB Los Angeles is a big deal, especially against the backdrop of Hollywood whitewashing and the long tradition of Asian American stereotypes used in comedy, often putting Asian American actors in positions of having to play stereotypical characters who are the butt of the joke. In addition to visibility, there is a power and freedom that comes from playing with improvisers with a shared experience. Cast member Zach Oyama noted in an interview that being backstage at UCB for Asian AF was "the first time I've been in this room and looked around and said, Oh there's only Asian people in the green room."[31]

Representation is important for many reasons, including the fact that it encourages others to join what has been an art form historically dominated by white men. Asian AF producer Will Choi began his improv journey after seeing Korean-American actor Steve Yeun performing, saying, "Seeing that he's doing it made me think I can do it too … That's the power of representation."[32] Choi's goal is for groups like Asian AF not to be necessary, saying,

> Right now we need it because of representation, but I hope there will be a day where it's like, 'No, you know what? This show does not need to exist anymore … Will that day come any time soon? I don't know. But I do feel like right now it's important, and I'm glad that we're doing it.[33]

Not only do they avoid the stereotypes and micro-aggressions that come with being the lone minority on a team, but they also get to showcase that Asian Americans are funny. They've also inspired and created several spin-offs: Filipino AF, South Asian AF, Gaysian AF, Voltron and Friends, and Polynesian AF.

The first two decades of the 21st century have seen an improv explosion. Well-established improv cities like Chicago saw a diversification of groups, playing styles, and structures. The growth of improvisation outside of the theatre pushed improv into new fields and introduced the philosophies and ideas of improv to millions via Applied Improvisation. International festivals became much more prevalent, which helped to spread improv across the globe. Improv's influence continued to expand beyond Chicago, as many of the world's most commercially successful comedians pointed to their improv training as central to their creative success. Improv's success on television, streaming, and podcasts brought improv to millions and helped the art form expand – including globally.

Notes

1 You might be asking, so why isn't this section The Third Wave? Good question. In part because many of the key Third Wave figures have already been included in other sections – The Annoyance, UCB – and because the Third Wave's influence carried on into the early 2000s and 2010s, lasting longer than the first two waves, and thus more difficult to narrowly pinpoint. Don't worry though, the Fourth Wave is coming.
2 "What is Applied Improvisation?" *Applied Improvisation Network*. https://www.appliedimprovisationnetwork.org/what-is-applied-improvisation-
3 Qtd. in Sarah Mahoney, "No Joke: The serious role of improv in medicine," American Association of Medical Colleges. 13 January 2020. https://www.aamc.org/news/no-joke-serious-role-improv-medicine
4 K.P. Boesen, R.N. Herrier, D.A. Apgar, R.M. Jackowski. "Improvisational exercises to improve pharmacy students' professional communication skills." *Am J Pharm Educ.* 2009 Apr 7; 73(2): 35. doi: 10.5688/aj730235. PMID: 19513173; PMCID: PMC2690892.
5 A. Mehta, D. Fessell. "Improvisation in the Time of a Pandemic: Field Notes on Resilience." *J Grad Med Educ.* 2022 Feb; 14(1): 13–17.
6 Lisa Howley, Elizabeth Gaufberg, and Brandy E. King. *The fundamental role of the arts and humanities in medical education* (Washington, DC: Association of American Medical Colleges, 2020).
7 C.J. Limb, and A.R. Braun (2008) "Neural substrates of spontaneous musical performance: An fMRI study of jazz improvisation." *PLoS one*, 3 (2), e1679.
8 M. DeMichele, and S. Kuenneke (2021) "Short-form comedy improv affects the functional connectivity in the brain of adolescents with complex developmental trauma as measured by qEEG: A single group pilot study." *NeuroRegulation*, 8 (1), 2021.
9 J.A. Mourey (2020) "Improv comedy and modern marketing education: Exploring consequences for divergent thinking, self-efficacy, and collaboration." *Journal of Marketing Education*, 42 (2), 134–148.
10 P. Felsman, C.M. Seifert, B. Sinco, and J.A. Himle (2023) "Reducing social anxiety and intolerance of uncertainty in adolescents with improvisational theater." *The Arts in Psychotherapy*, 82, 101985.
11 N. Keates, and J. Beadle-Brown (2023) "Improvisers' experiences across neurotypes of participating in improv comedy." *Advances in Autism*, Vol. 9 No. 3, 253–265.

12 Patti Stiles, *Improvise Freely: Throw Away the Rulebook and Unleash Your Creativity* (Australia: Big Toast Entertainment, 2021), 2.

13 Stiles, 3.

14 Stiles, 3.

15 Qtd. in Julie Kendrick, "Jill Bernard: The queen of improv," *Minnesota Women's Press.* 1 May 2016. https://www.womenspress.com/jill-bernard-the-queen-of-improv/

16 Qtd. in Matt Fotis, *Long Form Improvisation and American Comedy: The Harold.* (New York: Palgrave Macmillan, 2014), 136.

17 Qtd. in Meredith Francis, "A Comic, Modern-Day Retelling of Jane Austen," *Playlist, WTTW.* 8 January 2020. https://interactive.wttw.com/playlist/2020/01/08/improvised-jane-austen

18 "Properly Funny." https://improvisedjaneausten.com/.

19 Qtd. in David Peisner, "Boom Time: How a small theater in Amsterdam became the most influential American comedy factory you've never heard of," *Vulture.com.* 23 November 2020. https://www.vulture.com/article/boom-chicago-amsterdam-history.html

20 Qtd. in Peisner.

21 Qtd. in Peisner.

22 https://www.youtube.com/user/videosimprovaveis/channels

23 "Bio: Comedy + Black Excellence," *3peatcomedy.com*, 12 April 2018. https://3peatcomedy.wordpress.com/2018/04/12/the-journey-begins/

24 "Episode 236: 3Peat," *ImprovNerd.* 24 July 2017. https://jimmycarrane.com/236-3peat/

25 "Episode 236: 3Peat."

26 "Dark Side of the Room," Stumptown Improv Festival, Facebook Post, 2 July 2019. https://www.facebook.com/photo/?fbid=2288516061269805&set=pcb.2288545107933567

27 Qtd. in Matthew Love, "Improv So White? Yes, And," *American Theatre Magazine.* 13 March 2019. https://www.americantheatre.org/2019/03/13/improv-so-white-yes-and/

28 Qtd. in George Ko and Natalie Mark, "Race, Representation, and Laughs with Comedian Will Choi," *Giant Robot Media.* 25 July 2017. https://www.giantrobot.media/stories/2017/7/25/will-choi

29 The Comedy Comedy Festival was founded by Jenny Yang and features Asian American comedy.

30 Josie Huang, "Jokes aside, Asian-American comedians serious about visibility," *KPCC News*, 5 December 2016. https://www.kpcc.org/news/2016/12/05/66776/asian-american-comedians-improv-ucb-mainstage/

31 Qtd. in Huang.

32 Qtd. in Huang.

33 Qtd. in Kasia Pilat, "Comics of Asian Descent, Tired of Being Invisible, Put Themselves Onstage," *The New York Times.* 19 July 2018. https://www.nytimes.com/2018/07/19/arts/asian-af-comedians-upright-citizens-brigade.html

PART 7

THE INTERNATIONAL POWERHOUSES

This book has mainly focused on the US and Canada (and a little bit of the UK), but improv is a global art form. While so much of improvisation's history and development has happened in Chicago and North America, improv in the 21st century is global. In the same way that I began this book by saying this book is not meant to be a definitive list (and I've worked really hard and bent the structure of this series in knots to include more than 50 people), the improvisers included in the following three entries are not the definitive list of global improv.

This chapter is also structured differently than the others. I have broken the chapter into three entries, broadly categorized by continent – each one of which could fill its own Fifty Key Performers volume. Each entry here is an incredibly wide-ranging umbrella with a running list of performers and theatres, each highlighted in a brief snapshot. Everyone included (and many who are not) are all doing important, interesting, and influential work. As such, these entries should be used as a springboard for further scholarship and investigation rather than an ending point.

DOI: 10.4324/9781003359692-7

44. EUROPE

Improv in Europe is thriving, featuring the most well-established improv scene outside North America. Hundreds of theatres across the continent, dozens of high-level international improv festivals, and thousands of talented performers exist. Generally, European improv falls into one of three categories: Theatresports, The Match, or Chicago-style, though there is no shortage of other styles and types of improvisation – European theatre has never wanted for experimentation. The predominant style of each country is often tied to language rather than geography, with the French-speaking countries steeped in Match and the others more based in Theatresports or Chicago-style. Belgium, for instance, is deeply rooted in Match, while its neighbor, The Netherlands, is steeped in Theatresports and Chicago-style improv. While most groups perform in their country's native language, there is a lot of European improv done in English, especially at festivals, mainly for accessibility but also because many European groups and theatres have training roots in America, specifically Chicago. As such, some European theatres and groups are more American than European, like Boom Chicago. Others have weirdly embraced a Canadian hockey tradition via The Match despite little to no hockey tradition existing in their country. There are some basic generalizations about European improv – it is more physical than American (though much less physical than Latin American), the players are more inclined to work as a group rather than as individuals, and there is a greater emphasis on narrative. The truth, of course, is much messier. Improv styles and genres vary between countries, between groups in the same city, and between players on the same teams. There are easily well over 50 improvisers in Europe deserving of inclusion. So, again, while the mini-entries that follow highlight some of the different work and voices doing improv in Europe, they are not intended as a definitive crème-de-la-crème of European improv.

Germany boasts one of the world's most robust and well-respected improv scenes. There are hundreds of improv theatres across the country, thriving improv scenes in Berlin, Munich, and most major cities, top-of-the-line international improv festivals, thousands of high-level performers and teachers, and the improvised television show **Schillerstraße** (*Schiller Street*), which has been remade in dozens of other countries. While Theatresports-style impro is the leading form, dozens of theatres and groups do all sorts of exciting and experimental improv forms. One of the hallmarks of German improv would be experimentation – there is no shortage of new performances or forms on stages across Germany. As one of the earliest German improv theatres, much of German improv has been influenced by **fastfood Theatre**. The group was founded in Munich in 1992 by Karin Krug, Andreas Wolf, Roland Trescher, Susanne Brantl, Bernhard Ulrich, and Gabriele Heller. After taking an improv class while students at Ludwig Maximilians University (LMU) with Dr. Christopher Balme, the students immediately set to work establishing a theatre. A year after launching fastfood Theatre, they established the first improv school in Germany in 1993 – *Improschule*. Through its theatre and training center, the company has helped to shape the German improv scene.

Another of Germany's earliest and most influential improv groups is **Die Gorillas** (The Gorillas), named after Johnstone's Gorilla Theatre style. The company was founded in Berlin in 1997 by Thomas Chemnitz, Leon Düvel, Regina Fabian, Tom Jahn, Christoph Jungmann, Ramona Krönke, Robert Munzinger, Norbert Riechmann, and Michael Wolf. Initially performing in a Theatresports style, the group now performs in various styles. Expansion and experimentation underlie much of German improv, and Die Gorillas exemplifies that tradition. For instance, since 2001, the group has organized and hosted IMPRO, an international improv festival. While some groups come and perform, the festival is unique in that the main attraction is the collaboration of the international ensemble invited to the festival. So, instead of being a collection of improv teams and theatres from around the world, IMPRO invites (perhaps curates is a better word) a group of 20 international improvisers that they believe are interesting, exciting, and collaborative and puts them together in a series of different shows and formats across the festival. The festival has become highly regarded, and inclusion is a badge of honor.

Another aspect of German improv that is worth mentioning is that it has a vibrant collection of artist/scholars. It is home to many outstanding performers and one of the world's leading improvisation scholars and practitioners, **Gunter Lösel**. He is the Director of Performative Practice at the Zurich University of the Arts and the Artistic Director of Improtheater Bremen. He has written extensively about improvisational performance, most notably in *Theater Ohne Absicht* (Theatre Without Intention, 2004), *Der Heisse Kern Von Impro* (The Hot Core of Impro, 2015), and *Das Spiel Mit Dem Chaos* (Playing With Chaos, 2013). Lösel grew up in Germany and read Johnstone's *Impro* on a train ride, noting, "From that moment on, impro grabbed me and never let me go again."[1] Like many improv scholars, he is also an accomplished performer, working with Inflagranti, Stupid Lovers, Improtheatre Bremen, and Improtheatre Konstanz during his career. Before becoming the artistic director of Improtheatre Bremen in 2007, which focuses on long form style improvisation, he was a member of the 2006 German Theatresports National Team. Perhaps more so than any other country, Germany celebrates experimentation with improvisation. So, while there are traditional Theatresports theatres and companies across the country, tons of innovations and experiments are also happening.

Actor, writer, and improviser **Inbal Lori** began her improvisational career in Tel Aviv, Israel, in 2001, and like so many others, was first introduced to improv by Johnstone's *Impro*. After performing with her group 3Falling, she opened the improv school Impro TLV in 2013 before relocating to Berlin, Germany, in 2015 and continuing to teach and perform throughout Europe. One of her most popular shows is *Playing with the Enemy*, with Arab improviser Zaki Zakani. Harkening to improv's roots, Lori is unafraid of bringing politics and social issues to the stage, even when many theatres and groups actively avoid political content. She described her approach in an interview:

> For me the stage is a place of brutality, blood, tenderness, beauty but also ugliness … As artists we have the possibility to evoke thoughts in people. And if one tries to avoid such issues very 'correctly' and politely the outcome is, as we say in Hebrew, 'not milk and not meat.'[2]

She means that trying to be polite or politically correct can often lead to boring work when the theatre is intended to be an evocative space. Sometimes, that can be dangerous, but for Lori, playing things safely and boringly misses the point of the art form. That doesn't mean she doesn't care about humor or that everything is super heavy. As she says, simply sharing the stage with Zakani "is already a political act."

Poland may not be at the top of the list when folks think about European improv, but since its introduction in 2008, Warsaw has become an improv hotspot. The luminaries of Polish improv, the group **Klancyk,** was formed by students at the National Academy of Dramatic Arts in Warsaw. Not knowing much about improv, the group members eventually headed to Chicago to take classes at iO and The Annoyance. Upon their return, they helped create the Warsaw improv scene, including establishing a training school – Szkoła Impro. Improvisor **Malgorzata 'Gosia' Różalska** has a similar story. She was first exposed to formalized improvisation via an exchange program with the University of Northern Iowa. Upon returning to school in Poland, she began performing with friends.

> We had no idea what we were doing, but I'm so grateful for that. Nobody could tell us 'hey, what about the rules,' so we had to discover the rules ... and when Randy Dixon asked me – what is improv like in Poland – I said it's homemade.[3]

In part because she did not have formal improv training, she has become a self-described improv nerd, working to teach and learn improv in as many ways as possible. One such avenue is through the **Ohana Impro Project**, which brings together 50 improvisers throughout Europe to work together as a collective. The group meets three times a year, but the connections and exchanges go beyond the formal meetings. It is also a way to link improvisers from countries with emerging improv scenes, like Poland, with improvisers from countries with well-established improv traditions, like France.

As we've seen, The Match has dominated comedic improv in France since its debut in 1982 at the prestigious Avignon Theatre Festival. Since then, it has been THE improv staple in the French-speaking world, hockey and all. One of the leading figures in French improv is **Alain Degois**, aka Papy, founder and artistic director of The Déclic Théâtre (est. 1993). For decades, Papy has taught improv in schools and runs the Trophée d'impro, an improv Match tournament for student groups. In 2022, the prestigious Comédie-Française hosted the finals of the tournament, which, according to Papy, "is the first time in four hundred years that texts not validated by the reading committee will be played at Comédie-Française."[4] While The Match dominates French improv, there are many other styles and forms, with long form and musical improv becoming extremely popular in recent years. Another member of the Ohana Improv Project, **Flavien Reppert** began improvising as a teen and is the founder and artistic director of Le Théâtre de l'Oignon. Like many of his European contemporaries, he travels regularly, teaching and performing in 27 countries, performing in six different languages (French, English, German, Portuguese, Italian, and Spanish). A regular on the European and international improv circuit, he is a leading instructor and innovator, creating several forms and formats, including Random, which blends improvised music with improvised performance on a stage with random scenery.

Some of improv's earliest roots are in Italy, so it feels a bit wrong to say that contemporary improvisation began in Italy in 1988 with the formation of The Match style Lega Italiana Improvvisazione Teatrale (LIIT). On a trip to Paris, **Francesco Burroni** discovered the LIF, based on the work of Gravel and Leduc in Montreal. The LIIT quickly spread Match style improv throughout Italy, including the establishment in 2007 of the Improteatro Professional Association, a consortium of dozens of theatres, companies, and groups, as well as individual teachers and performers. One of Improteatro's affiliates is Teatribù in Milan, Italy, perhaps the most well-traveled improv company in Italy, performing at numerous improv festivals worldwide. One of the founders and artistic directors of Teatribù, **Fabio Maccioni** is one of the most well-known improvisers in Italy. A professor at the University of Milan, his format This Scene Was About … is a good example of Italian style improv (that isn't short form competition-style), which features a quick barrage of scenes where the previous scene inspires each new scene.

No one is more responsible for creating the Turkish improv scene than **Koray Bülent Tarhan**. One of the founders of Istanbul Impro, Tarhan is the author of the first Turkish improv book, *Dogaclama Icin Elkitabi* (A Handbook for Improvisation, 2013), created the first Kurdish language-based improv group in Turkey in 2015, and coordinates the Istanbul International Improv Festival. He is an actor, storyteller, and musician and is the Eastern European regional coordinator for the Applied Improvisation Network. First introduced to improvisation while at Ankara University and influenced by Johnstone's Theatresports, it wasn't until he attended an improv festival in Berlin almost four years after beginning performing that he first saw professional improvisation. Introduced to new styles and formats in Germany, he co-founded Istanbul Impro with a small group of improvisers, including his partner Zeynep Özyurt Tarhan. Istanbul Impro features many different shows, including improvised shows based on Anton Chekov's style and another based on Tennessee Williams's "unwritten" plays.

While there are several entries about improv in the United Kingdom already, I must highlight **Monica Gaga**'s work. It might be easier to list what Gaga doesn't do. Gaga is a regular performer at The Comedy Store Players and Hoopla Improv (London's oldest and most influential improv-only theatre) and producer of HELL YEAH!, the femxle-centred queer improv collective. Gaga is a cast member of numerous groups, including The Committee; the all-Black improv group Do The Right Scene (formerly known as Nu Z Land); Yes Queens; and the duo Derek's Mojo with Jodyanne Fletcher Richardson. A self-described British-born Black African queer host, improviser, facilitator, maker, and performer, Gaga has become a fixture of London comedy and a highly sought performer, host, and teacher. Gaga is a fierce advocate for diversity, equity, and inclusion in the improv community and regularly hosts events and runs workshops to make improv more inclusive and accessible for BIPOC and LGBTQIA+ performers. Along with Tai Campbell, Athena Kug-blenu, and other Do the Right Scene members, she co-runs regular workshops, classes, and performances at Hoopla for BAME improvisers (Black, Asian, Middle Eastern, and Minority Ethnic). Gaga also regularly teaches workshops at festivals and across the UK, including Wokeshops at Duck Duck Goose in Brixton. DDG's artistic director, Vic Hog, pro-posed the idea to Gaga to help the theatre more accurately reflect the community. Gaga accepted because,

> having been on the London scene for a while, I started to see cracks and would often hear people saying dumb shit on stage. Wokeshops seemed like an appropriate place for players to learn, be empowered and to delve into the more psychological aspects of improv.[5]

There is much more about European improv to say (and see). The many improv festivals held throughout Europe have become hugely important to the growth of improvisation and its simultaneous interconnectedness. While improv's roots are in the US and Canada, there are many exciting and interesting things happening in Europe that are influencing global improv. Interestingly, there is a kind of inverse relationship between America and Europe regarding theatre. American traditional scripted theatre has been heavily influenced by European theatrical traditions, only to have American styles and traditions become hugely influential in later years. In improv, the reverse seems to be true. European improv is heavily influenced by American improv, though styles and traditions (and experimentations) are emerging in Europe that are now influencing American improv.

45. LATIN AMERICA

As we've seen with Barbixas, improv is alive and well in Central and South America. The improv scene varies significantly between countries, within countries, and even within cities. The improv communities can dramatically differ in part due to political issues and unrest, which can quickly alter a country's social and cultural fabric. Despite political tur-moil, or in some cases in response to it (such as the work of Freire and Boal), high-level improv is happening in theatres across Latin America. The Match style of improvisation was the initial improv style in Latin America, beginning in Buenos Aires and then spreading. However, as with other areas, improv has grown in styles and genres to include more than Match. There are over-simplified generalizations about Latin

American improv, such as the notion that physicality is *much more* inter-twined into the process and performance of improv than in the US or Europe. Similarly, literary genre-specific improv in the US and Europe might focus on Shakespeare or Molière (or Ibsen or Tennessee Williams, etc.). In Latin America, magical realism is the dominant literary influ-ence, and as such, its tropes, style, and techniques influence much of the narrative-style improv in Latin America.

Buenos Aires is one of the world's theatre capitals, so it is no surprise that improv has deep roots in Argentina and that Argentinian improv would go on to influence most improv in Latin America. Like other Latin American countries, improv in Argentina has ebbed and flowed with the political climate, flourishing in times of stability and becom-ing more difficult in times of unrest. Even though Argentina is not a French-speaking country, improv in Argentina first began with The Match, which was brought to Buenos Aires in 1987 by French impro-viser Claude Bazin. The first Match performance was on July 4, 1988, which set the stage for improv in Latin America. From this initial foray, **Ricardo Behrens** formed the first Spanish-speaking Match league, la Liga Profesional de Improvisación (LPI), which has carried on The Match format since 1988. Initially working with Behrens in The Match format, **Fabio "Mosquito" Sancineto** would soon break away. While Behrens wanted to stick to the rigid structure of The Match (including all the hockey references), Sancineto wished to bring more style and playfulness to The Match and explore different types of improv. The two eventually split, with Behrens running LPI, which created a divide in Argentinian improv that was not unlike the divide in Chicago in the 1980s and 1990s. As a new wave of improvisers developed in the 2000s, the divide lessened, and groups began to collaborate more often, though The Match remains the dominant form of improv in Argentina and Latin America.

One of the most influential of the "new wave" of Argentinian impro-visers is **Omar Galván,** one of the most recognizable performers and sought-after instructors in the world. Like Jonathan Pitts' self-described walkabout, Galván tours the world on his Improtour. By tour the world, I don't mean he goes to a few international improv festivals. He spends at least half of the year on the road and working around the globe, hav-ing taught and performed on five continents and in over 35 countries. While he now resides in Spain, he is a major improv influence through-out the world, specifically in Latin America and the Spanish-speaking world, though, again, he travels pretty much everywhere. He is the au-thor of the first improv manual written in Spanish (and since translated into several languages), *Del Salto Al Vuelo – Manual de Impro* (From the Jumping to Flight), a wonderful guide to learning and performing improvisation. He organized the 1ˢᵗ Spanish-speaking "Impro World Cup" in 2004 in Mexico, co-founded Argentina's Sucesos Argentinos (1996), and is an accomplished and well-traveled solo improv performer. Influenced by Keith Johnstone, his work blends magic realism and narrative, focusing on blending artistic styles ("soundpainting") and poetic expression. Of the many forms he's helped create, his Impro Big Band Assembly is a good example of his experimentation and blending of styles. Using "soundpainting," Galván conducts a multi-disciplinary performance of improvised music, performance, song, and dance.

Improv in Latin America, as noted above, is often described as much more physical than improv in North America or Europe, where there is more reliance on language and verbal wordplay. Of course, this is an oversimplification, but **Felipe Ortiz** exemplifies movement in improv. Exploring improvisation through acrobatics, clowning, physical theatre, movement, and object manipulation, Ortiz highlights the physical and the body in his improvisational work. From Bogotá, Columbia, Ortiz discovered improv while in college. Initially studying industrial design, he was drawn to the theatre department and their work in movement. Without any real reference point and no true improv scene in Columbia at the time, his university group explored improvisational performance. They had not seen an improv show for nearly four years until they saw a show from a visiting Argentinian group.

He would go on to study Clowning and Buffon in Paris, and his work has become a mixture of movement, clowning, improvisation, and magical realism. He founded La Gata Cirko, La Gata Impro, and PICNIC Improvisación Teatral, which hosts an international improv festival each year. He has taught clowning and improvisation at the University of Bogotá. He has toured and taught internationally, including his solo clown show "La Cita," and his wordless improv show "Speechless," with fellow Columbian performer Daniel Orrantia and DJ Mama Cutsworth (Canadian Sarah Michaelson), which debuted in 2013 and has toured ever since. The show mixes sound with movement – from clowning to basic slapstick to dance. The show highlights the ways improvisation can facilitate communication without words, using "elements inspired by Buster Keaton's physicality or the magical realism of Gabriel García Márquez ...wrapped inside rich musical soundscapes."[6] The show features Michaelson creating the music while Ortiz and Orrantia explore storytelling through movement. Ortiz's highly physical approach to improv mixed with his circus and acrobatics makes his performances – and workshops – unique. His approach of leading with the body and movement starkly contrasts most US improv training and performance, which tends to privilege language and wordplay.

Perhaps one of the more provocative figures in improvisation, **Gonzalo Rodolico** is an innovator of solo improvisation, though he didn't start onstage alone. Based in Buenos Aires, he was part of the part improv part music show *La Celebración de lo Efímero*, which toured several international improv festivals from 2006–2008. His collaborators on the show were inspired by a performance of *La Impro Lucha* by the Mexican group Complot/Escena at the 2008 Impro World Cup in Chile. A mixture of wrestling, improv, and music, his collaborators were captivated by the spectacle, showmanship, and fun displayed in *La Impro Lucha*. Rodolico, however, was less interested in pursuing the style. So, he found himself rehearsing and working alone. Inspired by the solo work of Omar Galván, he began working on his solo show *Amorbo*. When he started working with musician Nico Deluca, he realized that "a solo show is not necessarily executed by one person."[7] At the same time, not having to compromise his vision drew him to solo work. The collaboration at the heart of improv for many, for Rodolico, was sometimes an impediment to his vision or truth. While his vision of improv might seem contradictory to the collaborative nature of the art form, he feels that working solo allows him to be his most genuine self and that "is the greatest act of generosity and exposition. You don't keep anything for yourself. You are there. Love it or hate it but this is my vision of the world."[8]

46. AFRICA, ASIA, AND AUSTRALIA

Australia has a long history of improvisation and is home to many theatres and international festivals. Still in its First Wave or early Second, contemporary improv in Africa and Asia is not quite as well established. While contemporary comedic improvisational theatre is just emerging, both continents sport incredibly rich and deep-rooted storytelling and performance traditions based on improvisational principles. In contemporary improvisation, we once again see the familiar pattern of American and Canadian styles being the catalyst for improvisational performance. As with Latin America, political stability or instability can play a role in the development of the arts and improv in any region or country.

Improv in Africa is not as widespread or popular as in other places, though there is still no shortage of improv. There are Match teams in many Francophone countries, such as Atelier Impro in The Republic of the Congo or T.I.M. – Troupe d'Improvisation du Maroc in Morocco. While Match is prevalent in many parts of Africa, it is hardly the only style. The Assembly in South Africa is a dedicated long form theatre, which is a branch of The Assembly in Toronto (which also has branches in Mexico and The Netherlands). As with Match, The Assembly represents one of the main ways improv is introduced in Africa and Asia. The importation of improv, whether by literal group, via the theories of Johnstone or Spolin, or through *Whose Line is it Anyway?*

An excellent example of a "home-grown" group influenced by North American improv is the Kenyan group **Because You Said So** (BYSS), which went from a one-off performance to one of the continent's most recognizable improv groups. Founded in 2014 by Jason Runo after he was laid off from his airline job (he would later become a beekeeper) and featuring June Gachui, Kevin K1 Maina, Patricia Kihoro, Justin Karunguru, Yafesi Musoke, and Mugambi Nthiga, the improv show has become incredibly popular, making its debut at the Kenyan National Theatre in 2018. Inspired by *Whose Line Is It Anyway?* BYSS was hugely popular in Kenya pre-pandemic and is largely credited with introducing improvisational performance in Kenya.

While we have already seen several Match, short form, and long form groups, I'd like to look briefly at the founder of Playback Nigeria, **Oluwadamilola Apotieri-Abdulai**. Playback Theatre was founded in the United States in 1975 by Jonathan Fox and Jo Salas. The basic idea is that an audience member or group tells stories from their lives, and then the improvisers re-enact them on the spot. There are many styles and uses of Playback Theatre – Johnstone's The Life Game is the most popular in comedic improvisational performance – but it tends to be used as a form of Applied Improvisation meant to enact social change and/or be a form of therapy. Inspired by the work of Augusto Boal, Apotieri-Abdulai's work primarily focuses on the therapeutic aspects of improvisation, helping people, mainly children and teens, overcome anxiety and other mental health issues. First established in 2002 as Theatre for Advocacy, Playback Nigeria grew out of this original organization and was transformed into Playback Nigeria after Apotieri-Abdulai finished his postgraduate studies in applied drama at the University of Witwatersrand in South Africa. Reorganized in 2017 as Playback Nigeria, the company became Nigeria's first professional improv company.

Improv in Asia is still in its early stages, though it has probably moved into its Second Wave. Again, styles and popularity vary from country to country (and city to city and person to person). As with so many other regions, much of Asian improv is rooted in the work of Spolin and Johnstone, or in the countries with French-speaking roots, The Match is popular. Several English-speaking theatres across Asia feature American, Canadian, and British ex-patriots performing, and while they help make up each country's improv scene, I have instead focused on groups and theatres created by citizens of each country, such as Silly People's Improv Theatre in the Philippines.

Gabe Mercado is helping to build the improv community in the Philippines. Naturally, his journey to bring formalized improvisational theatre and training to the Philippines started in Wisconsin, where, in 2001, he took classes from Paul Sills at the Wisconsin Theatre Games Center. In 2002, he founded the country's longest-running theatre, Silly People's Improv Theatre (SPIT) in Manila, which is still active and performs in Manila and around the globe. Reflecting on SPIT's success and his relationship with improvisation, he penned an essay answering the question, "Why I Do Improv," that captures the magic many improvisers and audiences feel, writing:

> An improviser cannot improvise a scene without an audience which serves as a demanding, sneering and jealous muse and partner. And it is that dance between audience and actor, that special moment when they see eye to eye and breathe each other's air and manage to not step on each other's feet – that's when the magic happens. And it's moments like that that improvisers create and live for and would absolutely die for.[9]

Well said. Thanks to the success of SPIT, he then became co-founder and CEO of **Third World Improv** (TWI), the Philippines' first and central improvisational training school. Education and teaching improv is as important to Mercado as performing, commenting on the creation of Third World Improv that "we felt that a legacy would not be complete if we did not pass on what we learned."[10] TWI's philosophy is "developing people," so their classes focus as much on how improvisation can help people outside of performing as it is in training improvisers. The tagline is also a reclamation, in much the same way Second City took an insult and turned it into their name by reframing the standard reference to Third World countries as "developing nations." In addition to sitting on the board of The Applied Improvisation Network, he is the founder of the Manila Improv Festival, so it is safe to say that Mercado has been a major factor in the development of improvisation in the Philippines.

Improvisational theatre in India is still relatively new and has only begun to grow post-pandemic. As with many places in the US and abroad, *Whose Line* was the main point of reference prior to the pandemic. The amount of improv during the pandemic that went online helped spread improv everywhere, especially in India, opening up different styles, genres, and possibilities of improvisation. Places like the Playground Improvisational Theatre and Comedy Collective in Delhi and Improv Comedy Bangalore emerged right before or right after the pandemic to create opportunities for performers. One of the key figures leading India's improv community is **Balasree Viswanathan**, artistic director of India's all-female group **The Adamant Eves**, one of the teams at Improv Comedy Bangalore. Viswanathan first began improv at the end of her graduate studies in the US. Wrapping up her Master's in engineering, she attended a few of the school's improv shows, joined some workshops, and did a few shows, then headed back to Bangalore with a desire to pursue improvisation. She quickly found Improv Comedy Bangalore and worked her way up to co-artistic director of the company and artistic director of The Adamant Eves. Her experience with the Eves mirrors many groups worldwide that feature an all-female (or Black or Asian, etc.) cast – the safety and trust allowed for more freedom. In an interview with *Status*, she said, "I felt a lot more comfortable and confident that that [being steamrolled by men] would not happen. The space felt safer and that was what I needed as a new improviser. As for stories, it naturally became more women-centric." She went on to say, "Good improv makes space. If you don't have space, it isn't good improv. Good improv makes space for different voices and experiences." [11]

The Tokyo Comedy Store began English performances in 1994, featuring stand-up comedy and improvisation, but in terms of Japanese improv, several women helped popularize improvisation in Japan. **Yuri Kinugawa** founded Impro Works in 1994, which was officially incorporated in 2009. Impro Works is based on the Theatresports model and is technically the longest-running Japanese improv company. In addition to her work with Impro Works, Kinugawa is an accomplished performer and teacher, serving as the Japanese team captain at the International Theatresports Championship and is a board member of the International Theatresports Institute. She also works extensively in applied improvisation, including doing the translation for *Applied Improvisation: Leading, Collaborating, and Creating Beyond the Theatre* (2018). The long-time artistic director of Impro Japan in Tokyo, **Naomi Ikegami** studied with Keith Johnstone at Loose Moose and then with Charna Halpern at iO in the

1990s before founding Impro Japan in 2001. An accomplished performer and teacher, she has appeared in shows across the globe and conducts hundreds of performance and business-style improv trainings each year. She has been the artistic director of Impro Japan for two decades, during which time she helped launch The Tokyo Improv Festival. Kinugawa and Ikegami are leading practitioners and advocates of applied improvisation and run training in Japan and abroad to help businesses, schools, and others apply the philosophies of improvisation to their lives and work off-stage. Improvisation in Japan, specifically in Tokyo, is much more extensive and diverse than two companies, but Kinugawa and Ikegami are at the heart of improvisation in Japan.

Hsiao-Hsien Wu is the founder and executive director of Guts Improv Theater in Taiwan, the country's first improvisational group. Opened in 2004, the group initially followed a traditional Theatresports format but began incorporating more long form styles, performing their first Harold in 2014. She studied theatre at the National Taiwan University of Arts and received her MFA in Theatre Management at Florida State University. She truly began her improv career in San Francisco, first taking a workshop at Berkely Rep (where she was an intern) and then studying more fully at the famed Bay Area Theatresports (BATS). When she was set to return home, she was depressed because "I kept hoping I would find an improvisational theatre group somewhere in Taiwan. But I never did." Rebecca Stockley, her teacher at BATS, suggested she start teaching improvisation in Taiwan, which she did at Shilin Community College in Taipei. While at Shilin, she came up with the concept and name for Guts, the idea being it takes guts to get up on stage and perform without a script.[12] Twenty years later, Guts is an institution, and Hsiao-Hsien is recognized as bringing improvisation to Taiwan. In addition to her work with Guts, she teaches improvisation at Taipei National University of Arts and translated Patricia Ryan Madson's *Improv Wisdom* and Keith Johnstone's *Impro* into Traditional Chinese.

At this point, you might be asking why Australia is grouped with Asia and Africa. Is it just the "A" continents?[13] No, though I do like alliteration. Australia forms a nice bookend for the International Powerhouse section because it has gone through every continent's journey. While improv is just starting to expand on the other A continents, Australia has a long track record, with Theatresports dating back to 1985. Debuting at the Belvoir St Theatre, the Sunday night improv shows quickly became must-see. Improv quickly exploded from Sunday night sell-outs to improv theatres, television shows, international tournaments, and festivals. Impro Australia, Improv Theatre Sydney, The Improv Conspiracy, and Impro Melbourne are highly regarded theatres, and there are several international comedy festivals in Australia and New Zealand.

Part of what makes improv in Australia unique is that improv thrived there in the 1980s and into the 1990s but then fell completely out of favor, only to be rediscovered again in the later 2000s, in large part thanks to the success of the semi-improvised television show *Thank God You're Here!* Debuting in 2006 and running for four consecutive seasons (renewed for a fifth in 2023), the show features four contestants (often established celebrities and actors) who each walk through a big blue door onto a "hidden" set. They are greeted by the improv cast, who are playing out a particular scenario, which is highly scripted, with the signature "Thank God you're here!" From there, the contestant must navigate the scenario. It plays out much like any short form guessing game where one player does not know the same information as everyone else and must figure it out from context clues and hints from the other players. After all four contestants play individually, they enter a final scenario together for the "all-in group challenge." The show's immense popularity in Australia and New Zealand led to a popular rebirth of improv. The show also spawned spin-offs in nearly 25 countries, including a rather disastrous American version that was canceled after seven episodes.

The re-emergence of improv in the late 2000s gave the region a kind of second take on the development of improv. So, while there is a lineage of improv that rivals their European counterparts, in some ways, the development of improv is more like that of Latin America or Asia, where improv began to explode in the 2000s. Theatresports style improv dates back to the 1980s, and Johnstone's theories heavily influence improv in Australia and New Zealand. In contrast, Chicago-style improv and other forms are much more recent, giving the area a duality of old and new. One of the foundational figures in Australian improv is **Lyn Pierse**, author of *Theatresports Down Under* (1995), the Australian improv Bible. Pierse has taught improvisation, specifically Theatresports and Johnstone, across Australia and New Zealand (and most of Asia), including long stints at the National Institute of Dramatic Art, Actors Centre Australia, and the Australian Academy of Dramatic Arts. Her work is largely responsible for the initial surge of Theatresports style improv in Australia and New Zealand and remains foundational for many improvisers and teachers working today. Her work continues to influence Australian improv, including at theatres trying to reimagine Australian improv in the 21st century, places like **Impro Melbourne**, which returned to Johnstone to re-learn and explore new styles and genres beyond Theatresports. Though many places still prioritize the Theatresports format, they began exploring new performance styles in the same way countries where The Match initially dominated began to expand and explore. The results speak for themselves, with Impro Melbourne standing as one of the most well-regarded improv theatres in the world and Australia and New Zealand currently sporting robust improv scenes.

As the last two Parts demonstrate, improvisation has grown exponentially. It is a true global art form that has heavily influenced many of today's most important comedic performers. Yet for all of improv's growth and increased accessibility, systemic and institutional barriers remain, many of which would be brought to the forefront during the pandemic and racial reckoning in the summer of 2020.

Notes

1   Gunter Loesel, "Life." https://www.gunterloesel.theater/en
2   Qtd. in Teodora Tzankova, "Inbal Lori interview about political improv between cliches and critical thoughts," *ImproNews(de).* 3 November 2017. https://www.impro-news.de/2017/11/inbal-lori-interview-about-political-improv-between-cliches-and-critical-thoughts/
3   Qtd. in Feña Ortalli, "Interview: Malgorzata 'Gosia' Różalska," *Status,* Year 7, Issue 77, November 2017, 10.
4   Qtd. in Sandrine Blanchard, "Theatrical improvisation makes its debut at the Comedie-Francaise," *Le Monde.* 31 May 2022. https://www.lemonde.fr/culture/article/2022/05/31/l-improvisation-theatrale-fait-son-entree-a-la-comedie-francaise_6128395_3246.html
5   Qtd. in Katasi Kironde, "The Black Women Transforming London's Improv Theatre Scene," Black Ballad. 2 January 2020. https://blackballad.co.uk/arts-culture/the-black-women-transforming-londons-improv-theatre-scene
6   "About," *Speechless.* https://speechlessimpro.wordpress.com/speechless/
7   Qtd. in Feña Ortalli, "Interview: Gonzalo Rodolico," *Status,* Year 11, Issue 121, July 2021, 11.
8   Qtd. in Ortalli, 15.
9   Gabe Mercado, "Why I Do Improv," *Third World Improv.* 3 July 2021. https://thirdworldimprov.com/why-i-do-improv-by-gabe-mercado/
10 Qtd. in Aih Mendoza, "Funny is a Side Effect: How Third World Improv is Developing People," *CNN Philippines.* 24 January 2018. https://www.cnnphilippines.com/life/culture/2018/01/26/third-world-improv.html
11 Qtd. in Feña Ortalli, "Interview: Balasree Viswanathan," *Status,* Year 10, Issue 110, August 2020, 13.

12 Qtd. in Kobe Chen, translated by Jonathan Barnard, "On Stage Without Scripts – Guts Improv Theatre," *Taiwan Panorama.* March 2015. https://www.taiwan-panorama.com/en/Articles/Details?Guid=cecabd52–9004-4512-bde6–61cb9ec50231&CatId=7&postname=On%20Stage%20Without%20Scripts%E2%80%94Guts%20Improv%20Theatre

13 Full confession, I assumed that Antarctica does not have a well-developed improvisational theatre scene, though I bet penguins are pretty funny.

PART 8

THE FOURTH WAVE

It is never a good idea to try and name a phenomenon while living through it, but I will do it anyway. As we've seen, the Third Wave of improv emerged in the 1990s as a reaction to the product-oriented improv of the 1980s (iO and ComedySportz) and the more rigid set of rules and structures to help improv transform from tool to performance product. The Third Wave similarly saw an expansion in improv style, the geography of improv, and the inclusion (sometimes unwillingly) of different voices. In many ways, the 2000s and 2010s were a sort of Third-And-A-Half Wave, where many ideas that sparked the Third Wave took shape and evolved. 3Peat and Asian AF, for instance, faced many of the same obstacles and issues that Oui Be Negroes faced 25 years earlier. The Pandemic and The Reckoning that accompanied it via #MeToo and the Black Lives Matter Movement in the summer of 2020, however, seem to have marked a change in the improv community (and, you know, the world). There were seismic changes in leadership at foundational institutions, and issues of racism and misogyny that had long been boiling under the surface were finally exposed to the light of day. We are still living through those changes (or lack thereof), so it is difficult to say that "we did it!" but it is important to mark how the pandemic and the first years of the 2020s have reshaped improvisation as we (maybe) enter the Fourth Wave of Improv.

DOI: 10.4324/9781003359692-8

47. THE PANDEMIC AND THE RECKONING

Perhaps you are reading this in 2054 and aren't aware, but a global pandemic in 2019–2020 (2021, 2022, 2023?) turned the world on its head. Like most of the world, an art form based on collaboration suddenly became isolated. The pandemic proved to be a considerable challenge both artistically and economically. In addition to the pandemic, the murder of George Floyd and the Black Lives Matter protests that followed in the summer of 2020 shined a spotlight on the racial inequities and injustices that have long plagued improv. These issues were added to the growing #MeToo movement that emerged in the late 2010s, bringing problems of sexism and misogyny to the forefront. To be clear, none of these issues began in 2020. Instead, they all came to a head in 2020. The pandemic and the reckoning that followed caused a seismic shift in the comedy and improv world, closing theatres and demanding change. In this section, I'd like to look at what happened, and then in #48, we'll look at some of the ways improv has responded by focusing specifically on iO and The Second City.

The pandemic caused nearly every improv theatre in the US to temporarily close in the spring and summer (and beyond) of 2020. One of the silver linings of the closures is that after a few months, a lot of improv and improvisers went online to perform, collaborate, and talk about improv. While some folks fretted about the best way to improvise online or worried that their shows sucked, none of that particularly mattered. This new online presence proved incredibly beneficial for many folks living in areas with no previous improv community or whose only source of improvisation was re-runs of *Whose Line is it Anyway?* Suddenly, the world's best improvisers were fully accessible online. As we've seen, this online presence was vital in spurring the development of improv in many countries around the globe. Performances, classes, and discussions were happening daily, and anyone with an internet connection could plug into the community. Ironically, so many personal connections occurred during a global shutdown, but from 2020–2022, they were vital in sustaining and expanding improvisation.

These performances, classes, and discussions helped to accelerate improv's development. In countries with established improv scenes, Zoom-prov worked to introduce new ideas, theories, and modes of performance and became a kind of "collaboratory." In countries and areas with less established improv communities, Zoom-prov became a catalyst, helping to create communities where none existed and accelerating the timeline for starting new groups. While books and television shows are helpful, there is no substitute for in-person instruction or discussion (even via Zoom). I'm obviously pro-books, but would you rather read *Impro* or take a masterclass from Keith Johnstone or Patti Stiles? Zoom-prov served a similar function as many international improv festivals, only with less drinking (well, on second thought, maybe not) and fewer barriers to entry. As accessible as many international improv festivals are, for improvisers with limited access to funding or institutional/governmental support, attending a festival in another country is simply impossible. Improvisers with family obligations or a work schedule or job that simply did not allow them to travel had been cut out, but suddenly, with Zoom-prov, they could join the conversation. While the online community was positive, much of what happened during the pandemic revealed and illuminated many of the problems in the improv community, specifically in terms of economics, race, and gender.

The pandemic and online improv made many of the world's best improvisers and top institutions accessible to millions. The pandemic also exposed some of the issues at these institutions. One was literal physical space. Before the pandemic, many of improv's stalwart institutions began massively expanding their physical footprint. iO, UCB, Second City, and The Annoyance all built or expanded their facilities, creating massive new spaces with multiple stages and classrooms (and bars and kitchens) at the cost of multiple millions of dollars. The theatres touted these as signs of improv's ascendance and prosperity. Even before the pandemic, some criticized these new spaces as too commercial or corporate – the antithesis to Brecht's "smokers' theatre." Much like The Compass Players experienced when they moved from a cramped bar in Hyde Park filled with University of Chicago students to a bigger and fancier North Side theatre filled with wealthy North-Shore Chicagoans in the 1950s, the vibe and the audience began to change. The cramped and "charming" spaces of the 1990s gave way to large and luxurious (for improv) spaces. The audiences started to become a bit less niche and more mainstream (which is not bad and undoubtedly good economically), but there were calls that improv had sold out. Whatever one's feelings, the new spaces were unquestionably a far cry from the cramped Brechtian cabarets at the heart of improv's roots. More importantly, these vast and costly spaces became economic weights during the pandemic. Frankly, many of them had been economic burdens from the start. Yes, there was federal and state pandemic assistance. Still, the price tags and taxes on these spaces became problematic – or, as some have argued regarding iO, perhaps became an excuse to close when the racial reckoning occurred.

The other economic issue during the pandemic, primarily spurred by the construction of these massive new spaces, was performer pay. Many improv theatres in the US do not pay their performers (while requiring them to pay for classes to be eligible to perform). The Compass Players paid their performers a weekly stipend, and The Second City followed suit (Second City is currently an equity house, meaning they hire union actors and pay them according to union-agreed pay scales). Despite this early tradition, most other US improv theatres, especially long form improv theatres, do not pay. ComedySportz pays, as do some Theatresports and Match venues. Since Theatresports is licensed and each theatre acts like a franchise, there is no set standard, though most do not pay performers, and outside of Second City, almost no improv theatres in the US pay a living wage. In the early days of the Second Wave of Improv, when teams were performing in bars or even when theatres had just acquired their first (very rough-and-tumble) spaces, it was clear that money was tight. That's not to say that performers should not have always been paid, but most performers understood that the theatres and administrators were not getting rich off their backs. Many improvisers felt as though they were part of the company and that their "free" performances (and free labor building, renovating, and staffing the new theatre spaces) were helping to build, maintain, and grow the theatre(s) and art form they loved so dearly.

With the new multi-million-dollar theatres and yet another generation of improvisers removed from the communal "let's build this thing together" ethos, it is not surprising that after spending thousands to take classes, these improvisers were less than thrilled with the "joy of working for free." Since so many of these theatres had become iconic, the assumption that one's performance was part of building the company from the ground up was no longer true. Instead, it had been replaced by the tried-and-true "this career exposure is priceless." As we've seen, many, many, many high-profile comedians started in improv, so the idea that performing at iO or UCB will help one's career is undoubtedly true, but that doesn't mean it has to happen for free. Even before the pandemic, many theatres continued to "preach" their economic vulnerability. By the summer of 2020, however, many performers found the calls of economic woe from leading institutions hollow. In "the good old days," the message came in the back of a bar after a show that had maybe brought in a few hundred bucks. Now, it was coming in a space with multiple theatres, multiple kitchens, and several bars, all housed in a building that cost millions of dollars to acquire and many millions more to renovate and furnish. iO, UCB, The Annoyance, and Second City had all expanded their physical spaces greatly since their inception, and each occupied a *performance complex* by the summer of 2020. One can certainly see how these new spaces were a substantial economic burden on the companies.

Still, one can also see how performers began feeling exploited by improv's economic model.

In addition to the massive new multi-million-dollar theatre spaces, most improv theatres had developed a pay-to-play system. Improvisers rarely audition "from the street" and then end up performing at iO or UCB (or any number of improv theaters). Instead, since the 1990s, the route to a theatre's stage has run through the theatre's classrooms. Improvisers would take up to five or six levels of classes, each level costing hundreds of dollars. Only upon completion, with some exceptions, would a student be *eligible* to be placed on a team – note there is no guarantee a graduate will get to perform outside of class shows. There are numerous issues with this structure, one of which helps to explain improv's overwhelming whiteness – the class-to-stage pathway is expensive and can be a barrier for many. While many theatres have instituted scholarships to help students pay for classes, or the more problematic "work for us for free and we'll give you classes" model, the simple fact is the classroom-to-stage model made improv inaccessible for many. It also meant that not only were improvisers not being paid for their work, but they were also often paying thousands of dollars *for the opportunity* to work for free.

For all the economic issues that the pandemic illuminated, very little would have probably changed at an institutional level without the Black Lives Matter movement. It is no secret that white men have dominated improv's history. Women and BIPOC (Black, Indigenous, and People of Color) performers have long felt ostracized and exploited. In the wake of the #MeToo movement in 2017, many of improv's gender issues began to come to the forefront. As noted in #16, iO West closed in part because of allegations of sexual misconduct by its leadership. Many women in improvisation have come forward over decades to share their stories of misogyny and sexual misconduct by male improvisers, often ones in positions of power. One of the issues exacerbating sexism and misogyny is the above pay-to-play structure. Because of this structure, improv teachers at various institutions often held positions of extreme power. Theatre leadership would often defer to teachers about who should be placed on a team, so it is easy to see how a male teacher might exploit that power over a female student or how a female student might not want to report misconduct for fear of it ruining her chances at making it to the stage. Exacerbating all of this was the rather putrid response of many in improv's leadership structure to sexual misconduct allegations. As much (or as little) as improv institutions worked to address these issues, little overt action was taken. Seeing that relatively little had been done to truly address issues of sexism and misogyny, when George Floyd was murdered in May of 2020, BIPOC performers came together to demand that the issues of systemic racism within improv's institutions finally be addressed.

Improv's racial reckoning began on June 3, 2020, when UCB's former diversity coordinator, Keisha Zollar, tweeted a thread about her experience in that position. While she did not name UCB in the thread, it quickly became apparent who she was talking about, and they acknowledged responsibility. Zollar wrote, "

> For years I worked as a Diversity Coordinator … where I was NEVER PAID in money for my work. Not one cent. I was offered 'classes' … I stayed cause I was hopeful that the next generation of comedians would be more diverse.[1]

Second City alum and member of 3Peat Dewayne Perkins responded to Second City's tweet supporting Black Lives Matter on June 4th, saying, "You remember when the black actors wanted to put on a Black Lives Matter Benefit show and you said only if we gave half of the proceeds to the Chicago PD, because I will never forget."[2] His thread "outlined several ways the theater fostered a racist environment for Black performers and said he 'had so much anxiety/fear built up from being in such a toxic predominately white environment.'"[3] Zollar's and Perkins's Twitter threads led to numerous BIPOC performers sharing their experiences, which painted a very bleak picture of how improv institutions have treated BIPOC performers for decades. While more performers came forward at the same time than ever before, many of the stories and experiences were not new. They had been shared previously, either met with little response or token measures like hiring an unpaid diversity coordinator. One difference in 2020 was the volume of responses simultaneously, and another was that several performers began calling for economic reparations. The most significant difference, however, was that the Black Lives Matter movement was creating a national conversation about race, so arguably, for the first time, improv institutions needed to respond.

UCB, Second City, and iO all had measurably different responses. UCB responded in a familiar way, with non-descript pledges and promises "to do better." UCB revealed they were trying to become a non-profit, though it was unclear how that would address any issues. They also promised that the UCB 4 would be turning over operations of UCB to a new yet-to-be-determined administrative board. As we'll see, iO's response was the most perplexing, while Second City's was the most immediately responsive.

On June 5, 2020, Andrew Alexander stepped down as Executive Director of Second City, pledging to divest himself from the theater (which he later did), writing in an open letter, "The Second City cannot begin to call itself anti-racist. That is one of the great failures of my life." He would go on to detail broad strokes about how Second City would try to improve, including hiring a BIPOC administrator to replace him. He also invoked the economic hardship of the pandemic, something we would see in UCB's and iO's responses as well, writing, "To make matters worse, the theater is struggling financially as a result of the ongoing COVID-19 closures...The company is not in a position to make major financial reparations at this time, if that is indeed what's being asked."[4] On June 8, a collection of Black actors and staffers, including Ashley Nicole Black, Amber Ruffin, Chris Redd, and Sam Richardson, wrote an open letter to Second City, writing, the "erasure, racial discrimination, manipulation, pay inequity, tokenism, monetization of Black culture, and trauma-enducing (sic) experiences of Black artists at The Second City will no longer be tolerated."[5] The letter further demanded changes to the theatre's structure, some of which were met (see #48), including hiring an outside HR firm to oversee hiring, hiring an independent BIPOC-owned diversity, equity, and inclusion firm, and putting more support in place for BIPOC administrators. The Second City responded on June 11, vowing to meet these demands and, "to be clear: We are prepared to tear it all down and begin again."[6]

The response from iO was ... convoluted. On June 9, 2020, the petition "I Will Not Perform at iO until Until (sic) the Following Demands Are Met" was published, accusing Halpern and iO of systemic racism. The petition demanded Halpern "must publicly acknowledge and apologize for the institutional racism perpetuated at iO as well as her individual history of racism."[7] The petition stipulated that iO decentralize its decision-making structure, actively work to include more BIPOC performers and create a safe and supportive environment for all performers. Responding to the petition, Halpern emailed the BIPOC comedy group Free Street Parking: "Thanks for your letter folks. I have always been open and interested in involving my community in change and growth in my theatre. One can't grow a business this big without doing that." She immediately pivoted and announced the permanent closure of iO, which was closed due to COVID, saying, "Its (sic) not looking like iO will be able to open its doors. The pandemic had made the financial struggle too difficult and I can't even see the light at the end of the tunnel at this point."[8] The announcement stunned everyone and was seen by some as a means to avoid the racial reckoning underway. Halpern responded, "If it were not for the pandemic I would not be closing. I would be meeting with the protesters." She again cited economics, further saying that "one of the demands was me to hire advisors, with a salary, and I wasn't going to be able to do that."[9] While Second City seemed to have a plan (or a plan to have a plan) to address racial issues, iO and UCB were shuttered without any clear plan, not just for dealing with systemic racism, but for ever opening again.

The following section briefly details the next steps taken at iO and Second City. But it is worth noting how seismically and quickly the racial reckoning rocked the improv community. Within a week, the future of UCB was murky, Second City's long-time owner and executive director was out, and iO had announced its permanent closure. Many of the issues raised in the racial reckoning remained unresolved, and outside of Second City, most remained un-responded to. How improv as a community would respond was also unclear (and is still unclear as of this writing). Let me be clear: while the time between Zollar's original tweet and Halpern's sudden closure of iO was incredibly quick, the issues raised in the reckoning had been present for *decades* – centuries within American comedy writ large. None of them were new, and none of them were being voiced for the first time. Just because some people heard them for the first time did not mean the issues were new.

48. THE NEW ARTISTIC AND EXECUTIVE DIRECTORS

As of this writing, we are still in the early days of the institutional responses to the pandemic and reckoning, though it is necessary to look at what has happened in response thus far. One reason for skepticism is that past issues of racism and sexism were largely dismissed, overlooked, or "solved" by hiring a diversity coordinator who has very little power or, in the case of UCB, isn't even a paid staff member. The Second City was only a few years removed from every BIPOC cast member quitting the theatre's 2015–2016 revue *A Red Line Runs Through It* due to a hostile racial environment, repeated verbal abuse from audience members, and a lack of institutional support, an experience detailed by cast member Peter Kim in a 2016 *Chicago Magazine* essay.[10] The pandemic and reckoning brought issues to the forefront. Not to be repetitive, but many of those issues existed and festered for decades, so it is perfectly understandable that many in the improv and comedy communities are skeptical that anything will change. Robin Thede voiced a popular sentiment during an interview about *A Black Lady Sketch Show*, saying, "First of all, *was* there a racial reckoning? There were protests and uprisings, but have people fundamentally changed how they think about race? Maybe some people, but by and large we have a lot more to do."[11] The changes made have varied across the improv community. While theatres across the country and the world are trying to become more inclusive institutions, I would like to look at the response of the two theatres at the center of it all – Second City and iO. As of this writing, UCB New York is still formally closed with plans to reopen in 2024 (a scaled-back LA branch reopened in late 2022), so any changes in their structure or operating procedure are still to be determined.

As noted above, long-time Second City Executive Director Andrew Alexander stepped down in June 2020 amidst charges of racism during his tenure at Second City. He put the theatre up for sale (a New York private equity firm bought it). Anthony LeBlanc replaced Alexander the next day as Interim Executive Director. A BIPOC Second City mainstage alum, LeBlanc only served briefly. Though his stint was brief, it was quite impactful. First and foremost, he stepped into a powder keg and helped steer Second City through the pandemic and its racial reckoning. LeBlanc helped to oversee many of the structural changes in hiring and helped lead Second City's immediate response in the summer of 2020 (both to the pandemic and charges of institutional racism), which included hiring a DEI partner and the establishment of standing DEI committees, securing a new HR partner that would develop the search criteria for new leadership job postings, and the hiring of a new Chief Operating Officer, Parisa Jalili, who had joined Second City the year prior as VP of sales operations.

The leadership team hired Jon Carr, the artistic director of Dad's Garage in Atlanta, founder of United Atlanta Improv, a cast member in the improv group Dark Side of the Room, and award-winning playwright. Unfortunately, Jon Carr would only stay in his position at Second City little more than a year, leaving after 14 months "due to changes in his personal life."[12] During Carr's tenure, there were not many changes to the creative structure of Second City's revues, albeit with a stronger focus on hiring and making space for more BIPOC performers. The fundamental changes were in the leadership structure and hiring practices, the incorporation of institutional DEI, and the restaffing of management. Ed Wells replaced Carr in 2022, who came to Second City from Sesame Workshop by way of the WWE (World Wrestling Entertainment). While Second City pledged to hire a Black Executive Director and did so with LeBlanc and Carr, Wells is white. Perhaps the most significant change/action under Wells' leadership was opening a new Second City branch in Brooklyn in the fall of 2023.

The changes on the creative side have been less sweeping than the restructuring and restaffing of the theatre's administration. Some of the changes were such low-hanging fruit that it is a little awkward to even write them down, such as hiring more diverse performers. Second City has tried to create more space for BIPOC performers, first and foremost by hiring more BIPOC performers for their mainstage revues – 2023's *Don't Quit Your Daydream* features three BIPOC performers in the traditional six-person cast. They've also created a BIPOC-only revue each February, though there has been little change in Second City's creative structure or process. Rather than changing the process, they have relied on change to come from having more diverse voices in the room while attempting to provide a more welcoming and supportive environment in said room. Since reopening, many of Second City's mainstage revues have been noticeably more diverse and generally well-received by audiences and critics. That said, there is still much work to be done. The underlying fear of many – at Second City and across the comedy spectrum – is that people will think the work is done and the issue is "solved" after making a few changes at one point in time.

Second City responded much more quickly than iO, putting plans in place almost immediately to address their issues. Again, how successful those plans and their implementation will ultimately be is still to be determined. iO, on the other hand, as we've seen, simply shut its doors, announcing its permanent closure a week after being openly charged with institutional racism. iO had no plan because its future was in doubt. For a while, the plan seemed to be "hope a rich alum like Tina Fey buys iO and reopens it." While that didn't happen, as with Second City, Halpern eventually put iO up for sale. Two Chicago real estate developers bought it in 2021, and plans began to emerge about reopening the theatre. During the year of uncertainty about iO's future, nothing was done to address the allegations against the theatre. While Second City hired an HR firm to evaluate complaints, re-evaluated the photos hanging throughout the building that mainly featured white performers, did an extensive deep-dive into their sketch archives to label offensive jokes and sketches, made their hiring criteria and practices more transparent for performers and administrators, and hired a more diverse executive staff, iO was still figuring out if it was even going to exist.

The new iO owners, Chicago real estate executives Scott Gendell and Larry Weiner, took a purposefully slow approach. One of their first moves was tapping The Annoyance Theatre's Jennifer Estlin and Mick

Napier to help guide iO's transition. In addition to charges of institutional racism, iO was also dealing with long-standing charges of sexual harassment and misconduct, exacerbated by Halpern's denial of many claims, including a high-profile claim in 2016 in which Halpern wrote on Facebook, "There are times when there are women who just like to either cause trouble or get revenge or just want attention so they make up stories."[13] Issues of sexism, misogyny, and sexual misconduct are hardly unique to iO. Still, they were part of the theatre's legacy and something the "new" iO wanted to address in its new structure. The other major administrative structural issue many performers wanted to address was how teams and performers would be selected. For years, Halpern held almost exclusive power in making, shaping, and cutting teams, which created an enormous power imbalance but also meant that many women did not go to Halpern with complaints about sexism or sexual misconduct for fear of retribution.

To provide transparency and create a more equitable power balance, iO would eventually hire co-artistic directors – Katie Caussin and Adonis Holmes. Caussin is a long-time member of the Chicago improv community, having performed at Second City, The Annoyance, and iO. Holmes is newer to the Chicago improv scene. However, he has performed at both iO and The Annoyance. He is one of Second City's Bob Curry Fellows, a program named after Second City's first Black cast member and meant to create more opportunities for diverse performers within Second City. Under Caussin and Holmes' artistic leadership, with new managing director Steve Plock and managing producer Kim Whitfield and with long-time iO and Chicago improv stalwart Rachel Mason leading the training center, iO reopened in late 2022, promising to make iO a more inclusive company. The owners hired Steve Sacks as CEO, saying, "What a great thing if we can actually pull off an iO that has all the good stuff and gets rid of the bad stuff."[14] The theatre has made more space for diverse voices at the leadership level and for performers. However, time will tell if there is any lasting reform at Chicago's iconic improv institutions or within the improv community.

One lasting impact of the pandemic and the reckoning is the displacement of Chicago as improv's undisputed epicenter. For decades, Chicago stood as the guiding light of improvisational comedy. Second City, iO, and The Annoyance stood above almost all other improv theatres worldwide. Aspiring comedians flocked to Chicago to learn and work, hoping to be the next comedy star plucked from Chicago or simply wanting to be part of a large improv community. This change has been slowly happening for years. Chicago has always competed with New York and Los

Angeles for comedic talent, and very few Chicago comics have turned down the bright lights and bigger paychecks when New York or LA came calling. A cycle of talent refreshment had taken hold in Chicago, where every few years, the brightest talents left Chicago for New York or LA and were replaced by new up-and-coming improvisers. That cycle was part of Chicago's allure – there was a path to the top that was constantly refreshing. That cycle still plays out in Chicago, though aspiring comedians no longer feel bound to come to Chicago. Part of that is due to the expansion of improv detailed in the previous chapter. One of the reasons that improv has expanded, as also seen in the previous chapters, is that folks left Chicago and took their improv training with them, or folks came to Chicago to train and then went back to their homes to start new improv theatres. Chicago's success, in some ways, made new rivals inevitable. Similarly, the expansion of improv has also been partly the exportation of Chicago-style improv.

The spread of Chicago-style improv (and other types of improv) means that Chicago no longer stands as the sole improv destination it once was. People can do improv, even Chicago-style improv (even at a very high level with lots of folks who did Chicago-style improv in Chicago), pretty much anywhere now. Zoom-prov did not create this change; instead, it illuminated it. The racial reckoning also cast a blight on Chicago that the city is still recovering from, shining a light on long-standing issues that had remained relatively hidden from much of the world. Its institutions were hardly the only ones accused of racism. Still, they were the most in the spotlight, partly because of their standing in the comedy community and partly because of iO's response.

To be clear, improv in Chicago is still some of the best in the world. Let me make a sports comparison in the spirit of improv's connection to sports. The situation is akin to USA Basketball at the Olympics. The US once completely dominated the globe – the 1992 Dream Team was unbeatable and light years better than the competition. That's no longer the case. USA basketball now has stiff and fierce competition. While Americans never expect USA Basketball to lose, sometimes it does, and those losses are no longer seen as catastrophic anomalies – the rest of the world simply got better at basketball. The pandemic and reckoning exposed issues within Chicago improv, much like the 2004 Olympics exposed USA Basketball's inability to do things like pass the ball, or shoot the ball, or play as a team. That exposure caused USA Basketball to re-evaluate its structure and processes, much like Second City restructured its administrative processes. Thanks in part to the changes it made, USA Basketball is the betting favorite for the 2024 Olympics, but it is no sure thing that they'll win gold.[15] Improv in Chicago sits in a similar position. It is still at the top of the improv world but needs to make institutional changes to adjust and adapt. Like USA Basketball, Chicago improv is no longer alone at the top.

49. THE FOURTH WAVE THEATRE

There are specific theatres associated with each wave of improv. The Compass and Second City with the First Wave, iO and ComedySportz with the Second Wave, and The Annoyance and UCB with the Third Wave. While Second City, iO, UCB, The Groundlings, and other major improv theatres re-configure and attempt to reboot, a new wave of theatres has emerged. As noted, we are only at the beginning of the Fourth Wave, so naming the definitive Fourth Wave theatres is a fool's errand. There are thousands of improv theatres worldwide and hundreds in the US. There are lots of exciting cities with long-standing or emerging improv scenes. Places like Portland with Curious Comedy Theater, Kickstand Comedy Space, Deep End Theater, and the Stumptown Improv Festival; Philadelphia has PHIT (Philly Improv Theatre) and the near(ish) by SteelStacks arts complex in Bethlehem, home to the SteelStacks Improv Festival; Atlanta has Dad's Garage, Whole World Improv Theatre Co., and a thriving arts scene; Denver's Rise Comedy (formerly Voodoo Comedy Playhouse) has made the mile-high city an improv hotspot; London has Hoopla Improv Theatre and one of the world's most vibrant comedy scenes – long story short, there is great improv all over the place. Many improv theatres are doing excellent work, and I would like to highlight one as an example of the Fourth Wave: Huge Improv Theater in Minneapolis. Huge is not the only Fourth Wave theatre; it exemplifies many things that constitute this new wave.

Founded in 2005 and formally incorporated in 2009 by Butch Roy, Jill Bernard, and Nels Lennes, Huge Improv Theater has become a fixture of Minneapolis's improv scene. The Twin Cities' first theatre fully dedicated to long form improv, Huge co-founded, co-produces, and has hosted the Twin Cities Improv Festival (TCIF) since 2006. Much like The Annoyance now operates, Huge does not produce all of the shows on their stage; instead, they act as host – providing space for independent producers, improvisers, and teams to perform. In addition to TCIF, Huge also co-hosts The Black & Funny Improv Festival and the Queer and Funny Improv Festival. Dedicated to creating an accessible and open environment, Huge also hosts several improv jams each month, each dedicated to making space for traditionally underserved performer groups, such as the Average Joes Jam for improvisers with disabilities, Queer Jam, BIPOC JAM, 40+ Jam, and the open to everyone Dino Jam.

Accessibility and transparency are key parts of Huge's operations. One of the most important ways they accomplish this is by paying performers. Each performance makes a set stipend amount based on the time slot and attendance, so unlike many similar theaters where the performers make nothing, Huge has been paying performers for quite some time. The sliding pay scale is available to all performers and is on the company's website, so everyone knows how the payment structure works. They also make the journey to performance as transparent as possible. Not all students will end up onstage at any theatre, but as we've seen with larger institutions like iO, *how* a student goes from student to player is not always clear. There are limits to making that trajectory a fail-safe blueprint, but Huge lays out the process from the start. Huge also helped to create the Student Bill of Rights, collaboratively developed with Pam Victor and the Improv Teachers' Support & Collaboration Group on Facebook.[16] Again, as we've seen, the teacher–student relationship in improv classes has been an area where some teachers, particularly male teachers, have abused the power imbalance. By laying out students' power (and the power teachers do *not* have), Huge is working to make their spaces more inclusive and accessible.

One of the key drivers of Huge's inclusive and accessible atmosphere is John Gebretatose, the theatre's co-executive director and director of diversity and inclusion. The co-founder of Blackout Improv and The Black & Funny Improv Festival, Gebretatose is an internationally known improviser and inclusion advocate. One of the more popular workshops that he has taught around the world is Hard Topics, which is, in his words, "designed to be the first step in having more of an awareness of the different stories we tell on stage and how we can create community to better approach those tough moments when—and hopefully before—they happen."[17] What makes Huge important is that many of these initiatives and programs were happening BEFORE the pandemic and racial reckoning. In many ways, Huge's structure can serve as a model for other theatres looking to be more inclusive. They also have publicly stood behind their inclusive and accessible ethos, most notably when it was revealed that the landlord of the building where they were initially located had donated money to white supremacist and former KKK leader David Duke. Huge responded immediately, issuing a formal statement that ended, "We would like to formally tell Nazis and the KKK that they can fuck straight off."[18] They began working immediately, broke their lease, and found a new home, which they moved into in 2023.

As noted above, many exciting improv theatres are working to shape the current Fourth Wave. As we look back in ten or 20 years, I'm sure there will be other theatres that emerged as defining and influential in improv's development. I expect Huge will continue to be amongst that group and at the forefront, but I doubly expect many other theatres and figures to become equally important.

50. THE PERSON YOU CANNOT BELIEVE I DIDN'T INCLUDE

I have inevitably left someone out who should be 100% included.

Umm, how do you leave out someone like David Razowsky? Or Jay Sukow? Or Asaf Ronen, Jet Eveleth, Craig Cackowski, Armando Diaz, Miles Stroth, Dan O'Connor, Rebecca Stockley, or Paul Vaillancourt? What about that other person who should be in the book, or at least in this list of people not in the book that should be in the book? How could I leave them out of the book or the list of people who were left out of the book?

How can I talk about The Compass and leave out Barbara Harris and Severn Darden? Or The Annoyance and leave out Jennifer Estlin, Faith Soloway, and Joey Soloway? iO without Noah Gregoropoulos? UCB and no Will Hines? A discussion of diversity in improv with no Bob Curry? Did you highlight improv teachers but leave out Aretha Sills, Michael Gellman, and Mary Scruggs?

What about Bay Area Theatresports? Or The Magnet or PIT in New York? Or Bad Dog Theatre in Toronto (formerly Toronto Theatresports)? Or Jet City Improv? Or the theatre that you perform at that is incredibly important to your community?

What about Carl and the Passions, J.T.S. Brown, or The Stepfathers? What about The Baldwins, Big Black Car, or Cook County Social Club? You left out Cook County Social Club? Seriously!?! Is Cook County Social Club not in this book?!?

What about Improv Everywhere? What about Mike Birbiglia's *Don't Think Twice*?

What about the other theatre theorists and practitioners beyond Brecht who utilized or influenced improvisational performance – like Konstantin Stanislavski, Jacque Copeau, Sanford Meisner, Jerzy Grotowski, Peter Brook, Joseph Chaikin, and Joan Littlewood?

What about all the journalists and scholars documenting this art form? You know, the ones providing an immensely valuable written record of the most ethereal (and overlooked) of art forms? Don't folks like Jack

Helbing, Tony Adler, Darel Jevens, Jason Zinnoman, and Feña Ortalli deserve some recognition? What about the scholars writing about improv, folks like Jeffrey Sweet – seriously, how does Jeffrey Sweet not have his own entry? – Sam Wasson, Theresa Robbins Dudeck, Jeanne Leep, Amy Seham, Nicholas Zaunbacher, Hillary Haft Bucs, and many others?[19]

There is undoubtedly a bevy of 15-year-old improv phenoms right now killing it in their high school shows who will transform the improv community and be included in Volume 2. Not to mention the folks in their 30s, 40s, 50s, and beyond taking their first improv class right now who will go on to successful and influential careers. It sounds like we might need a Volume 3.

There's a television show coming out soon or a film that will become a staple of the improv world – or something that exists right now that I missed or omitted. I promise to include it in Volume 4.

Suffice it to say that even after Volume 5 is released, there will still be people who deserve a spot because there are simply too many brilliant people working in this most collaborative art form to capture them all in one place.

Notes

1 Keisha Zollar (@keishaz), "To my comedy folk, a thread ..." Twitter.com. 3 June 2020. https://twitter.com/keishaz/status/1268226635800539138

2 Dewayne Perkins (@DewaynePerkins), "You remember when ..." Twitter.com. 4 June 2020. https://x.com/DewaynePerkins/status/1268617 150547128326?s=20

3 Megh Wright, "Improv Communities Demand Theaters Address Systemic Racism," *Vulture.com.* 18 June 2020. https://www.vulture.com/2020/06/ ucb-second-city-io-diversity-racism.html

4 Andrew Alexander, "A Letter from Andrew Alexander," The Second City. 5 June 2020. https://www.secondcity.com/updates-from-the-second-city-2020

5 Qtd. in Megh Wright, "Black Second City Performers and Alums Demand Change in Open Letter," *Vulture.com.* 8 June 2020. https:// www.vulture.com/2020/06/black-second-city-alums-open-theater-demanding-change.html

6 D'Arcy Stuart and Steve Johnson, "The Second City Response Letter to the BIPOC, Latinx, and LGBTQIA+ communities," The Second City. 11 June 2020. https://www.secondcity.com/updates-from-the-second-city-2020

7 Olivia Jackson, "I Will Not Perform at iO until Until the Following Demands Are Met." 9 June 2020. https://www.change.org/p/io-chicago-i-will-not-perform-at-io-until-until-the-following-demands-are-met

8 Qtd. in Jack Helbig, "iO past, present, and nonfuture." *Chicago Reader,* 4 August 2020. https://chicagoreader.com/arts-culture/io-past-present-and-nonfuture/

9 Qtd. in Doug George, "Chicago's iO Theater is shutting down permanently," *Chicago Tribune.* 18 June 2020. https://www.chicagotribune.com/entertainment/theater/ct-ent-io-theater-to-close-permanently-0819–20200618-2apv5ycvj5aeti665tg3uxagxy-story.html

10 Peter Kim, "Why I Left My Dream Job at Second City," *Chicago Magazine.* 26 October 2016. https://www.chicagomag.com/arts-culture/October-2016/Why-I-Left-My-Dream-Job-at-Second-City/

11 Qtd. in Rebecca Sun, "Robin Thede and Gabrielle Union on Improvising 'A Black Lady Sketch Show' Scene and Pivotal Platform 'ABLSS' Offers Black Actresses," *The Hollywood Reporter.* 18 June 2021. https://www.hollywoodreporter.com/tv/tv-news/robin-thede-gabrielle-union-a-black-lady-sketch-show-alblss-1234967687/

12 Darel Jevens, "Jon Carr leaves Second City after 14 months as executive producer," *Chicago Sun Times.* 23 February 2022. https://chicago.suntimes.com/2022/2/23/22948272/jon-carr-second-city-after-14-months-as-executive-producer

13 Qtd. in Nina Metz, "Women in improv comedy detail a culture of sexual harassment, silence." *Chicago Tribune.* 29 January 2016. https://www.chicagotribune.com/entertainment/ct-sexual-harassment-accusations-roil-chicago-improv-community-ent-0129–20160128-story.html

14 Qtd. in Wanjiku Kairu, "iO improvises its rebirth," *The Chicago Reader.* 15 September 2022. https://chicagoreader.com/arts-culture/io-improvises-its-rebirth/

15 You are undoubtedly reading this after the 2024 Summer Olympics – don't tell me who won, I want it to be a surprise

16 "Improv Students' Bill of Rights," Huge Theater. https://www.hugetheater.com/theme1/student-handbook

17 Qtd. in Feña Ortalli, "Interview: John Gebretatose," *Status,* Year 9, Issue 105, March 2020, 12.

18 Qtd. in Jay Boller, "Nazis, KKK 'can fuck straight off': Huge Improv Theater issues statement on controversial landlord, *City Pages.* 30 August 2017. https://web.archive.org/web/20181020084958/http://www.citypages.com/news/nazis-kkk-can-fuck-straight-off-huge-improv-theater-issues-statement-on-controversial-landlord/442153343

19 I'm so sorry to the Frolleague (friend and colleague – shout out to Cheryl Black) who I have unintentionally omitted. I will buy you a drink at the next conference.

INDEX

Note: Page numbers followed by "n" denote endnotes

he United States
Taylor Publisher Services

Printed in
by Baker &